Lands and Peoples

THE WORLD IN COLOR

VOLUME IV

THE GROLIER SOCIETY

NEW YORK · TORONTO

M

Volume IV

TABLE OF CONTENTS

Photo, V. S. Manley

A CARAVAN PASSING THROUGH BOLAN PASS TO AFGHANISTAN

In summer the parched traveler on Bolan Pass is met by the bitter smell of sagebrush and the blinding glint of heat waves on dry sand; and in winter by such an icy wind from the peaks that men and camels have frozen to death. But these disadvantages were as nothing to the danger of plundering marauders from Baluchistan that existed until the treaty of Gandamak (1879), which placed the Pass under British control. For there is one strategic point—at Sir-i-Bolan—where the passage makes it possible for a small band to hold up a caravan.

4

ARID AFGHANISTAN

A Nation of Highland Warriors

Laced by the principal trade routes of central Asia, Afghanistan sprawls atop a plateau between Iran and Pakistan. The dominating feature of the land, the Hindu Kush range, stretches its knobby fingers from the north far into the lower-lying deserts of the southern frontier. Valleys and high plains between the fingers are fertile. There is little rain and much snow, with fierce winds that race down from the north. The people of this bleak highland are today emerging from a pastoral way of life. New roads, dams, canals, schools and popular elections have brought with them the social ferment that marks all of Asia.

ASIA is the world's largest continent. It has mothered the wonderful civilizations of India and China, with which the travelers of the Middle Ages made us acquainted at the period of their decline. From west to east the continent stretches from the Suez Canal for 6,700 miles to Bering Strait, and from north to south it reaches from Cape Cheliuskin (Severo) for 5,300 miles to, approximately, Singapore. Its climate varies from the arctic to the tropical, and barring the islands off its shores, the continent presents a solid parallelogram scalloped with the peninsulas of Arabia, India, Indochina and Kamchatka. The Japanese archipelago is the largest of various offshore islands.

The northern Temperate Zone extends along southern Siberia, while fertile grasslands creep along the valley of the Amur and on to the Pacific. Central Asia is, however, an elevated tableland ranging from ten to seventeen thousand feet in altitude, which extends from the Pamir to the Gobi Desert with the Himalayas for its southern boundary. (The Gobi is only four thousand feet above the level of the sea.) This central tableland has lakes of salt. It shows evidences of having been visited by devastating sandstorms. Of what the sand may at the same time have destroyed and preserved, further reference will be made. The Himalayas, "the Abode of Snow," which contain the highest peaks on earth, are the dividing wall between the north and the south. To the north the climate is often unkind, and in some parts the people have been pinned

to the seeking of the bare means to existence. To the south abundance of food and ease of finding shelter have permitted the development of a high degree of civilization. Of rivers, China possesses in the Yangtse Kiang the longest on the continent. It is navigable for fifteen hundred miles. India's Brahmaputra, the Ganges with its tributaries and the Indus are among the great rivers of the world. The Irawadi is hardly less important. Of mountains and rivers Asia has a lion's share. She has not, however, many lakes.

Afghanistan is strategically one of the most important states in Moslem Asia. Though a Persian word for highlander may explain the term "Afghans," Afghan chroniclers call these people Beni-Israel and claim descent from King Saul through his grandson Afghana. The country borders on Iran, the Soviet Union, Kashmir, and the Northwest Frontier Provinces and Baluchistan of Pakistan. The land rises gradually from the stony deserts in the south to the Hindu Kush in the north, a continuation of the Himalayan system called the Roof of the World. The isolation of the people is due in part to the fact that the northern spurs of these mountains present impassable barriers; some peaks reach skyward twenty-four thousand feet and even some passes present the traveler with glaciers, nineteen thousand feet above the sea. This causes the climate to vary sharply not only from season to season but from noon to night. In summer the temperature sometimes rises as high as 100 degrees, but in winter the cold is correspondingly intense; an icy wind

GRACE AND DELICACY LAVISHED ON A TOWER FOR DEFENSE

The fort has long since been deserted, and the exquisite tower stands desolate. Afghanistan is scattered with ancient forts. It was the Bactria of Alexander the Great; Tamerlane swept over it; and the old silk route between Europe and the Far East led through the perilous mountains. Sometimes caravans returned with the rose-red balas rubies of Badakhshan (part of Bactria).

6

THREE LIONS

MERCHANTS PRAY IN THE BAZAAR

The Mohammedan religion requires its followers to worship five times daily: at dawn, after noon, before the sun sets, after it has set and after the day has ended. The worshipers face in the direction of Mecca and prostrate themselves on their prayer rugs. Friday is the "day of the assembly," when the people gather in their mosques to unite in prayer.

blows down from the snow-covered mountains and whistles through the narrow valleys, while the thermometer falls below zero.

Except for the military road through Khyber Pass between Peshawar and Kabul, the traveler must follow the valleys and climb the passes by the few rough trails that exist. Much of the region has seen few outsiders since Alexander the Great marched through the country in 326 B.C. on his way to India; and traveling is rarely undertaken even by the natives save in huge camel caravans well armed against brigands.

Deep canyons gash the central highlands. There is one defile between Kabul and Herat, ninety feet in width, that is bordered on each side by fifteen-hundred-foot limestone cliffs; for the same volcanic action that upheaved the Himalayas raised this region, fold on fold of sedimentary rock. In the mountains west of Kabul there are also great boulder bed terraces left by retreating glaciers.

The Afghans have been skillful in irrigating the narrow valleys, especially in the north where the villages are half hidden in spring by the blossoms of the orchard trees. The vineyards are famous throughout Asia, and the valley of the Herat is noted for its melons. From Kandahar great caravans take fruit down to Quetta, fortified town in Baluchistan that controls the Bolan Pass. All kinds of ordinary fruits are grown, besides mangoes and pomegranates. In both the south and east two harvests are gathered; the spring crop consists of wheat, barley and lentils, the autumn crop of rice, millet, corn and tobacco. Two other products of value are asafetida and castor-oil.

Afghanistan is comparatively rich in minerals, among which are gold, silver, coal, iron and lead, while the northern part contains copper. However, no organized attempt has been made to develop these resources.

Armed caravans with cattle, horses, and pack animals laden with fruit, silk, carpets, drugs, the wool and skins of the fat-tailed sheep and articles made of camels' and goats' hair make their way to Peshawar, Lahore, Quetta and Bokhara. They bring back tea, sugar, indigo and cotton goods—if the caravan is not plundered along the way by untamed hillmen.

The highlanders do not call themselves Afghans. Certain of the tribes speak

7

Persian, others Pushtoo, a Persian language to which a number of words from other languages have been added. The most important tribes are the Durani, a people of Persian origin, who have ruled Afghanistan since 1747; the Ghilzais, a race famous for their swordsmanship, who occupy the land between Kabul and Kandahar; the Hazaras, the descendants of Tatars who came from Mongolia and who are more trustworthy than the other Afghans, as some of them enlisted in the Indian Army as sappers; the Turkish Tajiks and Uzbegs of Afghan Turkestan, the former of which are sometimes employed as domestic servants and in other subordinate positions; the Aïmaks, also of Turkish extraction, who are found on the plains of the Oxus; and the strange Kafirs of Kafiristan in the Hindu Kush. The Kafirs are the descendants of the people who claimed to be compatriots of the Greeks and who gave Alexander and his army a royal welcome.

All of these tribes, save alone the Kafirs, who are ancestor worshipers, are Mohammedans and have in common certain customs, such as blood feuds, and reprisals; but they hate and distrust one another. Though there is a king, who is aided by a Parliament, his word is law only where it is supported by the bayonets of his soldiers. The Afghans are primarily a nation of horsemen. They also breed horses and annually send hundreds to India.

As a race the Afghans are tall, with hooked noses. Their long black hair is greasy. It is said that an Afghan is washed twice—at birth and just before burial. Their religion teaches them hospitality to the guest who has eaten with them; but an expert can steal a blanket from under a sleeping man without awakening him.

The Afghans, however, have no equals at guerrilla warfare. In a country where every man carries his life in his hands naturally everyone is a soldier, though discipline, even in the regular army, is extremely bad, according to Western standards.

The national costume consists of baggy, dirty-white, pajama-like trousers, a shirt worn outside them and a waistcoat, often elaborately embroidered, over which is sometimes worn a voluminous cloak. On the head is a kullah, or skull-cap, around which is wound a turban with ends falling down the back. The poor wear nothing on their feet or sometimes grass sandals,

BLACK STAR

CLOTHES MAKE THE AFGHAN MAN

While all Afghan children are well cared for, boys are especially cherished. A wealth of colorful embroidery decorates this good-looking youngster's turban and vest. He has probably already learned to ride horseback.

EDWARDES

A GLACIER of the Chitral border shows with unusual distinctness the deep trough cut by a wide river of ice moving forward only a few feet a day. Valuable timber is obtained from pine woods that cover the lower slopes of many of these high mountains. In some parts wild gooseberries, hawthorns and roses are met with at altitudes up to nine thousand feet.

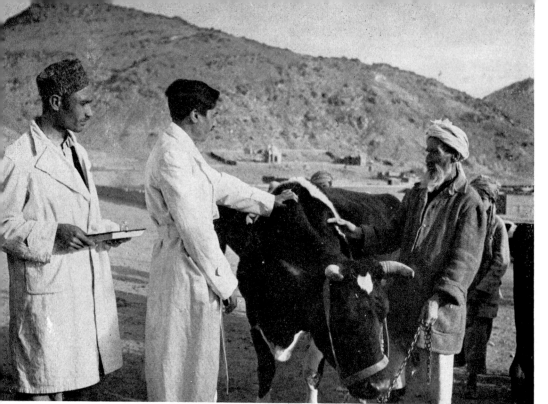

CATTLE VACCINATION—ONE STEP IN A GOOD HEALTH PROGRAM
Afghanistan's public-health program, started in 1943, was put on a sound basis in 1950 by UN advisers. Healthy cows mean germ-free milk, butter, cheese and meat.

THE WIDENED MAIN STREET IN KABUL IS COATED WITH ASPHALT
The once narrow, dark streets in Kabul have been transformed. They are now great, wide boulevards which gleam white and eerie at night under newly installed electric lights.

A TAILORED COAT OR A HOMESPUN ROBE SHUTS OUT CHILL WINDS

It was once said that to step across the disputed border from Pakistan into Afghanistan was to step back a century. Western overcoats are one of the many signs of modernization today.

11

MULLICK

FRUIT FROM KANDAHAR is sent all over Afghanistan, and even to the bazaars of Quetta, Baluchistan. The soil of Afghanistan is fertile but rainfall is scanty, so that irrigation is necessary in most parts. Each of these men wears a turban, the appearance of which is somewhat rope-like, wound around a skull-cap which is called a "kullah." This is the usual fashion among the tribes of the Afghanistan-Pakistan border. The fruit exposed for sale includes grapes, pomegranates, sugar melons and dates. The dates, however, come from Iraq, once called Mesopotamia.

AFGHAN WOMEN work very hard, and in consequence they lose their good looks at an early age. One of the hardest tasks that falls to the lot of a poor woman is that of collecting wood. Many miles of rough ground must have been covered by this woman before she gathered the unwieldy load that she bears upon her back, for the land except in the valleys is barren.

A STREET IN KABUL, CAPITAL OF LITTLE-KNOWN AFGHANISTAN

Kabul, in the fertile valley of the Kabul River in the eastern part of the Asiatic country, is hemmed in by mountains known as the Hindu Kush. Only 125 miles to the east is the historic Khyber Pass through which ancient hordes invaded India. The plains around the city are watered each spring by melting mountain snows, but winters are severely cold.

FOOD COOKED WHILE YOU WAIT IN KABUL, AFGHANISTAN

Where the summers are warm and dry and the pace is unhurried, a passer-by has time to pause and purchase food from an accommodating vendor. Afghanistan as a whole is still quite backward and undeveloped, and the only modernization that has been accomplished is in the city of Kabul. Since the turn of the century some industries have been established.

14

SKILLFUL METAL WORKERS IN THE BAZAAR AT KANDAHAR

Kandahar, a city of sixty thousand people, is the most important commercial centre of Southern Afghanistan. The Afghan, delighting in cultivating the land that he owns, despises shop-keeping. For this reason nearly all the merchants and craftsmen are foreigners from India or Persia, and the industries are not numerous.

but the wealthier classes affect richly worked leather slippers.

Outside the towns, such as Kabul, Kandahar, Herat and Ghazni, the Afghans live in fortified villages, with the local khan's or chief's, house, which usually has a high tower at one corner as the citadel and rallying point. The ordinary house is a single-story structure built of mud bricks, with a flat roof on which the family sleeps during the summer. The windows are without glass and have thick wooden shutters. The door is of rough timber and is secured at night by a heavy beam thrust through staples. No carpets cover the mud floor: a string bed or two and a pestle and mortar for grinding grain comprise the furniture. The kitchen is outdoors in a walled courtyard at the back and consists of a mud oven, a pot for boiling meat and a sheet of iron on which thin cakes of bread are baked.

Like nearly all Eastern races, the Afghans are kind to their children, of whom the boys are the more prized by the parents. Perhaps this is only natural in a land where every man is wanted for raiding or for protection against raiders and where the son must carry on the blood feuds of the father. Though elementary

STONE WATCH TOWERS, perched high upon such almost inaccessible crags, guard the passes leading into Afghanistan as well as many of the villages. Blood feuds are carried on all over the country, and the fierce mountaineers frequently raid the more peaceable villagers of the plains. Every man must, therefore, be ready to protect his property as best he can.

16

EDWARDES

IN MOUNTAINOUS KAFIRISTAN live the pagan Kafirs, about whom little is known, although it has been more or less established that they are descendants of a people who claimed kinship with the Greeks when they marched through the country to invade India. Notice how the conifers become dwarfed as the tree line ascends the frozen slopes of this rugged land.

17

education is compulsory and colleges have been founded at Kabul, the only education received by a large majority of the boys is instruction in the Koran from the village mullah, or priest.

Afghanistan is the region that dominates India's overland communications with Europe; its southeastern border is on the frontier of Pakistan. Actually there are two lines, the political boundary which is shown on maps, and an "administrative boundary" which runs irregularly about thirty miles east of the political boundary. The area between is known as tribal territory; it is governed by the tribes themselves. This has proved to be a convenient arrangement as Afghans are extremely sensitive about trespassing on their territory and the British can thus deal with raiding tribes without entering Afghanistan proper. The country is little developed as Afghans are suspicious of change. In their resistance to Western reforms, it was possible to remove Europeans from

Kabul by airplane, over forested ravines and precipices and snow-filled defiles, which have always made it easy for the Afghan mountaineers to maintain their independent ways against the inroads of civilization. In the meantime, it seems a matter for manslaughter to the Afghan Moslem who glories in his beard to be ordered to shave, while the substitution of the Western hat and trousers for the fez and the loose nether garments in which he is accustomed to sit cross-legged on the ground is an infringement of his ancient rights to which he will not be easily converted. The unveiling of his womenfolk, the forbidding of the court officials to have many wives, and the sight of his queen in Parisian short skirts was a shock ill calculated to bridge a gulf of thousands of years of conservatism in this regard. Manhood suffrage was, however, adopted as one step toward progress.

AFGHANISTAN: FACTS AND FIGURES

THE COUNTRY

Bounded on the north by the Turkmen Socialist Soviet Republic of the U.S.S.R., on the east and south by western Pakistan and on the west by Iran (Persia). The area is 250,000 square miles. The population, according to the latest Afghan estimate, is about 11,000,000.

GOVERNMENT

Since 1922, the government has been a constitutional monarchy with legislative power vested in a Parliament which consists of a king, a Senate and an Assembly. The Senate is made up of a maximum of 50 members nominated for life by the king; the Assembly of 171 members who are elected. The country is divided into 7 major and 3 minor provinces, each of which is under a governor. In 1926, the title of King instead of Amir was adopted.

COMMERCE AND INDUSTRIES

Most of the country is mountainous, but the fertile plains yield well with the assistance of irrigation. Two crops a year are harvested, one in autumn consisting of rice, millet and corn and the other in spring consisting of wheat, barley, peas and beans. Fruit and vegetables are abundant. Fat-tailed sheep furnish the chief meat diet. The fat of the tail is used as a substitute for butter, and the wool is the principal export. Horses, camels and goats are raised also. Minerals include copper, lead, iron, coal, gold and lapis lazuli. The chief industries are manufactures of silk, felts, carpets and articles from camels' and goats' hair. Exports, chiefly to India and Pakistan, are raw wool, manufactured woolen piece goods, fruits, vegetables, asafetida and other drugs, spices, cattle and hides, and the imports are cotton goods, indigo and dyeing material, sugar, tea, hardware and leather.

COMMUNICATIONS

There are no railways in the country, and there are practically no navigable rivers. Merchandise is carried by camel and pony on government trade routes. In the larger towns, there is telephone and telegraph service.

RELIGION AND EDUCATION

Nearly all of the people are Sunni Mohammedans. Elementary education is free and there are various special schools for higher education. Kabul has a university.

CHIEF TOWNS

Populations (estimated): Kabul, the capital, 206,208; Kandahar, 77,186; Herat, 75,632; Mazar-i-Sharif, 41,960; Jalalabad, 14,756.

India and Pakistan

Modern States in an Ancient Land

The subcontinent of India has drawn travelers to its rich shores for centuries. Men of war and men of peace have hurried there expecting wealth. They found glittering riches indeed—the fabulous diamonds of Golconda—side by side with cruel poverty. The ancient land has ever been one of extremes. There are soaring peaks in the north and vast plains farther south. There are jagged highlands and hills worn smooth by centuries of traffic. There are both soggy marshes, steaming jungles and arid fields, bone-dry deserts. No spot on earth receives so much rain as Assam, in the northeast; hardly any other receives so little as the broad desert of the Sind. The heart of almost every city is within a day's journey of jungle or desert or mountain. On the outskirts of Calcutta, wild beasts prey on man and his livestock, though trolley cars rattle less than a mile away. The contrasts are never ending in this home of two new states—Pakistan and India.

THE land of "purple Indian dusk, with its scent of sandal, incense and musk," of which Lawrence Hope has musically written, is the home of teeming millions of brown people who have only recently tasted the fruits of independence after centuries of foreign rule. For it is only since 1947 that the country has been divided into separate independent states. The largest and most populated is India; its people are mostly of the Hindu religion. The other, Pakistan, is split into two sections, with east and west more than a thousand miles apart. Mohammedanism is the principal religion of Pakistan. Though independent, each state remains a part of the Commonwealth of Nations.

India has been a ground of promise for hundreds of years. Before Columbus searched for the land of spices, it was India's fertile river valleys that tempted the Asiatic hordes from the arid regions beyond the Himalayas.

Before one can fully appreciate India's history, her people, her religion and her importance in the careful balance of world affairs, one must remember her geography. The middle one of three Asiatic peninsulas jutting southward, it is a country as large as continental Europe without Russia. For ages its natural barriers of high mountain wall and stormy tropic seas largely protected it from the influence of the rest of Asia.

Beyond the double mountain wall of the world's highest range lies the tableland of Tibet, on the east, with Afghanistan on the west just north of the Baluchistan States. Off the southern tip of the triangle that dips between the Bay of Bengal and the Arabian Sea lies the former Crown Colony of Ceylon, now a dominion of the British Empire. To the east lies Burma, which has become an independent republic.

India is divided into three regions geographically, that of the Himalayan highlands, that of the great river plains of Upper India, fertile with the silt brought down for centuries by the great Himalayan rivers, and that of the broken tableland or the Deccan of Central and Southern India. The one somewhat irregular wet season depends almost altogether on the southwestern monsoons or trade winds bearing moisture and discharging it along the Western Ghats and the eastern Himalayas. The latter region probably gets the heaviest rainfall in the world. For India has contrasts as sharp as those between arid Baluchistan and water-logged Bengal. During the winter months the winds are generally northeasterly and the weather prevailingly dry and clear. As summer approaches, the winds change; they come for long distances from over the Indian Ocean and arrive laden with moisture; and an early summer gives way to steaming humidity. These seasonal winds are the monsoons. When the rainfall is light, as in two areas in the south and northwest, there is famine, though a vast system of irrigation now reaches forty million acres in various parts of

THE PEARL PALACE of the Maharaja Sindhia of Gwalior stands in the middle of a beautiful park known to the natives as the Phul Bagh, which means the Garden of Flowers. The palace, with its massive buildings, its pavilions, pleasure grounds and ornamental lakes, is a residence worthy of the ruler of a native state so important as Gwalior. Within its walls are five old palaces, some of which were once of the greatest magnificence. This photograph was taken from the huge fortress which, perched on its high rock, frowns over and offers protection to the town of Gwalior.

THE FORTRESS OF DAULATABAD, the ancient Deoghur, stands in the territory of the Nizam of Hyderabad. It was built in the thirteenth century, and its defences were impregnable. The fort crowns an isolated granite rock, the sides of which have been made perpendicular to a height of a hundred feet all around. On the encircling plain beneath, one will find six lines of stone walls, and the bridge over the great moat leads to a passage cut through the rock. On the summit stands a pavilion and the citadel, which is reached by a flight of exactly one hundred steps.

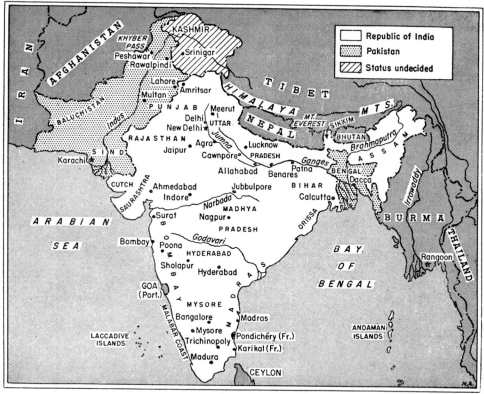

INDIA, RELIC OF AN OLD CONTINENT AND A VANISHED SEA

India. On the other hand, Bengal, Bihar and Orissa in eastern India suffer rather from flood and cyclone. At Darjeeling, the health resort of the hills, the rainfall ranges from 122 inches to the extraordinary figure of 229 a year and is even heavier on the lower Himalayas; and during freshets the eastern rice swamps become veritable fresh-water seas.

The Himalayas, rising in many peaks over twenty thousand feet in height, form a northern wall over which the ancient trade routes could advance only at certain high passes. Bolan Pass and a few others are still the gateway into Afghanistan, thence to remoter regions such as Russia. These mountains, peopled by certain Mongolian tribes, send down rainfall from both their northern and their southern slopes to the plains of India. Up in the northern tip, where the ranges bend almost like the top of a diamond, lies the Vale of Kashmir, and high in the eastern Himalayas, the independent states of Nepal and Bhutan. The river plains of northern India, wa-

tered by the rivers from the mountains, are rich with the deep alluvial loam and silt left by the receding waters that once covered all these lowlands.

Here was the theater of the ancient race movements, here still live representatives of the Aryan race, and here today exist the most densely populated provinces. These plains—including the Punjab, Sind, Rajasthan, Uttar Pradesh (the old United Provinces), Bengal, Assam—are watered by three great river systems. The tributaries of the Indus and the Sutlej start westward through the mountains, the Brahmaputra flows eastward, while the third river drains the southern slopes before it becomes the mighty Ganges. The Indo-Gangetic plain varies in width from ninety to three hundred miles.

It is the triangular tableland of the peninsula that has been the arena of the long struggle between the Aryans from the north and the aboriginal Dravidians now largely confined to the south. This Deccan region is tropical and is bounded on the

22

north by jungle-clad hills, while its sides are hemmed off from the ocean by the western Ghats, whose rivers flow across the peninsula to outlets through the more broken eastern Ghats. The Deccan includes the Central Provinces, Berar, Madras, Bombay and Hyderabad.

Everywhere in India there are tigers, though the big cats are now rare on the plains. They frequent the haunts of the deer and the wild hog, though they prey upon domestic cattle and occasionally one develops a taste for human flesh. Lions are rare, but leopards are common, as are the cheetahs used in hunting. Wolves are plentiful. There are several species of bears, and the disgusting hyena is rather common.

Elephants, which are found everywhere save in the extreme northwest, favor the hills, especially in the region stretching through Assam. Unfortunately, those in the Deccan have in times past not been protected by any game law; but now every-

where in India elephants are a government monopoly, for the docile great beasts are extensively used in the timber trade and in government transport. The rhinoceros is found chiefly in the eastern section. In the desert, camels are used and in many parts of India, domesticated wild asses are ridden by the natives.

India has a humped cow, and the gentle bulls that roam the city streets are objects of veneration not to be molested even when they block the traffic. The bison of the hills of the northeast frontier are domesticated for sacrificial purposes by the aboriginal tribes. Water buffaloes haunt the swamps, wild hogs come foraying from the jungle gloom, and there is a mongrel dog, the pariah, that runs wild, since no true Hindu will take life in any form. For the same reason the serpents, which find a fat menu in the billions of rats of all kinds, hang undisturbed from the forest trees, swarm into the village gardens and during the rainy season even crawl into

Manley

INDIAN POTTER MAKING FUNERAL POTS UPON HIS WHEEL

The potter often travels from village to village in India, supplying the needs of the people.
His vessels—selling for a penny or two for a penny—serve as urns in Hindu funeral services.
For cooking and eating purposes brassware is much more widely in use than the jugs and the
plates of the potter, yet he still manages to eke out a living from his travels and work.

SPLENDID SOLDIERS, such as these Marathas or Mahrattas of central and western India, in the seventeenth and eighteenth centuries conquered a number of states later under British rule. They were defeated by the British in 1803 and again in the war of 1816-18. The Marathas are a handsome group of Hindus and number around twelve million.

24

native dwellings unmolested. Most of these snakes are harmless to mankind, but the hooded cobra is deadly. Luckily it is industrious in reducing the numbers of the bandicoot, a three-pound rat highly destructive to crops. Resourceful monkeys chatter through the jungles.

Of the various deer, the sambhar and the antelope of the salt plains of the coast are the most numerous. In the high Himalayas an ibex, the barhal, or blue sheep, and a goat closely related to the chamois are important to native industries. Reddish wolves infest the open country, jackals yell hideously at night and packs of dholes, or wild dogs, hunt silently through the jungles. Crocodiles menace the ceremonial bather of the rivers. Fresh-water fish, especially carp and catfish, are so abundant as to be a staple food of the rice-eating natives. The English sportsman's favorite is a salmon-like species of barbel.

Peacocks, Parrots and Falcons

Of birds, there are numerous waterfowl and game birds, but when one thinks of India one thinks first of the parrots that flash colorfully through the jungle, the peacocks that strut in palace grounds and the herons that watch the streams for fish. There are several species of vultures, and many of eagles and falcons. The natives cage a sort of starling, the maina, that can be taught to say "Rama." Noxious insects, mosquitos or scorpions, according to the humidity of the region, and at times clouds of destructive locusts may be added to the debit side of India's wild life, and on the credit side the silkworm and the insect that produces lac.

Save in the mountains, we have a climate too hot, much of the year, for white men—too hot even for the natives to court exertion—but also a country wherein there is no need for man to exert himself to any great extent for food and shelter. Thus there is time for intricate religious observances. The fatalistic tendency has flourished in a country where the battle with the violences of nature has often been a losing one. As lately as 1905, a severe earthquake in Northern India caused the loss of between three and four thousand human lives. Two factors remain to be mentioned, the rigid caste system, by which the early Aryan conquerors have for the most part preserved their racial integrity, and the inharmonious element of the Mohammedan invaders whose religion is a militant one and diametrically opposed to the prevailing Hinduism.

Fair-skinned Aryan Conquerors

The race originally inhabiting this sub-tropical country was the stocky, flat-nosed, dark-skinned Dravidian. Long before the time of Christ, there came pioneering into Northern India, through the high and difficult passes of the Himalayas, conquering hordes of tall, fine-nosed, comparatively fair-skinned Aryans of the same stock from which sprang the races of Europe. For long ages the mountain wall and the stormy nature of the seas that sweep the remaining sides of the somewhat diamond-shaped country kept India to herself, save for the armies of Alexander, a few Chinese pilgrims and fierce invaders from the Mohammedan nations of the Middle East. The Mohammedan conquerors founded the Mogul Empire in the sixteenth century. But their power waned a century later when the trading empires of Europe set up strong colonies in India. Of the European nations, England was the most successful. Rule of her colonies was vested in the East India Trading Company until 1858. In that year rule was taken over by the Government in London. A regent of the Crown ruled in Delhi until 1947 when the two independent states, India and Pakistan, were created.

Land of the Five Rivers

Agriculture has always been the essential industry. The fertile plains of the five rivers, rich but requiring irrigation, have ever since been the bone of contention with invaders. Yet prior to the development of good roads the Punjab has been hemmed about on three sides by regions that offered no market for surplus produce and from which, in times of drought and famine elsewhere, no food supplies could be obtained. There has, however, always been travel via the Jumna and Indus.

THE DANCING GIRLS execute intricate movements without apparent effort, but the smooth flow of the steps is really the result of long training. The dances are usually in a slow rhythm and every gesture has a meaning, even the flick of a single finger. One performance is supposed to represent incidents in the life of Krishna, considered by the Hindus as the incarnation of God and worshiped as invincible in war and love. With his worship are associated brilliant color, the perfume of flowers, milk and honey and all things joyous.

CHARANS, village girls who perform folk dances and sometimes sing in the streets in various places in northern India. The slap of their sticks and the jangle of their many bracelets make a gay accompaniment; and the glint of metal, gauzy saris and widespreading skirts in all the hues of the rainbow add vibrant color to their graceful movements. Dancing of various kinds has always played an important part in the lives of the Indian people.

THE HEAD BOATMEN OF THE RAJAH OF MANIPUR

Attired in their national dress, with egrets in their turbans to indicate the prestige of their calling, these boatmen are ready for the annual water festival. Manipur, a northeast frontier state, has a caste system of its own, founded chiefly on a system of forced labor which has been abolished by the British. Their women hold an unusually high position.

The Punjab has a complex civilization. The majority of the Aryan invaders settled in the Punjab. Tribal feeling was strong, resulting in the early days in a joint ownership of the villages. Even today ninety per cent of the population live in villages where the communities are governed by a committee of elders and a village assembly. In these villages Hinduism arose with a caste system and rules of ritual but there have been several offshoots from the stem. The Mohammedan invaders came offering their faith with the sword, a faith that held the equality of all believers and substituted for idols, One Great God Allah. They made converts to Islam of most of the agricultural tribes of the western Punjab. Later the Sikhs, a church militant, developed from Hindu monotheism.

For a number of years India was fairly quiet under British rule. Discontent was growing, however, especially among the Indians who were educated in England, because the Indians had so little to say in how they were governed. The conflict between the Indians and the British became much sharper after World War I.

In the beginning Hindus and Moslems worked together, but later the Moslems withdrew from the group effort and began to demand a separate state, Pakistan.

Rodd

PROUD OLD CHIEFTAIN OF SIND WITH TWO OF HIS ATTENDANTS

More than half of the inhabitants of Sind, a province of Pakistan, are Mohammedans, easily distinguished from the Hindus by their dress and by the fact that the men usually wear turbans of a special pattern. With his symbolic turban and dignified bearing, this Mohammedan chief is a figure of importance.

At last, in August 1947, India became self-governing, though divided into two states along religious lines. In general, Pakistan includes the northeastern and northwestern portions of the Indian triangle; and the Union of India, the part that lies between. Both Pakistan and the Republic of India are members of the Commonwealth of Nations.

Let us now inspect the splendors of costume and architecture that would interest the tourist. To see the great Indian princes in their elaborate palaces, attended by fan-bearers and jeweled courtiers, makes us think that we might have been carried away on some magic carpet to the far-off times of the Arabian Nights.

One night in Mysore, the palace of the Maharaja was one bewildering mass of electricity. Every window and doorway was outlined, every tower and dome and turret was pricked out with those little white lights—there seemed to be myriads of them. All around the square before the palace were the buildings of the government, and they also were ablaze with

29

STONEWORK in the vast palace of Shah Jehan at Delhi. The work is so artistically inlaid that it gives the impression of painting, and Persian verses are inscribed in it. The magnificent building was once the residence of the Mogul Emperor's chief wife. As an empress, she had her own retinue of servants and guards, befitting her rank.

30

COMYN

FLORAL DESIGNS made of precious stones cover the marble pillars and arches of the Hall of Private Audience at Delhi. Here, among other priceless treasures, once stood the splendid Peacock Throne, on whose back two outspread peacocks' tails were worked in their natural colors in jewels. Through one of the arches of the Hall we see the Pearl Mosque

31

ORIENTAL SPLENDOR OF THE PROGRESS OF THE MAHARAJA OF GWALIOR THROUGH HIS CAPITAL

A column of armed men and elephants hung with rich trappings march in the royal procession of the Maharaja Sindhia of Gwalior, who himself rides in a carved howdah covered with gold and silks, borne on the back of an elephant. In this photograph we see his loyal, pageant-loving subjects crowding their balconies and the street known as the Sarafa, or merchants' quarter, in Lashkar, the capital of the state oí Gwalior. Lashkar is a modern city that has grown up near the old town of Gwalior, famous for its Jain and Hindu antiquities.

SUN-LOVING MAHA WOMEN AT THEIR HOUSEHOLD TASKS

The Mahas, who live in the Maratha country west of Central India, are privileged because their ancestors helped an emperor of olden times. They receive free bread every day, collect taxes and act as government messengers. The figures on the right of the door of this hut are for purposes of the Indian census.

Walker

BARE LIVING-ROOM OF A LOW CASTE FAMILY OF NORTH INDIA

There is little comfort in this Indian home. Behind the low wall against which the husband leans, smoking his native pipe, the household sleeps. The door behind the veiled wife, who is sifting grain, leads to the only other room in the house. The front is an ordinary oven commonly used all over India, by rich and poor alike.

BOURNE & SHEPHERD

AN EXECUTIONER of a maharaja's court in the days when the princes of India had absolute power of life and death over their subjects. This giant of a man must have been a terrifying figure, his bulk made even greater by armor studded with sharp spikes. His shield and curved sword must also have been wielded mightily in hand-to-hand combat.

34

PATHAN TRIBESMEN, men of the Afghan race, lovers of warfare and desperadoes, have long been a source of trouble on the mountainous northwest frontier of India. If attacked, they retire to their wild mountains. Because of their excellent marksmanship and skill in primitive warfare they are sometimes a match for the better armed attacking party.

Bushby

FRUIT AND VEGETABLES IN TEMPTING HEAPS ON THE STALLS OF AN OPEN-AIR MARKET IN OLD DELHI

Old Delhi (the capital, New Delhi, is located near by), with something like a half million people, has developed into a flourishing commercial city. Not only are its thronged bazaars and its craftsmen, celebrated for their work in ivory, wood and precious metals, a source of real prosperity, but biscuit and sugar factories, cotton and flour mills have been built. A residential university was established at Delhi in 1922, and there are about sixty newspapers and periodicals published in this important centre. We see above a tempting open-air market.

AN INDIAN MILKMAN ON HIS WAY TO MARKET

A crude trestle arrangement is rigged on the donkey's back so that the large brass jars are balanced on either side.   In the market places of many villages, milk is sold directly from such open vessels.   Those who buy bring their own containers.   Almost everywhere in India there are cattle, used for milk or as beasts of burden, not for meat.

DELHI'S GREAT MOSQUE, the Jama Masjid, is one of the largest mosques in all the Islamic world. Three domes of white marble rise from the roof. The two minarets are 130 feet in height, and from them a wonderful view of the entire city can be obtained. In days long ago, the huge doors of the main gateway were opened only to admit the Mogul emperors, and they are used now only on state occasions and by personages of great prestige; other visitors may enter only by the wicket. The mosque was built by Shah Jehan in the seventeenth century.

38

AT ALWAR, beside the still waters of the tank, is the marble cenotaph of a former maharaja of the tiny native state of Alwar. Blue pigeons flutter around the buildings, and gorgeous peacocks strut about the stone pavements. Children play upon the steps leading down to the water, while their elders gossip in the shade of one of the pavilions.

39

lights. The big square was crowded with thousands of people waiting cross-legged on the ground for a torchlight procession. It was a long wait—Orientals are never in a hurry. At last we caught the sound of music, and the procession entered the square.

A Maharaja's Gorgeous Retinue

There were companies of Indian soldiers in uniform, the Maharaja's own cavalry in white and gold and huge turbans, with leopard skins thrown over their saddle-bows; next camels striding along with noiseless tread; elephants, one behind another, their howdahs flashing with bright colors. At last came the Maharaja of Mysore dressed from head to foot in garments of cloth-of-gold, his necklaces worth a king's ransom and his silk turban brilliant with diamonds. How proud his elephant looked, as with stately tread he bore his master to the door of the palace! Then he paused, a ladder was placed by the attendants, and amid cheers the Maharaja alighted.

Many ruling princes of India have been incredibly wealthy. The Gaekwar of Baroda had a diamond necklace—almost a breastplate of gems. One of the diamonds was said to be among the largest in the world. Scores of others were the size of marbles. Nor was this by any means his most valuable necklace.

Splendor on a Budget

Powerful, indeed, were some of these princes. They were practically kings in their own dominions, though all of them recognized the British king as their overlord. They made their own laws, raised their own taxes, had their own prime ministers and Cabinet officers. Now the princely states have become parts of either India or Pakistan. Yet the rajas are supported by state grants of money. Their dignity and wealth have been respected and maintained.

Often the splendor of the rajas' palaces and retinues had been matched by their talents for efficient government. Such men now play important roles in the affairs of the new states.

The palace of the Maharaja of Gwalior stands amid groves and lakes in a park, most of which has been opened to the people of the district. Within the palace are lustrous Oriental rugs and rich tapestries, and other objects of art. There is a narrow gauge railway on the estate, as well as stables of horses and elephants and a fleet of motor cars. Another prince, the Maharajadhiraj of Darbhanga, has a private airfield on his estate in the province of Bihar.

Fond of Dazzling Spectacles

The Indian princes love display and often go about attended by companies of men in medieval dress or ancient armor. One of the spectacular scenes India witnessed in our century took place in Delhi in 1902. It was the great Durbar at which the Viceroy proclaimed Edward VII Emperor of all India. All the ruling princes were present, every one of them eager to outshine his rivals. The spectacle was dazzling. Proudly the slow procession of elephants, the largest India could produce, passed along the streets.

Some of them were covered with cloth-of-gold and ropes of pearls, others with dazzling emerald or crimson. The princes who rode upon those elephants were descendants of long lines of kings who had ruled great peoples, built up kingdoms and sometimes lost them, and created palaces and temples that rank among the most wonderful in the world.

More than nine hundred years ago, the Mohammedan hosts, led by Mahmud of Ghazni, called Mahmud the Great, burst through Khyber Pass. With green banners waving and the shouts of "Allah Akbar!" (God is Great) echoing from the crags, they swept through the defiles into India. During thirty years, Mahmud invaded India a dozen times or more. The Hindus fought bravely, but city after city was taken. Sometimes Indian women threw themselves into the burning ruins of their houses to save themselves from falling into the hands of the enemy. Mahmud, having thus spread the teachings of Islam by the sword, destroyed idols and overthrew temples wherever he went.

THESE OFFICERS are recognizable as members of the Sikh religion (founded in the 15th century) by their uncut beards, the ends of which are hidden by their turbans. The Sikhs, a Punjab religious community, are forbidden by their religion to cut their hair. The Punjab was annexed to British India following the submission of the Sikhs in 1848.

WADING THROUGH SALT

These salt beds are in Pakistan, near Karachi, the capital. The formation of such beds is a curious phenomenon of nature. Nearly all rock contains some sodium, which, as the rocks decay, is carried by running waters to the ocean or a lake. If the lake has no outlet, and is in a dry region where evaporation is great, eventually the salt forms deposits as shown above.

THIS IS INDIA BROADCASTING!

The very modern All India Radio Building above is one of the most attractive structures in the symmetrically laid out city of New Delhi. Founded in 1912, the city was built at the order of King George V as the administrative center of India. Its architecture is largely the work of Sir Edwin Lutyens and Sir Herbert Baker. It is now the government center of the new republic.

But as these first Mohammedans captured kingdoms in India and settled down in them, other Islamite conquerors swept through the passes and attacked them. States rose and fell; men were invaders one year, monarchs the next and fugitives the next. Until less than a century ago there was always war going on in some part of India.

These monarchs built themselves great castles. Wherever in North India we find a high, steep hill there are usually the ruins of some fortress on the top. One of these great fortresses was at Daulatabad in the Deccan. The steep sides of the round hill have been made perpendicular by being cut away at the base so as to form an encircling precipice. This is over one hundred feet high—a sheer wall of rock. Below this is a rock-hewn moat forty feet wide, and on the surrounding level plain there are six lines of high stone walls encircling the place and enclosing courtyards with barracks and stables for the horses and elephants.

Before every wall there is a moat. If invaders managed to force their way over the six moats and through those six walls—all stoutly defended by men and elephants—they at last found themselves before the great wall of rock that encircles the lofty citadel. To this there is only one entrance —a narrow bridge across the chasm, then a rock-hewn doorway into which only two men can enter abreast. Within, narrow stairways and passages are hewn out of the solid rock, up which the enemy would have to stumble in darkness—unless they had torches, which the defenders would strive to extinguish. Up they would climb harassed by showers of arrows and spears from defensive chambers cunningly cut in the rock.

Manley

CHILD OF A WANDERING BALUCHI TRIBE

This boy, who wears a charm around his neck to protect him from evil, is of the nomadic tribes of the mountains of Baluchistan. Being a Mussulman, he has to wear some form of trousers, *pa'ejámas*, in Persian.

If at last the invaders reached the place where the rock-hewn steps emerged upon the hilltop, they would find the only opening covered by a high iron door made redhot by a fire kept burning above it! The hill at that time must have been an impregnable fortress. On the lofty summit are some of the palace buildings in a nearly perfect state of preservation. At his imperial city of Agra, south of Delhi, the Mogul Emperor Akbar built a huge castle on the level plain. Its massive red sandstone walls are over a mile around.

THE HALL OF PRIVATE AUDIENCE, with its white marble arches and pillars inlaid with precious stones, shown above, is the most splendid of the many buildings contained in the fortress-palace built at Delhi by Shah Jehan, under whose reign, 1628-58, the Mogul or Mohammedan Tartar empire reached its height of magnificence. Shah Jehan held his architects in high esteem. He was evidently most proud of this audience chamber, since around the hall these words are carved: "If a Paradise be on the face of the earth, it is this, it is this, it is this."

THE TAJ MAHAL, near the city of Agra, is a 17th century tomb which took twenty-two years to complete. Precious stones have been inlaid the Emperor Shah Jehan erected for his favorite wife. It is considered in portions of the building and the tombs, the marble dome, walls to be the most beautiful building in all India. Leading up to the main and minarets, as the picture shows, **rest** on a **platform** of white marble entrance is a marble water-course lined with cypresses. The building eighteen feet high. The name Taj Mahal means "Gem of Buildings."

45

STATELY LAKSHMI VILAS PALACE OF THE GAEKWAR OF BARODA

This new palace of the ruler of Baroda, called locally the Gaekwar, is built in European style—which shows how the princes of India are being influenced by Western ideas. Although magnificent in its own way, the building differs greatly from other Eastern palaces, as, for instance, the elaborate royal dwelling at Mysore shown elsewhere.

Akbar's grandson, the famous Shah Jehan, turned the fort at Agra into a palace, building within its walls pavilions of snowy marble. In these courts of the harem there are huge screen walls of filigree work of marvelous delicacy, carved in solid marble, through which the imperial ladies could look out without themselves being seen. The bathing chamber is partly underground and all the light filters through a crystal cascade that flows down transparent steps into a marble bath, and is, in turn, reflected in the thousands of tiny bits of looking-glass with which the walls are covered.

But even this palace did not satisfy Shah Jehan. He resolved to build himself a new capital at Delhi and to embellish it with a palace such as the world had never seen. What remains of that palace to-day, especially the Hall of Private Audience, is enough to fill us with wonder.

It is a garden-pavilion built of white marble inlaid with precious stones. The original ceiling of solid silver has been stolen, but the frieze around it still bears the Persian inscription, "If a Paradise be on the face of the earth, it is this, it is this." In this chamber, nearly three centuries ago, Shah Jehan used to sit on his famous Peacock Throne.

It was in the form of two peacocks made of solid gold, their tails inlaid with emeralds. Above that throne was a canopy of cloth-of-gold fringed with pearls and supported by twelve golden pillars decorated with gems. The throne was taken from Delhi in 1739 by Nadir Shah, the robber chieftain of Persia, after he had captured the city.

But Shah Jehan built an even more beautiful building. His favorite wife died, and in his grief he resolved to build for her the loveliest tomb man's eyes had ever beheld. On the banks of the River Jumna, two miles below Agra, his engineers and artificers created one of the wonders of the world—the Taj Mahal. Companies of elephants brought the marble blocks, and for years the most skillful

46

MAGNIFICENCE OF THE MAHARAJA'S PALACE AT MYSORE

From all parts of the city of Mysore can be seen the golden cupola of the palace. The ornate structure is built inside a fort surrounded by a moat. In the palace is the hall in which the Maharaja, seated on his wonderful throne of ivory, silver and gold, showed himself to his people. The Maharaja of Mysore, reputedly the richest man in the world, died in 1940.

47

RUINED BIJAPUR, in Southern India, the capital of an independent kingdom for two hundred years, was originally called the City of Victory. The walls enclosing the town are about six miles in length, and inside these is the citadel. On some of the bastions are huge old guns. One, called Lord of the Battle Plain, is fourteen feet long. The mausoleum of the Mahomed

48

Adil Shahi can boast, in its great hall, the largest domed space in the world. After the city had been captured by the Mogul Emperor Aurang-zeb, of Hindustan, the third son of Shah Jehan, who supplanted his father, the buildings fell into the picturesque ruin shown above — until the British made it the capital of the district in 1883.

craftsmen expended on the building the finest work of which they were capable. At length the day came when the last scaffolding was removed and the Taj. stood out in all its loveliness. Shah Jehan, when an old and broken man, died with his eyes fixed upon it; and for ages to come men who love beauty will never be weary of gazing at it. "Go to India," said the great soldier, Lord Roberts. "The Taj alone is worth the journey."

To visit it, we would drive through long avenues of trees to a massive gateway that leads to the outer court. Around that court are red sandstone mosques. To the left is a gateway of sandstone inlaid with marbles and glazed tiles. Suppose we ascend the broad steps to the terrace before the gateway: instantly, through the arch, there opens out before us a vista of surpassing loveliness. The snowy mass of domes and minarets rises above greenblack cypress trees and marble water courses in a vision of loveliness. The monument stands in a tenacre garden, around which reaches, like a red sandstone wall, a succession of rest houses where pilgrims from a distance may find shelter for the night. Peacocks trail their gorgeous tails across the greensward. Now let us walk along those white marble paths beside

Rodd

BALUCHI OF A NOBLE FAMILY

With his coat embroidered with gold, his sword and his military bearing, this son of a chieftain of one of the leading tribes of Baluchistan makes a fine figure.

the lotus pools with their playing fountains. In the morning sunlight the Taj Mahal is dazzling. Within, a cool green light filters in through the marble work. Not a footstep is heard, for every visitor must leave his shoes outside. In the centre of the floor is the white marble cenotaph of the royal wife, and beside it, that of Shah Jehan. Their coffins lie in the marblevaulted chamber below. Around the cenotaphs is a screen that looks like marble lace.

At noon, the Taj is dazzling white; as the sun sinks toward the west it becomes golden, pink and crimson in succession, while the opposite side is bathed in purple shadow. When twilight deepens into night, the moon reveals new beauties: the Taj becomes a silver casket glistening with gems—a masterpiece by the artists of old India.

The palace at Udaipur has several arches reminiscent of the fabulous wealth of India's princes; for here some of them used to have themselves weighed with bags of gold and silver, which they would afterward give away, as the balance. But for every wealthy nobleman of this land of contrasts, there are hundreds of beggars: for every tinted palace there are thousands of wretched huts. Yet high or low, all are colorful.

INDIA'S SACRED PLACES

Its Marvelous Temples and Stately Mosques

Religion plays a large part in the daily lives of many of the people of India and Pakistan. The chief faith of those in the Republic of India is Hinduism; in Pakistan, it is Mohammedanism. There are also smaller religious groups: Sikhs, Jains, Parsees, Buddhists, as well as some Jews and Christians. In certain country districts, there are tribal religions. Each faith has its houses of worship—temple, mosque or church—many of them magnificent examples of architecture; and there are also a number of holy cities. This chapter deals with these sacred places, some of which were built long centuries ago.

ABOVE all other lands, India is famous for her mosques and temples. The temples are largely, though not wholly, those of the Hindus, the religion that claims over two-thirds of the people of India. The mosques are those of the Mohammedans, who number more than one-fifth of a total population of nearly four hundred million people.

The word Hindu was originally used by the Persians to indicate the dwellers along the River Shindhu (Indus), but has come to denote the modern phase of the varied social and religious institutions of India, with their rigid caste system and the bewildering distinctions as to the "twice-born" and the clean and unclean.

Jainism and Sikhism are religions that have developed from Hinduism. Mohammedanism is similar in many ways to the religion of the Hebrews. Buddhism challenged Hinduism for a thousand years; but after its golden age, in the third century B.C., under Asoka, it gradually declined. One can the better comprehend how the Hindu caste system was fostered when one recalls that, as the tall, fair-skinned, fine-nosed Aryan immigrants came in contact with, and subdued, the dark-skinned race it found dwelling on the northern plains, the need of preserving its racial type would have brought about severe restrictions as to intermarriage. Indeed, the Aryan type is still to be found (pigmented by the sun of many generations) in the northwest, in Kashmir, the Punjab and Rajputana. In Middle India, however, in the valleys of the Jumna and the Ganges, one finds in the lower social orders a considerable admixture of Dra-

vidian stock, while in Southern India the short, dark-skinned, broad-nosed Dravidian predominates. Incidentally, while these southern Dravidians theoretically acknowledge Siva and Vishnu, in practice they worship their village deities, often with the sacrifice of animals.

To return to Hindu belief: detachment from the world and the practice of renunciation and self-restraint are held to be conducive to a state of ecstatic communion with God. Indeed, Siva is called the great ascetic. But the rites of certain sects are erotic. Sanskrit is the language of the Hindu scriptures and it is interesting to reflect that the Sanskrit word, "varna," for caste, also means color.

In making a mental tour of India's sacred places, suppose we begin with the southern tip of the peninsula. From Ceylon one can approach by a train that crosses the causeways and bridges built across the sand-banks and coral reefs, which with the aid of a short ferry link up the chain of islets. On one of these small islands, known as Adam's Bridge, is a large Indian temple with colonnades of thousands of carved stone pillars and high towers. The Hindu sacred books tell how, long, long ago, a vast army of monkeys threw stones into the sea, built a causeway from India to Ceylon, and fought on it a mighty battle to help Prince Rama against his foes. The islets and reefs across the strait are said to be the ruins of that causeway, and this temple was built to commemorate the event.

The temple of Madura, on the mainland, which has a massive outer wall more than a mile long, contains a large

51

UPON SATRUNJAYA, the Holy Mountain at Palitana in Kathiawar, a peninsula of western India, stand eleven groups of Jain temples, each group of which is enclosed by a high battlemented wall. There are over five hundred temples and shrines in this city of the gods. The oldest buildings date from about the eleventh century. There are only about 1,250,000 Jains in India, but many of them are wealthy, and their temples are famous for their magnificence. The members of this religion will not take life in any form, if they can possibly avoid doing so.

© E. N. A.

52

AT SRIRANGAM, near Trichinopoli, is this great Hindu temple of Vishnu, undoubtedly the largest in the world. It has fifteen of the elaborately decorated towers such as we see in the photograph and seven large courts, one within another. In one court is the famous Hall of a Thousand Pillars, though the number is not quite correct. There are really about 940.

WITHIN THE HUGE CAVE-TEMPLE AT KARLI: INDIA'S FINEST BUDDHIST SHRINE

The plan of this edifice somewhat resembles that of a Christian church. Fifteen pillars hewn from the solid rock line each side of the nave. The capitals of these pillars show kneeling elephants with two figures upon the back of each. In the photograph we can see the wooden rafters, which are as old as the temple itself. Buddha is symbolically represented by the rock-hewn stupa at the end of the nave. At one time the temple glowed with banners hung from the roof, lamps set around the shrine beyond the pillars and the yellow robes of monks.

ENTRANCE TO THE KAILASA TEMPLE CAVE, ELLORA

Ellora, a village near Aurungabad city, is remarkable for its thirty-four cave temples, carved from the solid rock. One of the most majestic is the Kailasa Temple, lavishly adorned with statues of Siva, Vishnu, Lakshmi and other Indian deities. The courtyard is 156 feet wide and 276 feet long. The temple was built by order of Krishna I, who reigned from 760 to 783.

tank, "the Lake of the Golden Lotus," in which worshipers bathe. The pilgrims congregate on the long flights of granite steps that lead down to the water, and here perform their devotions, some reading the sacred books or sitting in silent meditation. Not far away is the holy of holies, a chamber in which is the image of the great god Siva. Europeans are not allowed to enter this chamber, but standing near the entrance one may catch a glimpse of the lamps burning around the image. One traveler bribed a priest to allow him to climb to the top of one of the high towers. He had to take off his shoes and leave them at the bottom. The stone passages were dark and infested with bats. But from the top, where he looked down on the vast temple below, he viewed its open courts shaded by palm trees, its labyrinths of colonnades, the square tank, the golden domes over the

THE JAMA MASJID at Ahmadabad, a city that was once the greatest in western India, is one of the loveliest mosques in the East. It was built by Shah Ahmed in the fifteenth century. The pointed arches and the elaborate decoration that covers every visible surface are typical of this period of architecture, which flowered in India during the reign of the Mogul emperors. Christians are allowed to enter mosques, but before entering one they must take off their shoes and leave them outside, as do the Mohammedans themselves.

AT MODHERA, in Gujarat, is this elaborately carved Hindu temple which was built in the eleventh century. It is dedicated to Surya, the Sun God, who is personified sunlight, vivifier of men, and who moves on a car drawn by seven ruddy mares, on a path prepared by Indra, god of the clear sky and the thunder. This temple is an example of Hindu craftsmanship.

THE GREAT TEMPLE OF JUGGERNAUT (VISHNU OR KRISHNA) ON THE BLUE HILL IN PURI, ORISSA

Juggernaut, a word derived from the Sanskrit for "Lord of the World," is another term for the Hindu god Krishna, and thousands of pilgrims come to Puri every year for his great festival. The idol is a roughly carved log of wood. It is dragged to the Garden House upon a huge long car, forty-five feet high, with sixteen wheels seven feet high. More than four thousand people often help to pull this vehicle and formerly, despite great care to prevent catastrophe, many used to be crushed beneath its ponderous wheels. This car typifies the moving world.

Walker

THOUSANDS OF PILGRIMS ENCAMPED BY THE GANGES AT ANUPSHAHR FOR A RELIGIOUS FESTIVAL

Whole families come from all parts of India to bathe in the waters of the Ganges during the great festival that is held every November at the new moon. They believe that as they cleanse their bodies in the holy waters so they free their souls from sin. As so often happens in the East, the occasion is also one of merrymaking, and all the attractions of a country fair are present. Water carriers and tradesmen mix with the crowds or set up shop in the shade of a tent. Their cries rise above the din as they cajole pilgrims to part with a few annas.

BUDDH GAYA, in Behar, is one of the most holy places of the Buddhist religion because there Gautama Buddha, the "Light of Asia" is believed to have received enlightenment. A huge pagoda marks the holy spot. The terrace, shown above, runs around the temple, and the strange stone ornaments on the right are shrines that have been erected by pilgrims.

KUTB MINAR, which is about eleven miles south of Delhi, is considered the most perfect tower in the world, and is one of the architectural wonders of India. It is built in five stories and rises to a height of over two hundred feet. The summit is reached by flights of steps. A cupola was added, but it was destroyed by an earthquake in 1803.

Comyn

IMPRESSIVE MANY STORIED TOWER OF THE GREAT HINDU TEMPLE AT TANJORE IN MADRAS

This thirteen-story tower, which is not unlike a pyramid in shape, is fully a hundred and ninety feet in height, and the entire upper portion of it is decorated with carvings. The temple, but little altered from its original form, is one of the oldest in Northern India. In the foreground of the photograph, upon a raised platform surrounded by carven pillars, is a nandi (bull) over twelve feet high and sixteen feet long. It was sculptured out of a block of black granite and is anointed with oil every day by the Faithful, so that it shines lustrously.

TEMPLE-CROWNED ROCK OF TRICHINOPOLY SEEN ACROSS THE TANK

Trichinopoly is on the river Cauvery, in Madras Presidency, and on the north of the town is a rock two hundred and seventy-three feet high on which stands the temple of Mathubuthesvara. The temple is reached by a covered passage, and in front of it is a stone bull which is covered with silver plates.

Lynde

A HINDU'S STRANGE SELF-IMPOSED FORM OF PENANCE

In the hope of obtaining special favors in the hereafter, this man has vowed to remain standing for seven years. He was afraid he might break his vow by falling down when asleep, so he supports himself by a board attached to the tree. In the foreground is a Yogi, or holy man, who spends his days in meditation and prayer.

THE HOLY CITY OF BENARES is in the United Provinces and stretches along the north bank of the Ganges River for three and a half miles. The city was probably founded about 1200 B.C. Splendid temples and costly palaces are reflected in the waters, as sacred to the Hindus as the Jordan is to Christians. Thousands of pilgrims come here each year to undergo

the rites of purification from sin. At intervals along the bank there are flights of steps by which pilgrims may go down to bathe in the water. The Hindus believe that to die in Benares and have one's ashes scattered upon the Ganges is to be certain of gaining salvation. The city is a maze of alleys, many lined by temples and shrines.

65

British Information Services

DOORWAY OF A HINDU TEMPLE IN JAIPUR

The structure is of white marble, and what look to be the leaves of real banana trees are really carvings in dark marble. Because of the hot climate, the clothing of both men and women is usually light in color. Some Indian fabrics, however, are in glowing jewel tones with metallic threads. The women are wearing saris, draped gracefully over their heads.

66

shrines of Siva and his wife, and rising above all, the gate-towers, all of them covered with carvings of gods and goddesses and of all kinds of strange animals, snakes and birds.

Two miles from the temple there is a lake with an island in the centre from which a graceful pagoda rises among the trees. A smaller pagoda adorns each corner of the island. Every January, at the time of the full moon, a festival takes place at this lake. The images of the god and goddess are brought on sacred cars from the great temple, thousands of worshipers pulling on the ropes. When the lake is reached, the images are placed on a decorated barge. In the evening the tank is illuminated with millions of lamps and there are fireworks, and, by torchlight, the god and goddess are pulled around the lake in their barge.

South India has many such temples and such festivals. On the island of Srirangam, in the Cauvery River, stands the largest temple in the world. It is more like a sacred city than a temple. Its outer wall is more than two miles around; it has seven courts one within the other,

Chirol

BEGGAR AND FOLLOWER OF VISHNU PLAYING UPON THE VINA

As a votary of Vishnu it is considered to be almost his duty to beg for alms as he plays and sings. He sits by the wayside with the sign of Vishnu painted upon him for all to see. The vina, believed by the Hindus to have been played by their gods, is made of a length of bamboo with a resonating gourd at each end.

© E. N. A.

THREE GATEWAYS give access to the courtyard of the Jama Masjid, and a long flight of steps leads up to each. Sometimes bazaars are held on these stairways and the tourist finds spread before him rugs, shawls and embroidered muslins, gold and silver filigree work, jewelry and carved ivory. It was on the site of the mosque that the Persian raider, Nadir Shah, watched while his army cut off over a thousand human heads. Nearby Chandni Chauk, the Silver Street of Delhi, 74 feet wide, is lined with warehouses and shops dealing in gold and silver work, and embroidery.

68

CANDLER

AMRITSAR'S GOLDEN TEMPLE is the sacred place of the Sikhs. It stands in the centre of the Pool of Immortality. The four doors are of silver, and white marble forms the lower portions of the walls, gilded copper the upper stories. Verses from the Granth, the scriptures of the Sikhs, are inscribed on the walls of the richly gilded and painted interior. A white marble causeway fully two hundred feet long, with ornate painted and gilded lamps on either side, leads to the temple. Foreign visitors may enter the building only through a north door.

69

a Hall of a Thousand Columns and fifteen towers. In North India the temples do not cover so large an area, but the really ancient ones are architecturally very wonderful.

Again, hundreds of years ago, a big cave would be made into a temple. One of the oldest of these, in the Western Ghats, is called the Karli cave. The rock-hewn front has suffered in the passing of centuries. Over the main entrance is a huge window by which the cave is lighted, and in that window there is a wooden screen more than two thousand years old.

Within, the rock is wonderfully carved, the cave containing forty-one huge pillars cut from the solid rock. It resembles the nave of some Norman cathedral, the more so because of its ribbed wooden roof which for two thousand years has defied the ravages of time. When this temple was used for Buddhist worship, the interior glowed with gold, and banners hung from the vaulted roof.

The rock temple at Ellora is called the Kailasa, after the heaven of the god Siva which the Hindus believe to be located among the eternal snows of the Himalayas. In the eighth century of the Christian Era, a Hindu king ordered the temple to be hewn from the mountainside to commemorate his victories. The rock has been cut away from around it so that it stands in a pit surrounded by walls of rock. Outside and in, every foot of its walls is carved. Around its base runs a border of elephants that seem to be carrying the temple upon their shoulders. It is probably the most remarkable example of rock-carving to be found anywhere.

India has many holy cities, such as Benares, Allahabad, Muttra, Nasik, Brindaban, Ajodhya and Conjeeveram. A city is sacred if it is connected with some event in the lives of certain incarnations of God, according to the Hindu mythology. Rama was born in Ajodha; Krishna spent much of his boyhood in Brindaban Every year these places are visited by thousands of pilgrims and some by hundreds of thousands. Every twelve years a great religious festival is held at Allahabad, where the waters of the Ganges and the Jumna rivers meet. "Allahabad" means the "City of God"; and it is aptly named indeed for it plays an all-important part in the religious activities of the Hindus. When the twelve-year festivals are held, the pilgrims gathered in the city are estimated to number three million persons, all of whom bathe in the river in the hope that they will be cleansed of their sins. At Allahabad the Ganges River is fairly wide and shallow; and pilgrims may wade out in it some distance.

All the rivers of the Indian peninsula are sacred to the

Screen Traveler from Gendreau

A FAKIR, OR HOLY MAN, LYING ON THORNS

"Fakir" is an Arabic word that means "poor," and especially "one poor in the sight of God." Mohammedans apply it to devout members of their religious orders. In India it is also applied to Hindu religious men. Some are wandering beggars who torture themselves.

PRIEST MAKING AN OFFERING TO A JAIN COLOSSUS IN MYSORE

This sixty-foot image of a saint of Jainism stands on the top of a solitary hill near Mysore. It is reached by a flight of nearly seven hundred steps. The figure was hewn out of the rock more than a thousand years ago. The priest is bringing a humble offering to lay at its feet, where a votive lamp is kept burning.

Hindus, but one of them is more so than the others—the holy Ganges, called "Mother Ganges." Of the sacred cities, one is more sacred than the rest—holy Benares, on the north bank of the Ganges. The sacred books declare that every step a pilgrim takes toward Benares causes his sins to fall from him like dust. To visit Benares is believed to bring salvation, and to die there and to be burned on the banks of the Ganges makes salvation doubly sure. In Benares, houses, palaces and temples are built up the steep bank, while along the water's edge run flights of stone steps from which the pilgrims bathe. For three and a half miles the city stretches along the bank of the river, and on the occasion of some great festival the river is black with bathers.

Within there are said to be over three thousand temples. There are also idols in the open streets, and it is not unusual to see a devotee prostrated before one of them, lying flat on his face across the nar-

BEFORE AN OPEN-AIR TEMPLE sits the keeper of the shrine, who tolls a bell the livelong day bidding passers-by to come to prayer. Lifelike masks, one black and one white, crowned with exotic headdresses, represent the gods. Spread before them are offerings of food, some of it in gleaming dishes and pots of copper.

row street. There are pilgrims wherever you turn, sprinkling holy water as they walk, hanging garlands of flowers around some idol, sitting on a bed of spikes or torturing themselves in ways that fill Westerners with amazement. Besides the greater gods many lesser divinities are worshiped.

The Essence of Hinduism

These Hindus believe in one Supreme "Essence" called Brahm that resides in everything. They do not think of Brahm as a personal spirit; they refer to it as "that."

They believe that Brahm has left the control of this world to three gods named Brahma (the Creator), Vishnu (the Preserver and Friend of Man), and Siva (the Destroyer). They believe that Vishnu and Siva have had many incarnations. They say, for instance, that Vishnu lived in this world as Krishna, as Rama, as Buddha and so forth. They believe also that these gods had wives and children. Some of the goddesses are worshiped as much as their husbands—for example, the beloved Sita, wife of Rama, and Kali, the wife of Siva. The exploits of the gods and goddesses are told in the Vedas and in the stirring epics of ancient Hindu literature. They were written in the Sanskrit language, which holds a place in Indian culture much like that of Latin and Greek in the civilization of the European peoples.

The Mohammedan Invasion

From the year 1001 A.D. onward, successive Mohammedan conquerors burst through the mountain passes into Northwest India. Each century brought fresh waves of Moslem invaders, and kingdoms rose and fell. In one invasion the ancient city of Delhi was captured, and on the ruins of one of its temples the conquerors built a magnificent Tower of Victory. Gradually the Mohammedans have settled in India until they form an important section of the community. They are a proud people, these Islamites, and they have much of which to be proud, for it was their ancestors who built the splendid sandstone and marble palaces at Agra and Delhi, to say nothing of the famous Taj Mahal. You may have read in the article on Arabia how Mohammedanism originated. The innate antagonism between the invaders and the native Hindus is evident when we recall that the Mohammedans believe in one God (Allah) whose prophet is Mohammed, who wrote the Koran under divine inspiration. They also believe in propagating their belief by the sword.

Their mosques are of great beauty. All the large mosques and many of the smaller ones have two minarets—tall, slender towers, from the balconies of which the call to prayer sounds out five times each day.

The Essence of Buddhism

Buddhism was founded in India but has almost ceased to exist in the land where it arose, though there are millions of Buddhists in Ceylon, Burma, Siam, Tibet, China and Japan. Its founder, Gautama Buddha, born supposedly between 552 B.C. and 562 B.C., is now claimed by Hindus to be an incarnation of their god Vishnu. Gautama, who is more fully explained in connection with China, taught the vanity of human desire. Declaring material things unworthy of men's love, he held that one must achieve a state where he wishes for nothing, before he can cease to be—that is, enter into Nirvana. He must become indifferent to pain, as to pleasure—a conception that accounts in part for certain practices. On leaving the body, his spirit enters into another form of life, wherefore to take life is sinful. The virtues of a Buddhist are purity, patience, contemplation and almsgiving.

There is, however, a religion in India very much like Buddhism that arose about the same time—Jainism. It has scarcely more than a million followers, but is represented by many splendid temples. In Mysore, on a hilltop, there stands a huge idol of a Jain saint hewn from the solid rock. It is nearly seventy feet high. For a thousand years that great image Vardhamana, the founder of Jainism, taught that everything—even trees and water—has a soul, which journeys from body to body; that no living creature must be killed; and that to escape from the toil of existence one must practice gentleness, liberality, piety and repentance. The growth of the philosophy of nonviolence in Indian public life and culture is allied with the inner spirit of Jainism.

About 1500 a great Indian teacher, or guru, named Nanak attempted to unite the Hindus and Mohammedans. Taking some of the best teachings of each, he

British Information Services
ENTRANCE TO A JAIN TEMPLE

This temple is in Calcutta. Outside and in, the walls are covered with intricate mosaic work in many colors. Jain architecture has enriched the artistic heritage of India.

founded a religion called Sikhism, whose holy book is the Granth. The Mogul Emperor Akbar gave the Sikhs a plot of land in the city of Amritsar. Here they built the tranquil Pool of Immortality, in which stands their Golden Temple.

As the years passed, persecution drove the Sikhs to arms, and they became a powerful fighting sect. Living together in the Punjab, they developed into a semi-religious, semi-military group; and their great leader, Ranjit Singh, the "Lion of the Punjab," became the undisputed master of that part of India. The Sikhs later formed some of the finest regiments in the Indian Army. A branch of the Sikhs the Singhs, when completely uniformed, wore five *kakkas:* topknot, comb, bracelet, shorts and a two-edged dagger. Today the Sikhs number about five million, and their homeland, the Punjab, is divided between Pakistan and the Republic of India. The modern Sikh rejects the caste system; and Sikh women have long been allowed equal rights with men. From the ranks of the Sikhs have come many administrative officials, Cabinet ministers and members of the professions.

Parsees, Followers of Zoroaster

On Malabar Hill, outside Bombay, there stand five grim buildings called the Towers of Silence, of which more anon. On their walls sit rings of vultures. Close at hand is another building called a fire temple. Here we meet a religion followed by the Parsees, whose prophet is Zoroaster, or Zarathustra. He was a Persian and founded the religion called Zoroastrianism in the seventh century B.C. He rejected the idea of a number of gods and concentrated on the spirit of good, handing down an orderly ethical system.

The Parsees believe in one God whom they call Ahura Mazda (Lord the All-Knowing). One strange custom distinguishes them from all other sects. Believing that earth, air, fire and water are sacred, they are in a difficulty as to the disposal of their dead, for the sacred elements must not be defiled. The dead are therefore carried into the Towers of Silence and placed on gratings where the bones are picked clean by the vultures.

Finally, let us go down the hill to the seashore. The sun is setting. There on the beach stand companies of Parsees praying, with their faces toward the setting sun. In their temples, they have sacred fires continually burning on the altars. The Parsees regard sun and fire as symbols of the great God who is the source of all light.

INDIA'S MILLIONS

In Crowded City and Jungle Village

Of our four articles on India, this one deals with the life of the people. The Indian of the large town, who lives in contact with the European and the marvels of Western civilization, is a very different person from the simple villager who may live a hundred miles or more from the nearest railway station. Besides the Indian races, there are such tribes as the Todas and Bhils, who were driven to the hills and jungles many centuries ago by their conquerors and are shy and usually peaceful folk. The peoples of India differ from each other as much as the nations of Europe, but, speaking generally, the ways of life in town or village are much the same all over the country.

THE orthodox Hindu traces the history of his land nearly five thousand years, but modern scholars place little faith in these legends. After 2000 B.C. Aryan tribes from the North entered India and finally subdued the aborigines such as the dark-haired Dravidians, but the first actual account gives as 557 B.C. the supposed date of the birth of Buddha. The country split into many separate states which made comparatively little resistance to Alexander the Great in 327 B.C. His successors attempted to maintain the Greek influence with indifferent success.

There were Arab invasions before 700 A.D., but about 750 the invaders were expelled. By 1001 the Sultan Mahmud of Ghazni had permanently established Mohammedan power on Indian soil. In 1398 Timur-leng (Tamerlane), the Tatar, defeated the King of Delhi and proclaimed himself Emperor of India, but his descendant, Akbar, was the real founder of the Mogul Empire. His reign was almost exactly contemporaneous with that of Elizabeth of England. His grandson Shah Jehan, who built the Taj Mahal, was supplanted by his son Aurungzebe (Aurangzeb), who raised the Mogul Empire at Delhi to its highest pitch of splendor, but afterward ruined it by over-expansion; and in 1759 Nadir Shah's Persian highlanders sacked Delhi, after which his viceroys formed provinces into independent states.

Meanwhile Vasco da Gama, sailing from Portugal, had reached India by sea. Portuguese, Dutch, French and English established trading posts and their rivalry led to armed conflicts in which final success came to England. The empire thus founded was at first administered by a mere commercial company, the East India Company, and the first governor-general, Warren Hastings, had to maintain British supremacy in the face of the hostility of powerful Mussulman sovereigns. His successors extended the area of British rule and most of the native states were brought under the control of the East India Company. There was much discord, however, and much fighting. The great mutiny occurred in 1857, and two years later the Crown took over the administration. Until 1947, more than half of the territory was administered by British officials. The nearly 700 native states of varying sizes were semi-independent under their native rulers, although the Indian government kept a watchful eye over them. The reigning King of England also had the title Emperor of India.

Not all of the peninsula of India was governed by the British. A small area under French rule comprises five colonies of which Pondicherry on the coast south of Madras is one of chief importance. Founded in 1674, it has been taken and later restored by the Dutch and the English in turn. Portugal claims territory along the west coast containing salt works and manganese mines. This consists of Goa, Damao—north of Bombay—and Diu, a small off-shore island. But British India comprised practically three-fifths of the peninsula, while the

Walker

AMONG THE MIGHTY HIMALAYAS, GUARDIAN MOUNTAINS OF INDIA'S NORTHERN FRONTIER

Along the northern frontier of India there runs that double wall of mountains, the Himalayas, which contains Mount Everest, the world's highest mountain, and many other peaks over twenty thousand feet in height. In these mountains live such hill tribes as the Ghurkas, Bhutias, Garhwalis and Kumaunis, and in the foothills are hill stations like Naini Tal, Mussoorie, Simla and Darjeeling, whither Europeans go in the summer. There are no roads in the Himalayas, but only tracks which have been used by the hill people for centuries.

DARJEELING AND THE SNOW-CAPPED GIANTS OF THE HIMALAYAS

Darjeeling in Bengal, situated on the lower slopes of the Himalayas, is surrounded by some of the finest scenery in the world. "Darjeeling" means "the place, or town, of the thunder-bolt," and from the ridge on which the town stands can be seen Mounts Everest and Kinchinjunga with their summits covered by perpetual snow.

Walker

SLOW BUT SURE WAY OF TRAVELING IN RURAL BENGAL

The two-wheeled cart is drawn by a team of water buffaloes, common beasts of burden in all the warmer parts of Asia. A water buffalo never hurries, but it is patient and dependable. This country road meanders past an artificial pond, in which water is stored for irrigation purposes. The old Province of Bengal is today divided between Pakistan and India.

78

LITTLE VILLAGE HIDDEN AWAY IN THE JUNGLES OF BENGAL

The huts in these jungle villages are all made of sun-baked mud and thatched with straw.
The peasants till their little plots of land, which they have won from the surrounding jungle,
untroubled by the changes that are taking place in the cities. Their chief complaint is the
leopards that infest these jungles and prey upon their flocks.

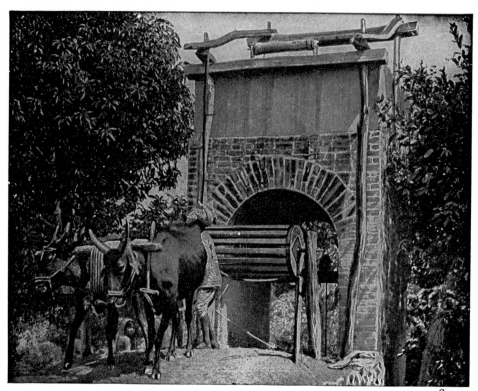

OX POWER FOR RAISING WATER FROM AN INDIAN BUNGALOW WELL

Every Indian bungalow has a well and oxen may be used to raise the heavy leather bucket. Here the bucket rope is attached to the yoke of a pair of oxen. When the bucket has been lowered into the well and filled, the patient beasts walk along a causeway, which is precisely as long as the well is deep, and so bring the water to the surface.

native states and agencies (of varying sizes and degrees of autonomy) occupy about two-fifths.

The government of India has been very complicated. There are nearly seven hundred semi-independent "native states," and all were, to some extent, under British supervision. A British official, called a Resident or an Agent, was stationed at the capital of each state, or group of states, but his power varied greatly. In some he was merely an adviser, in others he had almost complete control. British India, with around four-fifths of the population, was divided into provinces and administered by British officials, but these were not all of equal rank or authority. Slowly but steadily increasing authority was given to these divisions, though the Viceroy, as representative of the King was the final word.

In 1935, a new constitution for India was passed by the British Parliament. The constitution provided for a Federal Government in which the native states were to share. It also called for a Federal Legislature of two houses partly appointed, partly elected, to which the ministers were responsible. The constitution was regarded as the first step toward democracy through dominion status, or even complete independence. Later events proved the prophecy true, when the new states of India and Pakistan were formed in 1947.

Here we have a population roughly one-sixth to one-fifth that of the total population of the world, crowded into about one twenty-fifth of the land surface of the earth. There are, in much of India, on the average, more than 195 people to the square mile—as contrasted with approximately forty for the United States of America and less than three for Canada.

HARD-WORKING SEE-SAW THAT HELPS THE INDIAN CULTIVATOR

In those parts of India in which the rainfall is slight, the denkli, a kind of see-saw, is largely used to draw the life-giving water for the fields from the wells. The beam of the denkli has a bucket at one end and a weight at the other, like the shaduf, and a man at the point of balance, by rocking it to and fro, can raise and lower the bucket.

81

Assam-Bengal Rly.

NAGA VILLAGE IN THE WILD HIGHLANDS OF ASSAM

Grass mats form the walls of these thatched huts, which contain little furniture besides the beds—rough planks of wood—around the fireplace. Pigs are sometimes kept in the little enclosure by the hut, but the fowls roost on the rafters. Naga villages are generally built on hills, as the tribes at one time were continually fighting among themselves.

All of the invasions above mentioned, Aryan, Greek, Hun, Arab and Mohammedan, have left their traces in India, in blood, religion, manners and customs. As a consequence, there are about forty-five different races speaking many different languages and dialects. However, the Hindu caste system—which separates the people in rigid social levels—from the highest Brahmin to the humblest Untouchable—has been receiving attention of late. At the third meeting of the Indian Constituent Assembly just before the partition, the class term Untouchable was officially abolished.

The chief industry of India has always been agriculture. Seven people in every ten gain their living by farming; for the most part they are densely crowded together in the regions of plentiful rainfall. Modern methods of farming had been encouraged by the English, but most Indian farmers still use the primitive methods of their forefathers.

Increasing numbers of Indians are employed as industrial workers, chiefly in the larger cities. They are engaged in such varied pursuits as the weaving of cotton cloths, silk-rearing and weaving, carpet-weaving and metal-working.

India is thus a maelstrom of Hindus and Mohammedans, princes and paupers, half-wild hill tribes and highly organized industrial workers, Europeanized professional men and co-operatively-minded rice farmers. The differences have thus far been too great for any general body of public opinion to exist.

Both India and Pakistan have embarked on long-range plans for improving education, not only for children but also for the many adults who cannot read or write. Hundreds of teachers will be trained and national school systems will be organized to replace the present unrelated local systems.

There are some good modern schools, colleges and universities. Many Brahmins have been Christianized. Nevertheless, there is still a great amount of illiteracy among India's millions of people. It is estimated that only about fourteen percent of its total population is able to read and write. There are eight federal universities to which colleges are affiliated, besides a number of other universities, technical schools, law schools and medical colleges. Since 1920 India has made far-reaching changes in the realm of higher education. The report of a research commission on the University of Calcutta recommended the establishment of several additional universities, together with the more extensive education of women and the bi-lingual teaching of the more highly educated classes. The residential University of Dacca, founded in 1921 in Bengal, gives special attention to Islamic studies; the University of Rangoon, founded in 1920, has extension courses and courses in forestry, geology and engineering. At Agra University, established in 1926, women who have carried on private study are eligible for degrees; and Andhra University in Bezwada, created in 1926, among other activities promotes teaching in certain native languages.

However, as educational facilities increased, the people's dissatisfaction with their political position grew in proportion. The great Maharajahs, for instance, resented what they considered to be British interference with their ancient customs and beliefs.

Eleayas

NAGA WARRIORS ARMED READY FOR THE FRAY

"Naga" is a word meaning snake, and the Nagas are so named because they are snake worshipers. At one time these people were head-hunters who terrorized and preyed upon the gentle folk who dwelt on the plains below the hills of Assam. Their weapons are the javelin and a thick, heavy knife with a crooked end, and they carry large shields.

CAMELS AS DRAFT ANIMALS IN THE DESERT REGIONS   Talbot

In most of India oxen draw the heavy, springless carts, but in the desert of Rajputana, where water is scarce and underfooting soft, camels must be used. The cart that we see here is plying for hire, and can carry passengers as well as a heavy load of luggage, since it has both an upper and a lower deck.

Mahatma Gandhi initiated his passive resistance movement, but many acts of violence were attributed to it. Gandhi's program called for the settlement of religious differences between Hindus, Moslems and Sikhs; equality for all classes and women with men; prohibition of liquor; and the encouragement of spinning and weaving in the home by farmers and their families during periods when crops were poor.

The spinning wheel became the symbol of Indian independence, sponsored by the Indian National Congress, and soon the round white cap known as the "Gandhi cap" began to appear in the villages of the country. The famous spinning wheel later was to make its appearance on the flag of the Dominion of India as the nation's emblem of democracy.

There was restlessness also among the Moslems of India. They, too, wanted freedom but were unalterably opposed to any independence that would mean subjection to a Hindu or non-Moslem majority. The religious differences between Hindus and Moslems are deep-seated and there have been many outbreaks of violence. This antagonism has been one of the obstacles in the path of Indian unity. Indian nation-

alists, indeed, maintained that the British did their best to promote strife between Hindus and Mohammedans in order to keep India divided; but this claim seems to be rather far-fetched.

Though the Moslems were represented in the All-India Congress, their chief political organ was the Moslem League, led by Mohammed Ali Jinnah, who first proposed India's confederacy and later became the first governor general of the Dominion of Pakistan.

India's exports of merchandise in 1949 were valued at $887,550,000 and her imports amounted to $1,087,800,000. About one-fourth of India's trade is with the United Kingdom. Her sales to continental Europe, reduced during World War II, have been largely regained. Trade with Japan, one of India's important customers, has begun to reach pre-war volume. The United States and India maintain an interchange of goods.

Bombay, with its exceptionally fine harbor, has been for three centuries an important mart of trade. The Parsees represent the wealthy class. The port city, with its Western skyline and smoking factory chimneys, is lately making use of hydro-electric power for its in-

TWO OLD ENEMIES FACE TO FACE: THE COBRA AND THE MONGOOSE

As the snake-charmer plays his pipe, a long swaying form rises from the basket. At once the little mongoose is all attention, filled with fury at the sight. A mongoose in the yard of an Indian house is a great protection against snakes. It is usually quick enough to escape the vicious lunge of the cobra, and afterward bites through its neck.

85

MEMBERS OF THE WORLD-WIDE BROTHERHOOD OF BOY SCOUTS

The Boy Scout movement is popular even in India. The native lads there are as keen and alert at their drills as their fellow scouts in Great Britain and the United States. Their uniform is necessarily light, owing to the hot climate. Here we see some Boy Scouts of India carrying air-raid precaution equipment during a drill.

dustries. It has also been threaded by structures of lattice steelwork on which run the electric trains of the Bombay, Baroda and Central India Railway Company. The power is supplied by generating stations in the western Ghats a hundred miles distant. This is making commuting pleasanter and easier.

Though the rival port of Calcutta hums with the jute mills (which make bagging for the United States), the tourist will be less impressed by the commercial aspect of that city than by its colorful social life. The palace, once the official residence of the Viceroy of India but now occupied by the Governor of Bengal, is magnificent. The uniforms of the soldiers add color, and the officers appear at many functions in white uniforms with gold epaulettes. There are native chauffeurs in uniform, and no traveler can dispense with a "boy"

to act as servant and interpreter. He receives but thirty cents a day and feeds himself, but his needs are simple. Calcutta attracts large numbers of Anglo-Indians.

Both the Republic of India and Pakistan are well served by air lines. For instance, one can fly from London to Karachi, Pakistan, in thirty-six hours. There is also direct service between the United Kingdom and Delhi, Calcutta and Bombay; and India is on the flying-boat route to Sydney and Singapore.

Having taken a bird's-eye view of India's history, past and present, and of her industrial future, let us get out the magic carpet and make a personal inspection of her crowded city streets and jungle villages.

It is at dusk that the Indian cities become most interesting. In the heat of midday the bazaars—as the streets of shops are called—are almost deserted and the shopkeepers drowse among their wares. The bazaar of Muttra, a town in the United Provinces, is typical. The winding street teems with life, a moving mass of people hopelessly mixed with carts and animals of every variety. Humped oxen pull hooded carts through the crowd, men and women dodge under the noses of donkeys with bulky panniers or push their ways through the press, driven on by blows. The water-carrier with his dripping sheepskin, the pilgrim with his brass water-pot, the nearly naked coolie bearing a heavy load upon his head —people of every status jostle each other. In such a crowd it is impossible to make headway, even though the driver of your ekka, or high-wheeled cart, seated on one shaft, urges his pony onward by twisting its tail or by poking his bare toes into its ribs. In loud tones he shouts at people to make way for you. His shouts multiplied by a hundred or more are a constant refrain in the din that is so typical of a busy bazaar.

The determined cries from the side of the street—the cries of the ambitious shopkeeper, the shopkeeper who has never heard the word "no"—call your attention to the open-front shops. If his calls prove ineffective and you send your driver along past his shop, soon an eager boy will be behind your cart trying to bring you back. If not one, then another shopkeeper will lure you to his lamp- or torch-lit stall. Coins in the pocket and the sight of curious objects on the merchant's shelves often prove to be irresistible temptations. No one leaves a bazaar without first trying his bargaining skill. Once out of your cart you may wander through the maze of stalls for an hour or more.

Tom-toms and Smoking Torches

In those windowless shops the Kashmiri woodcarver exhibits his skillfully made fire screens and photograph frames; the brassworker sells his lamps, trays and bowls; the Afghan merchant unrolls his rugs; the goldsmith sits before his charcoal fire-pot smelting the precious metal

of his clients into necklaces, anklets or nose-rings. The seller of cheap bangles has thousands of glass bracelets arranged on the shelves around him. The sellers of sweetmeats and fruit and vegetables, the perfumers, the idol-makers, the garland sellers, the silk merchants—all are there.

The crowded bazaar is stifling and the air heavy with incense and perfumes. Hundreds of lamps flicker and smoke. We hear the sound of flutes and horns, and the beating of tom-toms. With smoking torches, and singing and dancing, a wedding procession moves slowly through the crowd. Some of the largest cities, as described elsewhere, are modern, but life in the villages remains about what it has always been.

Village Life in the Deccan

Some of the Indian villages are scattered over the cultivated plains; others lie hidden in the jungles or among the barren hills. Some villages consist of a mere handful of huts of mud or the branches of trees roughly woven together; others have streets of well made houses, with perhaps an ancient temple in the center of the town—all shimmering in the light of the hot sun.

Let us imagine ourselves in an old-fashioned bullock-cart, jolting slowly over the rough plain somewhere in the Deccan, in Southern India, to a village half hidden in a grove of mango trees. We meet the village boys driving the cattle to pasture, raising clouds of dust as they pass. Near the village is an irrigation tank—a sheet of shallow water. During the heavy rains this tank stores water which is used in the dry season. As we pass it we see the dhobies (washermen) soaking the clothes and banging them vigorously on the stones to knock the dirt out of them. It is terribly hot and a dozen water buffaloes are standing in the water with only their heads above the surface. At the village, under a big pipal tree is a mud platform on which the elders sit in council, to arrange matters of public business or to try some criminal. Near by is another platform shaded by the spreading branches of a sacred tree; upon it some of the village idols, with simple offerings of rice or milk or fruit laid out before them. In the courtyard the women of the house prepare the rice and curry for the next meal, wash the babies or polish the brass.

In some of the courtyards one may find villagers following their trades—the potters with wheel and clay, their newly-made vessels drying in the sunshine; the blacksmith with his fire and bellows; or the idol-maker giving a coat of paint to his wooden images. There may be several small temples in the village, and, if there are any Mohammedans, there may also be a small mosque from which the call to prayer is given several times a day. As the sun is setting, the cattle are brought home, and the smoke of many fires hangs like a pungent cloud over the village.

A favorite Hindu dish, correctly spelled mulligatunny, is a soup which may be literally translated as pepper water, as it is made of peppers boiled in water, though a flavor of garlic adds savoriness. Added to boiled rice and fried onions, it forms the staple dish. The native also eats his rice with hot curry sauce, or enriched with chopped egg, minced fish and lemon. Higher caste Hindus are vegetarians, and Mohammedans eat all meat with the exception of pork. The Indians of Bengal eat from banana leaves on ceremonial occasions, but ordinarily they use brass plates and bowls. They take food to their mouths with their fingers; forks are generally used only by Europeans.

Some miles from the village runs a high road, made by the government. It is usually wide, shaded by huge trees, that form an avenue through otherwise shadeless country. One side of this road is paved for quick-moving traffic, but the other side is sandy and is used by the bullock-carts, the pack-oxen and strings of camels. India has more than two hundred thousand miles of good roads. Per-

Bailey

MONKEYS BEGGING AT A RAILWAY STATION

The small Bengal monkey is regarded as semi-sacred by the Hindus and the animals are impudent, as they know they are safe from molestation. They beg for sweets and fruit, and chatter and grin angrily if nothing is given to them. Europeans sometimes keep them as pets, but they are quick-tempered and can bite viciously.

A SLEEPY TAILOR LETS HIS SIGN SPEAK FOR HIM

The Arabic script makes the same announcement as the English letters. Mohammedans in India speak a language called Urdu, which is written in Arabic script. Hindustani, spoken by many Hindus, is written in Sanskrit script. Both Urdu and Hindustani, however, are used generally as secondary languages among speakers of India's hundreds of dialects.

89

WASHERWOMEN IN INDIA, a country where laundries are few, sociably take the clothes down to a river, where they soak and wring them, then beat them upon stones. They certainly get the dirt out, but the process is hard on the garments. However, they dress chiefly in calico, a kind of cotton fabric that takes its name from the city of Calicut. Brass jars like those you can see on the bank serve Indian housewives in many ways, often to carry water. While they are still quite young, girls learn to balance the jars on their heads.

THE PEARL MOSQUE at Delhi was built in the seventeenth century as a private chapel for the Emperor Aurang-zeb, third son of Shah Jehan, who usurped the throne in 1658, after murdering two brothers and imprisoning his father. The mosque is of marble wonderfully carved, and decorated with colored designs. It lies within the walls of the fortress-palace.

91

Kenneth Comyn

IN THE PADDY FIELDS OF SOUTH INDIA; PLANTING THE YOUNG RICE SEEDLINGS SEPARATELY BY HAND

In India it is possible to cultivate crops all the year around; for so long as they are watered, they can defy the heat of the summer. Two crops a year are not unusual. In Northern India a corn crop is not infrequently followed by a wheat crop, while in Southern India two and sometimes three rice crops are grown. The finer varieties of rice are raised from transplanted seedlings; and as the rice usually requires that its roots stand in water during a part of its growth period, the fields are leveled, embanked to retain the water, and finally flooded.

haps the finest is the Grand Trunk Road which runs from Calcutta to Peshawar, a distance of fifteen hundred miles. Yet there are still vast areas of country with no roads at all.

Who has not heard of India's jungles? The name suggests to a good many people an impenetrable forest with tangled undergrowth. Yet the word is applied to any uncultivated land. Some of the jungles, like those of the Ganges delta, are covered with long grass and other vegetation through which tigers roam. In other places the jungles are great plains, with little grass and very few trees, and with masses of granite strewn about or piled up as though by the hands of a giant. Here and there are low bushes among which leopards prowl, and masses of cactus, aloes and prickly pear, under which deadly snakes have their holes. On the rocky hills there are bears and in some parts of the country there are wolves.

Every night the voices of the jackals and hyenas curdle the blood of the hearer.

Here snakes are far more dangerous to human beings than tigers. Every year about twenty thousand people are killed by them, whereas tigers and leopards together claim only about a thousand or twelve hundred victims. The commonest snake is the cobra, one of the most poisonous. Unless a remedy is applied at once, its bite is certain death.

In some of the jungles and mountains, there dwell small tribes of people who hunt their prey with bows and arrows; and, in inaccessible regions in Northeast India, they still practice head-hunting and sacrifice human beings to their gods. On the other hand, some of these "jungle tribes," like the Todas of the Nilgiri Hills, are quiet, peace-loving people. These hill tribes are believed to be descended from the people who inhabited the country before the Hindus.

H. S. Talbot

SCORES OF COOLIES TOILING AT THE WORK OF A CRANE

Machinery has by no means entirely replaced man power in India, as may be seen from this photograph of a gang of Bundanis carrying a stone beam up to the top of a building in process of construction in Gwalior. As many as 128 men have been harnessed to a single beam slung by ropes from poles borne on the men's shoulders.

MUSICIANS AND DANCERS travel all over India and give their performances in the open air, in theatres or at private houses. The music of the players with the queer, stringed instruments in the photograph would seem to our Western ears nothing but a succession of more or less unpleasant squeaks. The man in the red turban, standing between the two girls, has two small drums on which he plays a monotonous accompaniment with his fingers. These traveling troupes also perform plays, which are usually symbolic of religious conceptions.

GHURKA (or Gurka) WOMEN come down from the fastnesses of Nepal with their husbands, who enlist in the Indian army. With their children the women live in special quarters inside the lines of the Ghurka regiments. The Ghurkas are of Hindu descent but have much intermingling of Mongolian blood. The Ghurkas' soldierly qualities are celebrated.

THE GREAT COMMERCIAL CITY OF BOMBAY SEEN FROM MALABAR POINT

Bombay is the industrial centre of India and its port facilities are modern. In its harbor one can see the flags of many nations, in peacetime, for this is a trade centre as well as a stop for tourists. From this world port cotton goes to England and returns as calico. Back Bay, at the seaward end of Bombay Island, has the shape of a half-moon, with Malabar Hill at one tip and Colaba at the other. The five Parsee Towers of Silence are at Malabar. The island of Bombay is one of a group of twelve formerly separated from one another and the mainland by channels

ECHOES OF THE SEA, CHEAP

The shell vendor of Karachi will sell you, in a beautiful pearly package, "the awful mysteries of the tide, the misty sea, profound and wide." The quotation is from Eugene Field's *The Wanderer*. Of course we know that what we hear, when we clasp a shell to the ear, are faint near-by sounds murmuring in the resonator, the shell. But the poetic fancy is more charming than the truth.

FRUIT-SELLERS abound in India because many of the people eat practically no meat and their meals consist chiefly of fruit and vegetables. Fruit is fortunately to be had in great abundance and is very cheap. If we gave this man a small coin he would give us as much as we could carry away in our arms for he has no paper bags for his customers.

INDIAN CRAFTSMEN are noted for their skill in making ornaments of gold, ivory, brass and silver. Their occupations are hereditary, and sometimes one family has carved ivory for hundreds of years. Unfortunately, many of the fine native handicrafts are now in danger of dying out as much cheaper articles are produced by the factories.

To reach the Himalayas one crosses the foothills, then ascends steep trails that cross range after stupendous range. At every turn one has a new view of towering heights and mysterious gorges. At sunset, the vast chasms are dark and only the peaks catch the light. The snowy heights above one flush rose against the sky. As the shadows deepen in mysterious twilight, the towering heights glow crimson until they seem to be on fire.

THE REPUBLIC OF INDIA: FACTS AND FIGURES

THE COUNTRY

The country that was formerly a part of British India became a republic and a full member of the Commonwealth of Nations in January 1950. It is bounded on the north by Sinkiang and Nepal, on the east by Pakistan and the Bay of Bengal, on the south by the Indian Ocean and on the west by the Arabian Sea and Pakistan. The area is 1,220,011 square miles; population (estimated), 360,185,000. The Andaman and Nicobar Islands are a part of the Republic.

GOVERNMENT

The government is composed of a president, two houses of Parliament—(upper) the Council of States and (lower) the House of the People—and a number of advisory ministers. The president is elected by members of Parliament and the various state legislatures and serves for five years. He may be re-elected. Members of the Council are elected by the members of the state legislatures, and members of the lower house are directly elected by the people on the basis of adult sufferage.

COMMERCE AND INDUSTRIES

Agriculture is the chief occupation supporting more than one-third of the population; chief crops: tea, rice, wheat, sugar-cane, oil, seeds, cotton (second only to the United States), jute and rubber. Much land is under irrigation. The most important minerals are coal, petroleum, gold, lead, manganese, silver, tin and copper. Chief factory industry is spinning and weaving cotton and wool. Metal-working, woodcarving and silk-raising are also important. Chief exports: raw cotton, tea, jute and rice. Chief imports: manufactured cotton, sugar, metals and machinery.

COMMUNICATIONS

Railroad mileage, 40,524, mostly government-owned and operated. Length of telegraph lines, 97,583 miles; telephone exchanges, 2,747.

RELIGION AND EDUCATION

According to the latest census, India has 254,930,506 Hindus, 92,058,096 Mohammedans, 6,316,549 Christians, 5,691,447 Sikhs, 1,449,286 Jains, 114,890 Parsees, 232,003 Buddhists, 22,480 Jews and 409,877 of other religions. There are 164,552 recognized institutions of learning, including primary and secondary schools; colleges and universities; technical, vocational and teacher-training schools. A 16-year plan to modernize education systems was begun in 1948.

CHIEF TOWNS

Population: Delhi (including New Delhi, capital, and suburbs), 521,849; Calcutta, 2,108,891; Bombay, 1,489,883; Madras, 777,481; Hyderabad, 739,159; Ahmedabad, 591,257; Cawnpore, 487,324; Amritsar, 391,010; Lucknow, 387,177; Howrah, 379,292; Nagpur, 301,957; Agra, 284,149.

FRENCH AND PORTUGUESE INDIA

France and Portugal retained their colonies in India when the latter became an independent republic in 1950.

PAKISTAN: FACTS AND FIGURES

THE COUNTRY

Formerly a part of British India, Pakistan became a dominion in the Commonwealth of Nations in July 1947, as a result of the Indian Independence Act of the same year. The Dominion consists of two separated areas in the northwestern and northeastern parts of the Indian subcontinent. Western Pakistan includes the former states and provinces of Baluchistan, Punjab, the Northwest Frontier and Sind. Eastern Pakistan includes East Bengal and most of Sylhet, a former district of Assam. The total area is 360,007 square miles and the estimated population is 70,103,000.

GOVERNMENT

Following the partition, a Constituent Assembly was formed to govern the Dominion and draw up a constitution. When the constitution has been ratified, it is planned to elect two houses (upper and lower) of Parliament. The principal officers of the present government are the governor general and prime minister.

COMMERCE AND INDUSTRY

Pakistan is principally agricultural, growing wheat, rice, jute and cotton. Industries include cotton spinning and weaving, milling and food processing. There are large railway shops and foundries in the western zone.

COMMUNICATIONS

Railroad mileage, 6,678; there are telephone and telegraph services and an air service.

RELIGION AND EDUCATION

The population is 70 per cent Mohammedan. There are 2 universities, at Lahore and Karachi.

CHIEF TOWNS

Karachi (capital), 359,492; Lahore, 671,659.

KASHMIR IN THE HIMALAYAS

The Loveliest State in India

If India may be described as irregularly diamond-shaped, Kashmir lies in the northern peak of the diamond, walled in by the highest mountains in the world. The lovely land of Kashmir is not only one of the most important states of India, possessed of a semi-independence under a separate ruler, but it has the finest climate, and part of its people—the Brahmans and the Rajputs—are of Aryan blood. The richness of this country has through the centuries attracted to it such conquering races as the Moguls, the Pathans and the Sikhs. Every summer large numbers of European officials, merchants and others go there to escape from the heat of the Indian plains.

WE can get the best idea of Kashmir, which lies to the north of the sun-scorched Punjab, by thinking of it as three parallel strips lying northwest and southeast. First comes the range of the Pir Panjal, the barrier that separates the happy valley, as the land has been called, from India; then the valley itself, the plain of Kashmir, which is called the nearest approach on earth to the Garden of Eden; and last, the chain of sheltering hills which rise in tiers of extraordinary grandeur up to the mountain wall on the north.

Kashmir has been likened to an emerald set in pearls, for the valley is always green, and during nine months of the year the inner circle of hills that rings it about is white. Farther north lie the eternal snows. Nanga Parbat, 26,620 feet, is visible from certain points in the valley, and K2, or Mount Godwin-Austen, 28,278 feet, the second highest mountain in the world, can be seen from a spot only a day's journey distant.

The Pir Panjal, the southern wall, through the passes of which Kashmir is entered from the plains of India, is the most delightful playground in the Himalayas. In it there are open spaces, where we can gallop over downs of short turf and through forest glades. We can look down into the green valley over meadows dotted with clumps of birch, maple and pine, and as we walk along we crush the flowers which grow so thickly.

But it is not the flowers alone that make the land so beautiful. Nearly every mountain range in a temperate climate, given sufficient rain, is more or less a garden. It is the position of the garden that gives the Pir Panjal its unusual beauty. To say that it commands a wide view of the plains is to convey little.

From most Indian hill-stations or their neighborhood one gets an extensive view of the plains. But the plain on which we look down from Gulmarg, in the Pir Panjal, is a mountain plain, another garden under the rock garden, quite different from the sunburnt expanse of the plains of the Punjab. The green and golden valley of Kashmir is over eighty miles long and from twenty to twenty-five in breadth. It lies at an elevation of some six thousand feet above the sea. In it are all the fruits of the earth and there is no corner of it which is not beautiful.

From the Pir Panjal the traveler does not look out over an endless stretch of country as he does from the southern slopes of the Himalayas. The Vale of Kashmir owes most of its loveliness to the fact that it is not very large. If a mist hid the lakes and mountain buttresses, it would still make a picture of unforgettable beauty and mystery. But when the mist lifts and we can see all, we understand then why the valley with its encircling hills is famous as the most wonderful natural garden in the world.

The visitor to Kashmir seldom sees the Pir Panjal in spring. Up to the end of the second or third week of April, Gulmarg, a favorite resort, is uninhabited. All through the winter the huts lie deep in snow. It is only in July and August when the valley grows hot and mosquitoes be-

KASHMIRI WOMEN, whether rich or poor, display in their costumes a fine sense of color harmony. In India one can generally tell from an individual's dress not only her social standing, but her native place and her religion, while one is informed of her race from her mode of hair dressing. These women are obviously high-caste ladies of leisure.

CHILDREN OF NORTH KASHMIR, with their delicate features, are charming in their bright, gold embroidered clothing. Most Hindu children go bareheaded, but as this brother and sister are dressed in their best clothes, the little girl wears a light shawl on her head and the boy has a magnificent turban. The Hindus of North Kashmir are a fine race.

SUSPENSION BRIDGE OF ROPES OVER THE JHELUM AT URI

The crossing of the river is made on a swinging seat which, hung to one rope, is drawn along by another. Though Kashmir is making electric power from the swift current of the Jhelum River, many such primitive bridges are to be found along its course. Here one works oneself along by hand power.

come a nuisance that folk flock to this upland town. The place is nothing more than a huge inn—a collection of tents and huts, the Maharaja's palace, the Residency, where the prime minister and his government work for the season.

We might leave Kashmir without setting foot in the Pir Panjal and still think of it as the most delightful country in the world. The road from the railway at Rawalpindi, in the Punjab, to Srinagar drops into the Jhelum Valley below Murree and follows the bank of the river, cut into the edge of the cliff, until it comes to Baramula under its cedar forest and enters the Vale of Kashmir.

In the last few miles before Baramula the torrent becomes a wide, placid stream; the valley broadens out into rich cornfields and pastureland; walnut, willow and elm enfold snug villages. At Baramula the Jhelum becomes navigable.

Baramula is the gateway of Kashmir, and the visitor can leave the road and continue his journey to Srinagar, the City of the Sun, in a houseboat. He will be poled and towed to the Wular Lakes and Manasbal with their mountain background.

UNATIONS

KASHMIRI WOMEN EXAMINING SILK COCOONS IN SRINAGAR

Long noted for their fine shawls, the people of Kashmir are now turning their attention to the weaving of silk, as industrialization advances on the Indian continent. Srinagar, in a valley surrounded by the snow-covered Himalayan Mountains, is the summer capital of Kashmir. Over the countryside around the city grow the mulberry shrubs on which the silkworms feed.

THE HEAD OF A TRIBE OF WANDERING MUSICIANS

The people of Kashmir enjoy folk music and dancing, and tribes of wandering musicians, called Bhands, help to keep the old tunes and steps alive. Usually they roam from village to village after the harvest is over, for then the people have more leisure. This man, the leader of a Bhand, plays an instrument that looks something like a modern oboe.

NOT TIME BUT MAN DESTROYED THIS LOVELY TEMPLE

The beautifully carved structure was built at Martand some time in the eighth century A.D. and dedicated to a Hindu sun-god. At that time most of the people were Hindus. By the fourteenth century, Mohammedan rulers had gained the upper hand. It was by the orders of one of the most fanatic of these Moslems that the lovely building was demolished.

MOHAMMEDANS AT PRAYER IN THE COURT OF A SRINAGAR MOSQUE

Today about three-fourths of the people of Kashmir follow the Mohammedan faith, though for many years the rulers have been Hindus—a situation that has caused friction and has kept old grievances alive. In 1952, however, the monarchy was abolished. This action was passed by a convention meeting in Srinagar, presided over by a Mohammedan prime minister.

ONE OF THE SEVEN QUAINT BRIDGES THAT SPAN THE JHELUM RIVER AT SRINAGAR

The road from the railway at Rawalpindi to Srinagar follows the banks of the Jhelum until it comes to Baramula in its forest of cedars. While the former torrent widens to a stream navigable by houseboats, the valley through which it flows gradually flattens into corn-fields and flower-enameled pasturelands. Arrived at Srinagar, we find that canals flow through the city like streets and the better class of dwellings have carved lattice windows and ornamental balconies, with gently sloping roof gardens. There are two mosques, Jami Masjid and Shah Hamadan,

UNATIONS

A LADEN BARGE ON THE JHELUM RIVER AT SRINAGAR

The river is not very wide as it passes through the city, so bridge construction is simple. There are seven wooden bridges like this. In Kashmir, the Jhelum is called the Veth River.

A TURBANED SIKH WEAVER DISPLAYS HIS FINE WARES

The world's finest shawls are produced in Kashmir as are also some high quality carpets. The shawls for which Kashmir is so famous are woven of silk as well as of wool spun from the fleece of goats bred for this purpose. The merchant is demonstrating the exceptionally fine quality of the fabric he is holding by pulling it through a small ring.

Women and children crowd the balconies and river steps. They wear a long garment in bright colors with loose, turned-up sleeves. The Kashmiri women are pretty and the children are often beautiful, with regular features, fair complexion and large, bright, black eyes. Their hair is worn in long plaits, bound with coarse woolen threads and tassels. Their lives are hard, however, and they soon lose their good looks.

Srinagar lies between two hills. On the top of the one to the north is the straggling, yellow fort of Hari Parbat; that to the east is the Takht-i-Suleiman, or "Throne of Solomon," rising a thousand feet above the plain. The Dal Lake washes the bases of both hills, and both are reflected in its clear waters. It is a spring-fed lake and the water is as clear as crystal. The surface, five miles in length and two and a half in breadth, is broken by belts of gigantic reeds, bulrushes, floating gardens and islands.

There are gardens of cockscombs in the dry patches between the dykes, a rich warm glow of color, and fields of bright marigolds, which the true Hindu plucks daily to strew on the altars of the god Siva. At every turn in these creeks there is a new glimpse of the hills. The Nishat, Shalimar and Nasim gardens,

© Underwood & Underwood

THE WINDING JHELUM SEEN FROM THE "THRONE OF SOLOMON"

Srinagar lies between two hills, one called the "Throne of Solomon," on the east, and one the Hari Parbat on the north. On the Throne of Solomon is a magnificent temple of stone, said to have been founded in extremely ancient times, although the present buildings are probably not more than four hundred years old

MONOTONOUS TASK ENLIVENED BY MELODIOUS SONG

Mortar work in India is an agreeable occupation. Around and around the bullocks travel, causing the great stone wheel to revolve and grind the mortar. Their master alternately whips them and sings to them in a cheery, humdrum manner, the grating of the wheel his only accompaniment, but song relieves the monotony of labor for man and beast.

on the shores of the lake were made by the Moguls, who were the rulers of India for over two hundred years. The Nasim, or garden of breezes, is famous for its "chenars," or plane trees, planted by the Mogul emperor Akbar in the sixteenth century. All these gardens are built on the same plan. A spring-fed canal runs down the centre, dropping from terrace to terrace by a series of cascades into reservoirs in which fountains play. The walls of the canal are of marble or old limestone, and have niches for lights, which glisten on nights of festival behind the falling water.

The Nishat Garden is finer than the Shalimar. Its terraces slope down from the steep rocks behind it to the green shores of the lake, so that the last pavilion, covered with roses and jasmine, overlooks a bed of lotuses. The Pir Panjal, twenty miles beyond the opposite shore, forms the southern screen.

From Bandipur on the Wular Lake, we may climb the zigzag path to Tragbal over the Burzil and Kamri passes to Gilgit and the Pamirs. Ten days out of Srinagar, camp can be pitched under the Tarshing Glacier at the foot of Nanga Parbat. Or a visit may be paid to the cave of Amarnath, the natural temple of Siva under the snow. According to Hindu mythology, Siva is a god who forms the supreme Trinity with Brahma and Vishnu. Siva is the destroyer of this life or the re-creator of a new form of life.

Or leaving the houseboat at Ganderbal, after seven days' march one crosses Zoji-la, which is 11,300 feet high, the lowest pass in the northern wall, and is well on the road to Leh in Ladakh a province of Kashmir which makes an ideal contrast to the barrenness left behind. Some of the pleasantest haunts of the side valleys may be reached in a morning's walk from the houseboat.

Islamabad, at the eastern end of the valley, where the Jhelum ceases to be navigable, is a favorite camping ground. Within a circle of a few miles lie the blue springs of Bawan, the Mogul Garden of Achibal, the rock caves of Bomtzu, the monastery of Eishmakam, and Martand, the ruined Temple of the Sun.

The valley is strewn with ancient temples. Martand is believed to date from about the eighth century A.D., during the period of early Hindu civilization in Kashmir. The ruins are of a bluish-gray stone with a tinge of pink.

The temple stands on one of the flat ridges peculiar to the plain. In the valley on either side a river appears and dis-

appears among villages set in poplar clumps and groves of walnut and willow, and one can look down on a well-irrigated plateau, where fields of purple amaranth and the green and chocolate colored rice crops stretch away to the yellow hills. The glittering waters run underneath the road, feeding the rice fields and turning little mills. Such is the valley in spring. In summer Dal Lake is ablaze with tall pink lotuses, acres of them, through which a channel is with difficulty preserved for navigation. By July or August most of the visitors will have gone to the upland plateaus, either to Gulmarg or to the

THE FORT-CROWNED HEIGHT OF HARI PARBAT BEYOND SRINAGAR

When Akbar, the great Mogul emperor, conquered Kashmir, he built the fort on Hari Parbat. After Akbar had consolidated his power over the greater part of India, he instituted a number of improved social laws. He forbade the marriage of boys under sixteen and of girls before fourteen and tried, among other social reforms, to stop widow-burning.

ETERNAL SNOW ON THE LOFTY MOUNTAIN PEAKS THAT RING THE LOVELY VALE OF KASHMIR

The Jhelum River valley is hemmed in by the Himalayas and the Hindu Kush. Snow covers the awesome ranges nine months of the year, and on the highest slopes it never melts. The valley is six thousand feet above sea level, while the mountains tower four miles above the plain.

COZY HOUSEBOATS AFLOAT ON THE JHELUM RIVER IN THE VALE

The custom of living on houseboats in the Vale of Kashmir was begun by English visitors from India many years ago. At that time no foreigners were permitted to erect houses in the vale.

VARIETY OF DWELLINGS ALONG THE RIVER BANK AT SRINAGAR

In contrast to the homes in the picture above, these houses seem ramshackle. In fact, the vale has so many lovely lakes and waterways that houseboats are the preferred dwellings.

DAUGHTER OF THE HEADMAN OF A VILLAGE

A Kashmiri beauty wears a pale silk scarf draped over her head, the better to set off her lovely dark eyes. The trousers are really full—perhaps four or five yards at the waist before being gathered in.

and orchards of apples, quinces and cheeries are reflected in the lake.

It is interesting to watch the sheep being washed at the autumn shearing in Islamabad. They are dragged out of the stream and their hind legs are held up while the relentless wooden scoop scours their fleeces. Fine cloth is woven from this sheep wool.

However, the once famous Cashmere shawls are made from the wool found beneath the hair of the Kashmir goats. Some of these shawls, which many people treasure today as family heirlooms, have an embroidered border. This kind of needlework is a specialty of the region around Srinagar.

Both industry and agriculture are on a small scale. Most of the Kashmiri own or rent tiny farms on which they raise rice, wheat and other cereals for their own use. Some fruit is grown for export and canning. The chief industry is sericulture—raising silkworms—which dates back to the fifteenth century. Wool and silk are spun and woven at home.

Srinagar is a center for wood-carving, carpet weaving, silver and copper articles and papier-mâché, as well as the embroidery mentioned above.

There are no railroads in Kashmir itself, but the Jammu-Pathankot motor highway links the state with the railroad system of India. The Banihal cart road, about two hundred miles long, connects Srinagar, which is the summer capital, with Jammu, the winter capital.

Kashmir was once part of the Mogul Empire; and in the late 1700's it came under the rule of Afghans. In 1846 the former state of Jammu and Kashmir was created when a Jammu chieftain, Gu-

camping grounds in the valleys of the northern tributaries of the Jhelum, where wild goats, bears and deer still haunt the silences. By October the air is nipping,

lab Singh, a Hindu, acquired the Vale of Kashmir. The dynasty founded by Gulab was a benevolent one, and the people gained a measure of freedom. Nevertheless, as a large majority of the Kashmiri are Mohammedans, they have never been altogether happy under Hindu maharajas. Discontent became more vocal during the 1920's and 1930's. One popular demand at that time was for a government by legislature rather than by royal decree.

Thus Kashmir, with a Hindu ruling house and a Mohammedan people, became a disputed area in August 1947 when the subcontinent was divided, largely along religious lines, and the two new countries of Pakistan and India were created. The Maharaja was free to join Kashmir with either country. At first he hesitated, but in October 1947, as armed tribesmen poured into Kashmir from Pakistan, he hastily acceded his state to India. Immediately the Indian Army took over the defense of Kashmir and troops were flown in. India placed the dispute before the United Nations in January 1948, but all during that year Kashmir was the scene of bitter strife between Indian and Pakistani divisions. In January 1949, a United Nations commission finally succeeded in bringing the undeclared war to a halt. Since then a number of efforts have been made to get India and Pakistan to agree on conditions whereby the people themselves could decide their own fate by popular vote.

Love

STREET CORNER IN ISLAMABAD, ONCE THE CAPITAL OF KASHMIR

Islamabad's importance has gradually declined, though it is even now the second most important town in Kashmir. It was once known as Anant Nag, after its sulphurous holy reservoir, which still contains swarms of sacred fish. The town contains a fine mosque and shrine and an old summer palace, besides shawl and chintz factories.

HIMALAYAN DANCING BEAR EARNS A FEW COINS FOR ITS MASTER

The traveling showman seen above obtained this good-natured beast in the Himalayas, where bears, both brown and black, are to be found among the dense forests. It now helps him to gain a few annas or pice, the small change of India, from villagers and townsfolk, who are ever willing to watch dancing bears, jugglers, acrobats or trained monkeys.

THROUGH THREE FORBIDDEN LANDS

Man and Nature in Tibet, Nepal and Bhutan

In this chapter, we are to read about three countries, which all lie together, where few travelers have been welcome. If we look at a map of Asia, we find that India and Pakistan are shut off on the north by the Himalaya Mountains, beyond which lies an immense and little-known territory called Tibet. For many years it was really an independent country, with a government by priests, although nominally it remained an outer dependency of China's. However, in 1951, the Chinese Communists marched in and made it Chinese territory in fact. The smaller independent mountain states of Nepal and Bhutan stand between Tibet and the Indian subcontinent and are separated from each other by the even smaller Indian state of Sikkim.

A PREHISTORIC sea, the Middle Ocean, once separated China and Northeast Asia from the Deccan of India. (Salt water fossils have been found at what are now altitudes of four thousand feet.) In time a gigantic mountain ridge, the Himalayan, was built up by geologic upheavals. Now peaks from three to five and a half miles high, with level valleys high between the ridges, drop abruptly on the south to the plains of India. On the northern side we have the plateau of Tibet, a land of mystery high under the shining snow peaks. A land dry and barren but affording pasturage for the flocks of the fiercely independent Mongolian tribes who dwell there. Their religion is Lamaism, a faith reminiscent of Buddhism, in which the Dalai Lama is believed to be a reincarnation of Buddha.

The Lamas for years permitted none but the Chinese to enter the capital, Lhasa. Explorers were turned back at the rude forts along the route, or were murdered, and China prevented any trade with India. In 1904 the government of India succeeded in sending a mission to Lhasa to establish trade relations directly with Tibet; the Dalai Lama fled, and three Tibetan marts for Indian goods, Gartok, Yatung and Gyantse were agreed upon. Thereafter caravans of pack-sheep and of yaks crossed with Indian cattle began winding over the fourteen- to eighteen-thousand-foot passes, usually to a point near Darjeeling, to exchange raw wool for cotton piece goods and other commodities. By 1908 Tibet further agreed

that it would consent to no foreign interference without the consent of the British. When, in 1910, the Chinese sought to reinvade this hidden land, the British extended their protection, and the Dalai Lama sought refuge in India. He returned to Tibet in 1913, declared its independence of China and established an arsenal at Lhase. Nonetheless Tibet remained a nominal dependency of China's.

Chinese Communists marched into the outskirts of Tibet in 1950; and in May 1951, they announced the "peaceful liberation" of Tibet through a political settlement. Thus the Red flag was planted on the "roof of the world" and the Communist conquest of the Chinese mainland was completed. There were promises that the position of the Dalai Lama would be maintained and that religious freedom would be protected. At the same time the Communists called for a return of the rival, pro-Communist Panchen Lama, who had been in exile in China.

Between Sikkim and the Yatung Valley of Tibet there is a gap in the mountain wall. A trip through it to Tibet is like stepping back into the fifteenth century. High above the plain of Lhasa, the capital, towers the Potala, a fortress-palace. Tibet is a land of praying wheels. These are turned by wind or water and contain strips of thin paper on which is printed the Buddhist mystical prayer "Om Mani Padme Om!" (Ah, the jewel in the lotus, ah.) As these wheels revolve, the prayer is thus thought to be repeated countless millions of times. Small prayer wheels are carried in the hand by nearly every-one, and one passes long rows of them attached to the walls of houses and mon-asteries.

Another device for the easy production of prayer is the pole twenty or thirty feet high with thin strips of muslin nailed to it which flutter in the breeze, and upon which is written the same sacred text. These are the praying flags, or "horses of the wind."

The "chorten"—a pyramidical shrine for offerings, often built over the relics of some Buddhist saint—and the "men-dangs"—long walls in the middle of the road, built for the most part of stones on which is inscribed the same Buddhist prayer—are so common that one comes to look on them as natural features of the country.

Flowery Valley and Bleak Waste

In May the Yatung valley is beautiful; on the sides of the mountains the red blooms of the rhododendrons can be seen among the pine trees; the rocks in the stream are covered with moss, which forms a bed for gentian and anemones, celandines, wood sorrel and irises. But a few miles beyond Gautsa, near the meeting place of the sources of the Ammo-Chu River, one passes the last tree, at an elevation of thirteen thousand feet. Beyond there is nothing but desolation.

The Chumbi valley leads into the higher tableland, where you first see typical Tibetan scenery. The climate for the greater part of the year is terribly severe and the shaggy-haired Tibetan yak is the only beast. A numbing, grit-laden wind blows over the high plains and in Janu-ary the thermometer falls to 25 de-grees below zero. The traveler goes for sixty miles through this wasteland be-fore he sees the first solitary willow in the valley of the Paina-Chu.

Rare Pieces of Cultivated Land

In the valley of the Paina-Chu the traveler comes upon the first of the plains where the ground can be cultivated. There are very few of these in Southern Tibet, but every bit of them is used to grow food for men and beasts. After three days' traveling one again enters the treeless region, and on the fourth night camp is pitched in the snowy range of Noijin Kang Sang, nearly one thou-sand feet higher than the top of Mont Blanc. The Karo-la or Karo Pass, over sixteen thousand feet in altitude, lies under the summit of the range twenty-four thousand feet and magnificent gla-ciers come down to within five hundred feet of the track. Then the road de-scends to the basin of the great Yamdok Tso, the Turquoise Lake, a wild and beautiful stretch of water, with arms winding into the mysterious crannies of hills which perhaps no white man has ever trod. The road to Lhasa runs along the edge of the water for a long way and then goes up the ridge to the north to the Khamba-la, twelve hundred feet above the lake level.

The Great River of Tibet

The path makes a sudden turn, and the traveler looks down into the great trough where the Tsang-po river cuts through the bleak hills and desert tablelands of Tibet from west to east. This is no de-tached oasis, but a continuous strip of rich vegetation. The Tsang-po and its tributaries have drawn to them half the population and the greater part of the merchandise of Tibet. A mysterious river, in parts unexplored, it was only re-cently discovered to be a part of the Brahmaputra, which flows through Assam.

The river is crossed by a ferry at Chaksam, where it flows so swiftly that it is dangerous for boats; yet the Tibetans in their light craft made of hides can go up or down the river for a distance of one hundred miles. It is the main way for traffic in the country and is crowded with boatloads of pilgrims in seasons of fes-tivals. A hundred miles upstream the Tashi Lama of Tashi Lunpo holds court. He is the "Great Precious Teacher," the second of the Grand Lamas of Tibet, con-sidered even holier than the Dalai Lama himself, whose power is political.

Lhasa, the City of Mystery, blessed by

A DEVIL DANCER who takes part in one of these religious dances makes himself look as dreadful as he possibly can. With the grotesque mask and head-dress that he is wearing, the lama, as monks are called in Tibet, is here supposed to represent the sort of fiend that Tibetans will meet in the next world if they do not lead righteous lives in this one.

121

the Buddha, and the Potala, the palace in which lives the Dalai Lama, lie three days' hard travel beyond Chaksam. Lhasa is hidden from sight until one has a view, at about seven miles distance, of the Potala, which seems to be a golden dome standing out on a steep rock in the centre of the valley. To the south the Chagpo-ri, another such rock, rising from the banks of the Kyi Chu, is crowned by a yellow fort and the Lamas' Medical College. The narrow ridge between this rock and the Dalai Lama's palace is bridged by the Pargo Kaling, a typical Tibetan chorten, through which is cut the main gateway into Lhasa.

Lhasa, like all Tibetan towns, is filthy beyond description. Undrained and unpaved, the streets are pools of stagnant water in which pigs and dogs search for refuse. Even the Jokhang, the cathedral, the holy of holies, is dirty.

From the outside nothing is splendid in Lhasa except the Potala, which rises high above the miserable huts at its foot. The palace catches the eye at once. It is not a palace on a hill, but a hill that is also a palace. The rock is merely the foundation stone. It is difficult to discover where the rock ends and the building begins. High above the causeway one face flashes white in the sun, a stretch of nine hundred feet of bare wall without a break, then at the height of a church steeple row upon row of windows, thousands of them, oblong openings which look like dominoes. On top, in the centre of this massive block of rock and brick,

TEMPLE AND TIERED BUILDINGS IN THE CITY OF PATAN

On the left is a temple with lions guarding the flight of steps leading up to the entrance, and on every side are buildings with two or three roofs, which are found only in Nepal. Patan is situated not far from Khatmandu, the capital of Nepal, and, owing to its shape, is believed by the Newars to be the wheel of Buddha.

STRANGE STONE FIGURES BEFORE A TEMPLE IN BHATGAON

When the Newars ruled Nepal, Bhatgaon was one of the capitals, the others being Khatmandu and Patan. Many of the fine buildings are now deserted, as all the officials live in Khatmandu. Flights of stone steps lead up to the larger temples and palaces, on the stairs of which are carved figures of animals and quaint human beings.

THE NA-CHUNG MONASTERY has many colored prayer flags hung in strips across its courtyard. On each flag is printed a prayer which, the Tibetans say, is prayed whenever the wind flutters it. The monastery is just outside of Lhasa in a gully overgrown with trees, and the monks have added to the beauty of the spot by planting beds of flowers. But this is the headquarters of the chief magician of the country and, while his monastery is beautiful outside, the walls within are covered with grotesque paintings of tortures.

124

THE ROYAL PALACE of the Maharaja of Bhutan is a spacious fortress called Tongsa Jong.
The word "jong" means fort, both in Bhutan and Tibet, and, like many in the country, this
one is built up the side of a hill in a series of courtyards which are commanded by towers.
Note the beautiful windows and the eaves which remind one of those of Swiss chalets.

A TIBETAN NOBLEWOMAN AND HER SON WEAR FESTIVAL FINERY

During the summer festival in Lhasa, capital and holy city of Tibet, a gracious lady and her son display richly woven and bright colored silks. There is little weaving in Tibet. Fine fabrics, as well as tea, rice, porcelain, cotton and cereals, come to the isolated land from China. Until the Chinese Communists took control in 1951, Tibet also traded with India.

126

TEMPLE BUGLERS PLAY ANCIENT INSTRUMENTS FOR A LAMA DANCE

The bleak Himalayan Mountains shelter many monasteries within their fertile valleys. The ancient horn, or bugle, plays an important role within these orders. The buglers summon the monks to prayer with a series of shrill blasts. Low, monotonous melodies may be played for medi-tation, and the same horns provide fast, blaring accompaniment for a festival or dance.

THE POTALA (fort, palace and monastery) is one of the most curious buildings in the world. For centuries it was never seen by white men, with the exception of occasional solitary travelers. It houses the Dalai Lama, whom Tibetans believe to be an incarnation of Buddha, who is successively re-born in one body after another. High up the white fortress walls are

pierced by row after row of windows. Above can be seen the Phodang-marpo, the red-painted palace of the Dalaï Lama, down the front of which hangs a vast curtain of yak hair screening the holy of holies. The roof of the palace is gilded and flashes in the sunshine. The holy city of Lhasa, filthy and unpaved, is out of sight to the right.

THE RANEE OF NEPAL SEATED AMIDST THE LADIES OF THE COURT WHO WAIT UPON HER

The figure of the Ranee is completely hidden by yards and yards of material, which are spread out over the sofa. On her head is a wreath of flowers which is beautifully modeled in silver and gold. In public she is always escorted by her ladies-in-waiting, who carry fans of pea-cocks' feathers and fly-whisks. The attendants at either end of the row are holding the state umbrellas. Those of the Nepalese women do not wear trousers. Instead, they have skirts which are like balloons, as the material is arranged over a light framework.

John Claude White

STALWART LIFEGUARDSMEN IN THE BODYGUARD OF THE MAHARAJA OF BHUTAN

The Maharaja of Bhutan keeps a company of bodyguards to protect his royal person. They are armed with swords, which, we notice, they wear on the right hip, whereas the British regiments use the left. The shields are made of hide, with metal bosses for extra strength, and each war- rior's headpiece is of steel swathed in bright colored silks. The scab- bards of the swords are of silver. The wonderfully patterned garment worn by the king, who stands in the centre of the picture, is of Chinese brocade. It is called a boku.

131

THE MAHARAJA OF BHUTAN, Ugyen Wangchuk, whose death occurred in 1926, made a fine figure seated among councilors. Around his neck is the broad ribbon, supporting a medal, that shows him to have been a Knight Commander of the Order of the Indian Empire, an honor conferred upon him for helping the British Mission that went to Tibet.

THE SPIRIT OF BUDDHA is believed by the Bhutias to have entered the body of this gorgeously robed young man in the centre of the picture, just as the Tibetans hold that it dwells in their own Dalai Lama. The youth is called the Avator of Thaling because his monastery is at Thaling, in Bhutan. The old man on his right is his teacher and guardian.

133

LUNCH TIME AT AN ENCAMPMENT AMONG THE GRAND SCENERY OF MOUNTAINOUS BHUTAN

When the British Resident of Sikkim went to Bhutan to confer the Order of the British Empire upon the Maharaja, the Expedition had to be a large one on account of the wild state of the country. The party is here seen camped on a plateau fifteen thousand feet above sea level. Beyond are some of the wonderful mountains of Bhutan, the slopes of which, covered with forests lower down, are at this height becoming bare as the summits are approached. The coolies, or native porters, are sitting down for their midday meal.

A FEARSOME FACE DECORATES THE TOWER OF A BUDDHIST TEMPLE

There are some 2,700 shrines in the Khatmandu Valley and thousands of priests of both Hindu and Buddhist faiths. The Buddhist temples here, unlike those elsewhere, do not house relics of Buddha. Instead they are apt to have five shrines to the Dhanibuddhas, the five saints below Buddha. Most of the temples have dome-shaped roofs with lofty spires.

135

THE DHARM RÁJÁ is a king without power, as the real ruler is the Maharaja. But when acting as the temporary head of the Buddhists, as shown here, he appears gorgeous in yellow brocade, while behind him and before hang gorgeous banners worked with fabulous beasts. On the table are the drum, bell and vessels of silver and gold used in Buddhist services.

stands the Phodang-marpo, the red palace of the priest-king, in tiers of bright crimson. The present Dalai Lama is a child born in western China in 1935. The Tibetans firmly believe that he is the fourteenth incarnation of Buddha. Until he is eighteen a regent will rule.

The outskirts of Lhasa make up for the dirt and unsightliness of its streets. It is a waterlogged city approached from the west by a stone road raised over a marsh. The visitor passes beautiful spots in the Tsang-po valley and lower down the Kyi Chu, but these are only patches of fertility and he does not expect to see the wide belt of green by which Lhasa is encircled—willow groves divided by clear running streams, swaying poplars, walled-in parks with palaces and fish ponds, marshes where the wild ducks, left undisturbed, have become bold, and barley fields stretching away to the hills.

Warrens of Tibetan Lamaseries

The lamaseries outside the city are almost hidden by trees and their golden pagoda-shaped roofs have a green background formed by the base of the mountains. Each is a little town in itself. In design the Tibetan lamaseries are all much alike, a warren of monastic buildings, temples and narrow streets, perched in white tiers on stone terraces built out from the rocky sides of the hill, honeycombed with passages, halls, chapels and cells. In the dark and grimy recesses of the temples loom the great gilded Buddhas, life size, covered with precious stones, especially turquoises. The smell of the butter lamps before the altar is almost suffocating; their smoke has hidden the showy paintings on the wall. It is a relief to look through the dark pillars to the cloistered courtyard and quadrangle outside, where the sun is shining and flowers bloom in the garden. The truth is that Lamaism has sunk back into the worship of spirits supposed to live in all manner of objects. Every rock and cavern is marked with superstitious emblems.

There are happier sides to the picture. Most travelers in Tibet will remember being entertained by jolly abbots in the Rongbuk valley, where the Everest Expedition discovered that the mountain sheep, tamed by the hermits, would come to feed out of their hands.

An Inhospitable Land

The only Tibet known to travelers over the Indian frontier is but a narrow strip of green country at the beginning of a mountainous desert. Central and Northern Tibet form a vast and cheerless tableland. From the passes north of Lhasa there is a view of mountains stretching away in endless ridges. This is only the beginning of the wilderness, which continues to the borders of Mongolia and Chinese Turkestan.

At the eastern end of the Himalayas, north of India, is the mountainous state of Bhutan which likewise is closed to the traveler. The land consists of range after range of mountains between which lie narrow valleys watered by fast flowing streams. The best idea of Bhutan can be had by imagining it to be a gigantic stairway leading from the humid plains of Bengal to the chill tableland of Tibet.

Bamboos and tree ferns are found in the lower valleys and oaks and rhododendrons cover the sides of the mountains up to a height of eight thousand feet, at which point they are replaced by dark forests of pines and firs. Unfortunately for the traveler, owing to the damp atmosphere, a leech is waiting on nearly every leaf that overhangs the path, ready to attach itself to any living creature that passes. Besides these pests, there are many kinds of stinging and biting insects in this every way inhospitable land. High up on the sides of the mountains can be seen the great Buddhist monasteries.

Guarding many of the passes, especially those leading to Tibet, are great fortresses, each of which contains a central citadel occupied by the governor and his family. Both the monasteries and forts have overhanging eaves to shed the snow and wooden galleries like those of Switzerland.

A Tortuous Approach

Bhutan is usually entered from Buxa, Bengal, whence the road bends and twists

John Claude White

TRUMPETERS AND DRUMMERS OF A BHUTAN FORT TURNED OUT TO WELCOME BRITISH GUESTS

To receive the British Mission to the Maharaja of Bhutan one of the forts which the Expedition visited turned out its band in welcome. The trumpeters are clothed in scarlet uniforms, and it will be noticed that they stand barefooted in the snow. The drummer is clothed in green, and next to him comes a man who beats upon a gong. Behind the group are two riding mules with gorgeous trappings as a present for the visitors. Mules are used in the country for riding, as they are more sure-footed than horses on the mountain trails.

138

John Claude White

A PARADE OF BHUTANESE MUSICIANS AND A GROUP OF LAMAS AT A RELIGIOUS DANCE

In the top photograph we see the private band of the Maharaja. There are trumpeters in red, drummers in green, and a choir of singing girls. The lower photograph shows lamas in their robes of Chinese silk, their masks in this case made of *papier-mâché*, though usually these hideous objects are of wood. The weird devil dancing practically consists of a series of shufflings and turnings. It is performed outside a "gompa," or temple, to the accompaniment of prayers and of the band (seen on the left). and may last for four days.

like all Himalayan trails until it reaches Punakha, the seat of government. There is another way into the country up the valley of the Manas River, which rises in the Tibetan lake, Yamdok Tso, and flows across Bhutan from north to south; but as yet practically nothing is known about the northern and eastern borderlands.

The Bhutias, as the inhabitants of Bhutan are called, have built their little villages chiefly in sheltered spots where they can grow wheat, barley, millet, mustard and chillies. Owing to the steep nature of the country they make their fields in series of terraces, each of which is supported by a stone embankment, which may be as much as twenty feet in height. The farmers cultivate no more land than is absolutely necessary, because

when there is anything left over to sell, it is likely to be taken from them by the lamas of the nearest monastery or by the governor of any fort in the neighborhood.

The government of the country was originally in the hands of the Dharm Raja or spiritual head and the Deb Raja or temporal ruler. To-day the Dharm Raja has little authority save in matters of religion. An hereditary Maharaja is the executive.

Until the end of the last century there was no real form of government, the strongest governor making war on the weaker ones and acting as a king in his own district, while the poor people were robbed and oppressed by everyone. The first Maharaja was Sir Ugyen Wangchuk, who was elected in 1907. He had to fight hard to make the governors recognize his authority.

John Claude White

THE LATE MAHARAJA AND SOME MEMBERS OF THE ROYAL FAMILY

His Majesty is standing on the top step and to the left of the group. Next him is his sister, her grandchild and her daughter. Seated below are the king's two daughters. A male and female retainer complete the party. The Maharaja's sister looks after the food and clothing of the royal household, which numbers several hundred people.

LAMAS WHO BEAT TIME FOR THE MASKED DANCERS

There are devil dancers in Bhutan and also in Tibet, and the same sorts of instruments are used, the trumpet, drum and cymbals. The drum-sticks are of metal and shaped like question-marks. The noise is not unpleasant but to Western ears, monotonous. There is no attempt at a tune, but just a rhythm to keep the dancers in time.

The huge monasteries are mainly responsible for the backward condition of Bhutan, since into them go so many of the nation's best men, who might be better employed in farming, trading or preventing raids on the northern and eastern frontiers. The Maharaja has, however, done much to break the power of the lamas and to check the abbots of the lamaseries, who were once continually intriguing with the Grand Lama of Tibet.

The inhabitants of western Bhutan are like the Tibetans in appearance, and equally suspicious of strangers. They have to work hard in their terraced fields, which are sometimes swept away down the hillsides by the terrible storms that break over the mountains. Since the officials receive no regular salary, they take what they can get from the people of the district, who can do nothing to protect their property. Eastern Bhutan is practically unexplored. To the west of Bhutan, and only separated from it by Sikkim, is the independent state of Nepal, which stretches along the Himalayas for a distance of five hundred miles. The whole country is a wild tangle of mountains, the only flat space being the valley of Nepal, in which stands the capital, Khatmandu. Outside this valley there are no roads, no towns, not even large villages. Although Nepal is under the protection of the Indian government, the only white

KHAMBA JONG, ONE OF THE HUGE FORTRESSES OF TIBET

There are few more desolate places than the plain which stretches away before the great fort of Khamba. It stands fifteen thousand feet above the sea, and about one hundred miles from Mount Everest, which can be seen on a fine day. Here and there amid the expanse of bowlders grows a little coarse grass that provides food for the hardy Tibetan yak, and over all the dust is blown by the cold, strong wind.

THE NEW YEAR FESTIVAL AT TASHI LUNPO MONASTERY

Tashi Lunpo, whose abbot is seen on a subsequent page, is built by the banks of the great Tsang-po River to the west of Lhasa. It is, next to the Potala at Lhasa, the holiest monastery in Tibet, and there are always tremendous crowds who gather at the festival of the New Year, which is known as the "Losar," for the celebration of which there is a fortnight's general holiday.

NEPALESE WOMEN WHO BELIEVE YOU ARE WORTH WHAT YOU WEAR

The inhabitants of Nepal are known in general as Paharis, or "dwellers in the cliffs." They are divided into various tribes such as the Bhotias, the Gurungs and the Magars. The Bhotias are a nomadic tribe and their women, as shown above, adorn themselves with ornate jewelry made of coins. The size of the family fortune may often be gauged by the decorative display.

PANNIERED DONKEYS AND A CHORTEN IN A TIBETAN VILLAGE

A chorten is a Buddhist shrine with a chamber that houses a relic. A spire or an umbrella may surmount it. This old chorten has been made into a gate, a rather unusual use.

144

SPREADING EAVES AND A PRAYING STATUE IN KATMANDU

The capital of Nepal is a city of temples—most of them dedicated to Siva, one of the Hindu
trinity. The architectural design is unique and is called Newar, or Mongoloid Nepalese.

145

men allowed into the country are the Minister, who is the representative of the government, and the officers commanding the Minister's escort. Indeed, few white men have ever seen the mountain fastnesses outside the valley which so nearly constitutes the state itself. This valley was originally the bed of a lake 4,500 feet above sea level; and a legend relates that when the lake drained away, its waters

Georg Haeckel

ONE OF THE MAGICIANS WHO TERRORIZE TIBET

A magician's duty is to discover any demon supposed to be doing harm, and to drive him off by magic. Before Buddhism was established in Tibet the country had a religion of its own called Bon. This had much to do with demons and ghosts, and when the purer faith was introduced, aspects of the Bon religion became mixed with it.

were released by the god Manjusri, who cleft the rim of mountains with his sword. The chasm thus made is alleged to be the Kot-bar or Sword Cut, and much of the ancient art of the region represents Manjusri, the patron saint of Nepal, with uplifted sword. Geologists offer the theory that the lake burst its boundaries during some violent earthquake and escaped into what is now the Baghmati river. A ropeway was made in 1927 to carry goods to the valley from Raxaul.

There is a narrow strip of cultivated land where the foothills of the Himalayas slope down to the plains of northern India. Beyond lies a belt of jungle twenty miles wide known as the Terai, one of the finest regions for big game hunting in the world. After passing through the Terai the traveler is faced by a succession of mountain ranges which extend clear to Tibet, the highest peak being Mount Everest, 29,141 feet. It stands on the frontier between the two countries. This highest known summit in the world was never attempted by climbers until 1912. There are several other mountains over 20,000 feet high.

Percy Brown

TIBETAN ARCHER-MUSKETEER AT A SHOOTING COMPETITION

Every year there is a shooting competition in the Tibetan town of Shigatse. Competitors are armed with bows and prong muskets. The prong can be let down and used as a rest when the musket is fired from the ground. But in the competition each man rides at full gallop past two targets, shooting with bow and gun alternately.

C. SUYDAM CUTTING

HEAPED CLOUDS AND JAGGED MOUNTAIN MASSES IN TIBET

The forbidding aspect of the "roof of the world" can be seen even at this comparatively low level. Yet the mystery and solitude of the country continue to challenge the imagination of man and have lured him to some of his boldest ventures. The crude little boat on the river is made of wood covered with the skin of the yak, the animal of a hundred uses in Tibet.

TIBET, NEPAL AND BHUTAN: FACTS AND FIGURES

TIBET

Though nominally an outer dependency of China for many years, Tibet was considered an independent country for all practical purposes. All this changed, however, when the Communists gained control in China. Red Chinese troops marched into the outlying reaches of Tibet in 1950; and in May 1951, the Chinese Communists announced that the theocratic (by priests) government of Tibet had surrendered. The country is bounded on the north by Singkiang, on the northeast by Tsinghai, on the east by Sikang, on the south by Bhutan, Nepal and India, and on the west by India. The frontiers are not definitely established; but the estimated area is 469,294 square miles; and the population is about 3,700,000. The capital is Lhasa, which has a population of about 50,000. The prevailing religion is Lamaism, a variant form of Buddhism. Some agriculture is carried on, and barley and other cereals, vegetables and fruits are grown. Minerals include gold, borax and salt. In the pastoral regions sheep and yak, buffaloes, pigs and camels are raised. The most common industries are wool-spinning, weaving and knitting, and the making of images and other decorations for religious use.

NEPAL

An independent kingdom in the Himalayas, bounded on the north by Tibet, on the east by Sikkim, on the south and the west by the Republic of India. The estimated area is 54,000 square miles, the population about 7,000,000. The capital, Katmandu, has a population of about 108,805. Most of the people are Hindus.

The government, nominally under the Maharaja, is actually a military oligarchy. All power is in the hands of the Prime Minister. The chief products are rice, ginger, sugar, tobacco, potatoes, fruits, cattle, hides, gums, oil seeds, jute, timber and saltpetre. There are valuable forests in the southern part. Chief exports are cattle, hides and skins, opium and other drugs and the imports are cotton, silk and woolen piece goods, leather, brass, iron and copper wares. There are two railways, totaling 58 miles in length.

BHUTAN

A state in the eastern Himalayas, bounded on the north and east by Tibet, on the west by the Tibetan district of Chumbi and Sikkim, on the south by the Republic of India. The area is about 18,000 square miles, the population about 300,000. The religion is a Tibetan form of Buddhism. The government is under a hereditary Maharaja. Chief products are rice, corn, millet, lac, wax, different kinds of cloth, musk, elephants, ponies and silk. There are valuable forests. Muzzle-loading guns and swords of highly tempered steel are manufactured. Other manufactures, including woven cloth and wooden bowls, are for home use.

BURMA ON THE BAY OF BENGAL

A Land Where Women Are Independent

Burma, formerly a part of the Indian Empire and later a British Crown Colony, since the end of the second World War has become the republic of the Union of Burma. It is a land where the women occupy an unusually privileged position. They dress like men, smoke cheroots, conduct shops and forego chaperonage. Burma is a land in which the means to a livelihood is easily procured and people devote much time to the building of their Buddhist temples. "The temple bells are ringing," sang Kipling of Mandalay, " . . . An' the dawn comes up like thunder outer China 'crost the Bay." Here, too, elephants are used in the hills as beasts of burden. Burma is also the home of the Padaungs of the colder north, the Lihsaws who live just across the frontier from Yun-nan, and the Akhas of the Shan States.

BURMA, formerly an important province of the Indian Empire, lies on the Bay of Bengal, between Assam, Tibet and China, Indo-China, Siam and Malaya. Ranges of hills running south from the rim of the Tibet plateau make traveling wearisome in the eastern portion of the country. Anyone who wishes to cross these hills must continually descend into deep valleys, then ascend four thousand feet or more.

Burma proper lies in the valley and basin of the Irawadi, one of the world's great rivers. Its basin forms one of the three natural divisions of Burma, of which the other two are the Arakan with the Chin hills, and Tenasserim with the basin of the Salween. The Irawadi is navigable for about nine hundred miles. After a journey of a thousand miles it carries down so much silt that it yellows the Bay of Bengal. It has an average breadth of a mile and a half, but below Rangoon it sometimes reaches for several miles from shore to shore. Its swift currents then prevent ships from anchoring and people must go ashore in small boats. Indeed, when it overflows, at the rainy season, it becomes ten miles wide at certain points. Up and down this great highway passes a large portion of the commerce of the country, notwithstanding that a railway runs more or less parallel to it for much of the way. All the wealth of Burma comes down the Irawadi—teak, oil, rice, indigo, ground nuts, jade, amber, rubies, silver and, not least valuable, rubber. Upstream go manufactured goods, foodstuffs, milled rice and other of the necessities of life for the Burmese and also the European inhabitants. There is a large local trade in silk, "ngapi" (pickled fish) and "let-pet" (pickled tea).

The only towns of importance are Rangoon, Moulmein and Mandalay. Rangoon, situated in the delta of the Irawadi, was the British capital and chief port. It boasts a model jail, which can accommodate three thousand. Moulmein across the Gulf of Martaban, was the first British capital. The old native capital of Upper Burma is Mandalay.

Burma is rich in forests. Reserved forests alone, maintained principally for timber, cover 31,637 square miles. Her extraordinary fertility is due in part to her more than abundant rainfall. That of the Arakan along her upper coastline and Tenasserim, the coastal strip that depends from the south of Burma between the Gulf of Siam and the Indian Ocean, averages two hundred inches in a year—nearly five times, that of, say, New York—while there is ninety inches in the Irawadi delta. In the mountains of the extreme north, however, lies a zone as dry as California.

Unlike the Hindus, the Burmese are generally supposed to have migrated from Western China to the headwaters of the Irawadi, as did the people of Tibet. Their language is monosyllabic, though it depends a very great deal less than the Chinese on intonation. The alphabet, on the other hand, shows evidence of having been borrowed from the Aryan Sanskrit

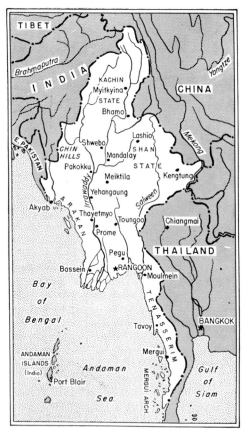

TIBET

Brahmaputra

INDIA

KACHIN
Myitkyina•
STATE
Bhamo•

CHINA

Yangtze

Shwebo
CHIN
HILLS
Pakokku

Lashio•
SHAN
Mandalay
STATE
Meiktila
Yehangaung

Mekong

Kengtung•

E. PAKISTAN

Akyab•

Thayetmyo
ARAKAN
Toungoo
Prome

Salween

Chiangmai

Pegu•

THAILAND

Bassein•
★RANGOON
•Moulmein

Bay

of

Bengal

Tavoy•

BANGKOK

ANDAMAN
ISLANDS
(India)
Port Blair

Andaman

Sea

Mergui

TENASSERIM

MERGUI ARCH.

Gulf

of

Siam

HOMELAND OF THE BURMESE

of India, and it is true that the Buddhist scriptures of Burma came from Southern India and Ceylon.

Protected by hilly walls, the Burmese maintained their independence for centuries. Then during the nineteenth century wars were fought with the British which resulted in making Burma India's largest province. It really began with a dispute over the Arakan and Chittagong, which generated such ill feeling in Burma that she eventually made preparations to invade Bengal by way of Manipur. This invasion the British prevented by occupying the strategic port of Rangoon in 1824 and advancing up the Irrawaddy. As a consequence, the disputed Arakan came under British administration, together with Assam in the north, and Tenasserim in the south. Further territory in Lower Burma was acquired in 1852. The third

change came in 1886, when Upper Burma was annexed. Burma became a Governor's Province of India in 1923. In 1937 it was separated from India and became a Crown Colony of the British Empire. Burma was conquered by the Japanese in 1942 after a brief campaign.

After the Japanese surrender in 1945, agitation for independence grew. Conferences in London between Burmese independence leaders and British government officials led to the formation of a Constituent Assembly and finally, in January of 1948, complete independence.

Burma is chiefly agricultural and its prime export is rice. The tourist will enjoy visiting the ricemills, the teak sawmills and lumber yards in which elephant labor is employed, and perhaps the petroleum refineries, which represent a third important industry. Just below Rangoon, at Pazundaung, on the Irrawaddy, stands a ricemill so vast that it turns out tons of rice a day. To it float barges loaded with the "paddy" (unhusked rice) which has been garnered with a hand-sickle, often by coolies from Hindustan. From the barges, heavy basketloads are carried on the head or shoulders to the mill. The paddy is first run over sieves and shakers to remove dirt and grit, then passed between grinders which remove its outer husks and leave a brown "natural" rice more wholesome than polished, where rice is the mainstay of the diet. This brown rice is run through pearlers to remove the clinging inner husks, then through sieves to grade it for the storage warehouses.

The humming teak sawmills at Rangoon employ hundreds of elephants, for teak is heavy. The hard wood preferred for Oriental temples and carved furniture is so heavy that in the green state it will not float. It grows in the hills amid bamboo brush, and elephants are used first to drag the logs downhill through the heavy undergrowth. Young bulls rounded up from the wild herds of the North Burma forests are chiefly used for this work because first it is easier to train the young animals, then because their tusks are useful as levers for picking up logs and for carrying them about the lumber yards. The great beasts appear to have almost human intelligence as they kneel before a log, thrust their tusks beneath it midway, then steady it with their trunks as they move it. When the rivers are deep, they can swim about, pushing the logs to place as directed by the drivers who sit on their heads. When the creeks are as "sludgy, squdgy," as Kipling's poem describes them to be, the elephants can go into mud knee-deep to float the logs in what water there is. In return for this labor, which would be impossible to any other living creature, the pachyderms must be kept scrubbed and curried, fed on tons of hay and bran, with perhaps rice and molasses for dessert, and given frequent holidays. The wild herds of the jungle are conserved by a commissioner of elephants who corresponds in importance to the forest supervisors of other countries.

Burma is one of the important oil producers of the world and supplies a good proportion of the lamps of Asia. The Burma Oil Company has huge refineries at Syriam and elsewhere, and its own fleet of oil tank steamers. Burma also has some of the finest and largest jade mines in the world and sells quantities of the costly transparent jade to wealthy Chinese for jewelry.

In Rangoon, natives of India, Chinese, Malays and Europeans jostle one another. White men find it too hot to walk, and unless they have their own automobiles, patronize the "gharries" (pony cabs) or street cars, which have second-class compartments. A few natives ride bicycles; others draw carts in competition with humped cattle. The city is a religious centre because it contains the famous Shwe Dagon pagoda.

In the country districts, the houses are built of bamboo, with palm leaves to thatch the roofs and matting to paper the walls. Rice flourishes in the fields and delicious fruits grow wild. There is thus little inducement to thrift. When a man becomes wealthy, he buys jewelry for his wife and daughters, gives feasts to his neighbors or builds a pagoda that he may acquire merit for a future existence.

Scott

BURMESE MEN WEAR SKIRTS

Shirt-like nether garments are worn by both men and women in Burma, but turbans are favored by men only. Burmese men are lazy and leave the work for the women to do.

Notwithstanding, the women are exceptionally capable and energetic. In Rangoon certain of them have even been appointed to the Rangoon judicial court. Every Burmese woman is a born shopkeeper: every girl wants to manage a stall in the bazaar. Once she has gained her desire, she will sit there above huge baskets of grain or lengths of colored silks, smoking a cheroot as long as a school ruler. This business capacity of the women is the more surprising in that, until recent years, there was no education pro-

NIMBLE FINGERS AND POTTERY PLATES

The worker above is turning out Burmese pottery which, while sturdy and durable, is not as artistic as many of the other native wares. The people of Burma are highly skilled as weavers, sculptors and gold and silver smiths, and they also produce interesting brass and lacquer work. They like to adorn their houses and boats with their own ornate wood carvings.

vided for girls. If the husband is idle or ailing, the wife can divorce him. But he may claim his freedom if the wife gives him no sons.

In most of the out-of-the-way villages there may be a "pongyi kyaung," or monks' house, and the drone of voices coming from it will lead us to the schoolroom, where a dozen boys are shouting out the letters of the Burmese alphabet.

When Burma attained its independence, the school system came under state control. It includes primary, middle and high school grades. Primary education is free. In secondary schools, Burmese is the language of instruction, with English required as a second language. Rangoon is the seat of the University of Rangoon as well as of the University for Adult Education for those who do not qual-

152

WHERE THE MARK OF BEAUTY IS A VERY LONG NECK

The principal adornments of the women of the Padaung tribe are brass rings or coils worn around their necks, arms and legs. They start with one ring of the collar when they are very little girls, and add to this as they grow older until the later ones rest upon their shoulders. The practice results in grotesquely elongated necks, regarded as a sign of great beauty.

153

A SPIRED PAGODA ON THE TOP OF A HILL NEAR LASHIO

Burma is often called "the land of pagodas," for the charming structures dot the countryside.
They are not temples, but reminders of Buddha, erected to gain merit for the builders.

A SERENE LANDSCAPE OF ROLLING HILLS IN UPPER BURMA

Northern Burma is plateau, though it is not a perfectly level one but rises as high as five thousand feet above sea level. The little-known Padaung people inhabit this region.

ify for the former. The Intermediate College at Mandalay now confers degrees and is due to become a university.

In Burma every name has a special meaning, and some of them are very quaint. A boy, for instance, may be Mr. Grandfather Elephant or Mr. Crooked and even Mr. Like-his-Father; and a girl may be called Miss Dog's Bone, Miss Naughty, Miss Rabbit or Miss Affection. A custom, however, decrees that the children must have names beginning with the initial letter of the day on which they were born. This rule is considered im-

BLACK STAR

DANCERS AT A PWE—THE MOST POPULAR FORM OF AMUSEMENT

There are several kinds of *pwè*, which may include acting and singing as well as dancing. These dancers are wearing exquisite *longyis*—draped skirts using five yards of cloth.

TUSKERS TAKING BAGGAGE UP TO THE HILLS

In the hill country of the Southern Shan States elephants are the only pack animals that can negotiate the steep paths up to the villages. For various reasons the tribesmen keep these paths as secret and difficult as possible, and so bad are some of them that a baggage elephant has consumed fourteen hours in covering four miles and a half.

portant, because boys and girls born on certain days may marry only those born on other days.

The days of the week are each connected with a particular animal. The children thus have birth animals as people have birthstones. Monday is represented by a tiger, Tuesday by a lion, Wednesday by an elephant, Thursday by a rat, Friday by a guinea-pig, Saturday by a dragon and Sunday by a fabulous creature, half bird and half beast.

When a girl reaches the age of eleven of thereabouts her ears are pierced with great ceremony. The friends of the family are invited to a feast by the customary method of sending around packets of pickled tea. It is the girl's début. She may scream when the silver wires pierce her lobes, but the process will not have ended until—perhaps a week later—the holes are large enough for the insertion of large jewels.

The corresponding ordeal for the boy is even more painful, for he is tattooed. All Burmese have their legs tattooed from knee to thigh in such a way that, from a short distance, it looks as if they were wearing dark blue tights. The process is so agonizing that only a part can be undergone at a time, and a boy has to show his manhood by bravely enduring the pain. Anyone who shirked would be a coward.

Every boy also has to go into a Buddhist monastery for some time before he can assume the status of a man. He puts on a yellow robe like those worn by the monks, and conforms to the rules of the monastery while he is there. This does not mean that he will become a monk, though many do so. There are thousands of monks in Burma, supported by the community.

Men and women dress so much alike that at first it is difficult to distinguish between them. Both wear cotton or silk skirts and little white jackets, but the men's skirts for ordinary wear are shorter and more sack-like. Their skirts, or *putsos,* for gala days, however, are made of many yards of the richest silk. The women's gala dress, which reaches to the ground, is tightly girt about the body. The great distinction in the dress of the two sexes is that the men are never seen without their headdresses, or "gaung-baungs" while the women wear nothing on their heads. Their glossy black hair is coiled on top, with an orchid or some other blossom hanging down over the right ear. The men wear their hair long also, but a Burman with a beard is unknown, and very few of them have even a moustache.

The best way to see the Burmese in their fine clothes is to go up to one of the great pagodas on a festival day, for then

156

men, women and children give themselves up to devotion and merrymaking.

The chief place of worship is the great Shwe Dagon, or Golden Pagoda, of Rangoon. It stands on raised ground, and long flights of steps lead up to it on four sides. At the foot of the main steps two enormous white beasts with glistening red eyes and mouths ever stand on guard.

Placed at the sides of the steps are stalls with wax tapers, lotus, frangipani and jasmine, gold leaf and sweetmeats. These are bought by the people flocking to the shrines. Each flight leads up to a platform (larger than a city block) from the centre of which rises the golden spire of the pagoda. On its top rests a gilded cage set with jewels and hung with hundreds of pure golden and silver bells, which tinkle in the breeze.

All around the base and at the edges of the platform are shrines, some of them decorated with teakwood carvings. Others are covered with a mosaic of bits of colored glass which glitter in the sun; others still are gilded over. There are posts topped by the sacred goose, there are almost life-size carved elephants, and there are bells which swing between two posts. As a Burman passes one of these bells, he will pick up a deer's horn from the pavement and strike a note to let the good spirits know he is there.

The whole scene is gay beyond description. Here a fortune-teller cries out that he will tell your fortune by a cast of the dice. There, in the shadows before a gleaming alabaster or brass figure of the Buddha, are wax tapers stuck on the ground and piles of flowers, and before them men and women crouch devoutly.

Mandalay is a Mecca for Buddhists. It must have a thousand pagodas, of which the seven-roofed Arakan is considered the holiest. It contains an image of Buddha said to be the only one ever made during his lifetime. The larger sections of the heavy brass figure proved so difficult for the workmen to handle that, it is related, Buddha himself came to their aid. This revered statue was brought to the capital city in 1784.

Only two meals a day are eaten by the people of Burma, except by the monks, who may not eat after midday. Boiled rice is put on a large platter from which all help themselves, and little saucers of such condiments as curry, onions or chil-

Parry

SOLEMN CONSECRATION OF A PAGODA SPIRE

Every pagoda in Burma is surmounted by a "hti" or umbrella spire formed of concentric rings of gilt ironwork tapering to a rod. Kneeling monks pray before the hti, surrounded by gifts of rice and fruit. When bamboo scaffolding has been erected the spire is hoisted into place by many willing hands, and more prayers are offered when in position.

A YELLOW-ROBED PRIEST AND SHWE DAGON PAGODA, RANGOON

The most sacred shrine of the Buddhist world is a solid stupa (mound) of brick—built over
a relic chamber—covered with gold leaf. The place of worship is the surrounding terrace.

PIX

A GIGANTIC SITTING BUDDHA IN A SHRINE NEAR RANGOON

Rangoon is famous for its numerous shrines dedicated to Buddha, the most famous being the Shwe Dagon shrine that dominates the city. Hundreds of Buddhas are grouped about its spire.

159

IN RANGOON: AN OFFICE BUILDING THAT LOOKS LIKE A PALACE

Rangoon is one of the most modern cities in the Far East. Among its many fine buildings, some
are as Oriental-looking as one would expect but others show Western influence.

A BURMESE VARIATION OF A GONDOLA IN RANGOON HARBOR

The water taxi, with upcurved bow and stern, is somewhat like a Venetian gondola. Rangoon
has another feature in common with Venice; it is built largely on filled-in swamp.

A DRUGGIST'S STALL IN A CROWDED BAZAAR OF RANGOON

Looking for all the world like someone ready for baking, a Rangoon druggist studies the passing
scene from his ovenlike stall, a cubicle at the entrance to a market building.

Courtesy, United China Relief

LOOKING DOWN ON THE FAMOUS BURMA ROAD

The Burma Road twists and turns on a series of ridges in the mountains of Yunnan Province. At points along the road a driver can look down and see seven layers of the same road wind down the precipice beneath him. Chinese labor, with primitive tools, built this road in less than two years; and before the Japanese captured Burma, it was the main supply route for China.

POST OFFICE AND TRINITY CHURCH IN THE STRAND, RANGOON

Rangoon, owing to a bend in the Rangoon River and a large creek at the confluence of the Pegu and the main stream, lies surrounded on three sides by water. Wharves line the bank, and behind them runs the Strand, which contains the chief public buildings. The low white building seen behind the bullock cart is the post office.

162

lies are served with it. The Burmese eat with their fingers. They roll a ball of rice neatly between finger and thumb, take a little condiment and then place the morsel in the mouth. When everyone has finished, each in turn goes to the water-butt by the door to drink.

One of the most popular forms of entertainment is the plays, or "pwes." These take place as often as not out of doors. They are free, for they are given by some wealthy man for the entertainment of his friends and of anyone else who cares to come. They are very long, sometimes lasting more than one day, and the spectators come and go as they please. The plays are usually legendary tales about princes and princesses. The actors wear old-fashioned court costumes and make long speeches, but there is always a clown to relieve the tedium and, judging by the laughter, he is really funny. Sometimes performances are given by marionettes cleverly worked by strings.

The people of the hill country are quite distinct from the Burmese. The Shans, a fair, sturdy race, are the largest tribe, but the Karens, who are divided into Red and White Karens, are nearly as numerous. There are also many other tribes, of which the best known are the Padaungs and Palaungs, the Akha, Lihsaw, Lahu and, in the north, the Kachins. Many of the Kachins live in districts which lie beyond the jurisdiction of the government, and they have so-called slaves, who are

© E. N. A.

THATCHED HOUSES OF NAINSAN, CAPITAL OF A SHAN STATE

Native houses in the little Shan villages are built of bamboo and thatched with elephant grass, and the settlements are sometimes enclosed by bamboo palisades which keep the cattle out by day and in by night. The Northern and Southern Shan States, lying between Eastern Burma, Northern Siam and China, are the remnant of a once powerful nation.

really domestic servants and are quite well treated by their masters.

The hill country, which lies between Burma proper and China, has recently been given back to the tribal chiefs, who rule independently within their own states.

Of all the odd customs observed by these hill races, none is more strange than this: when a Padaung girl reaches the age of seven her neck is encircled by a brass coil, which is extended from time to time. These coils are never removed, and as the girl grows older her neck is naturally stretched by the rings until she looks like a Jack-in-the-box, with the lid permanently drawn back. The more rings a Padaung woman carries, the more fashionable she is considered to be. The limit is somewhere in the neighborhood of twenty-seven. The last rings are larger than the others and they rest on the shoulders. Coils of brass similar to those worn on the neck are also worn on the arms and legs. This custom of adorning the body with metal rings is common to many of the tribes of Burma's hill country. Among some of these tribes (among the White Karens, for example) rattan rings replace the brass ones.

The costumes of these races are very picturesque. They weave and dye their own cloths. Reds and blues and trimming made of white strips or of seeds are enhanced by all kinds of strange and often very effective ornaments made from the silver that is found in the hills.

The peoples of Burma believe in good and bad spirits. Much of their lives is passed in endeavoring to propitiate the bad spirits, and in most of the villages in the hill country may be found tall spirit-posts, at which sacrifices are frequently made. It was formerly believed that photography had been devised as a magic method of capturing them. But so great has been the appeal of the beads, hand mirrors, tobacco tins and other bribes that to-day the difficulty is to keep the entire village from crowding before the camera.

BURMA: FACTS AND FIGURES

THE COUNTRY

Bounded on the north by China and Assam; on the east by China and Siam; on the south by the Bay of Bengal; and on the west by Assam and Pakistan. The area, including the Shan States, is 261,757 square miles. The total population of Burma is estimated to be about 18,674,000.

The present republic of the Union of Burma included the six northern and 28 southern Shan States. Britain retains rights of defense of the republic.

GOVERNMENT

The Union of Burma gained its independence on January 4, 1948. Burma had been under British rule since the first Burma War of 1826, and was administered jointly with India until 1937. In June 1947 Burma's Constituent Assembly voted for the establishment of a republic, and a treaty agreeing to this was ratified in London in October, 1947.

COMMERCE AND INDUSTRIES

Essentially an agricultural country, about 85% of the people living on the land. Rice is one of the most important crops. In the dry zone, sesamum, millet, peanuts, cotton and beans are cultivated. Some rubber is produced. The most important mineral product is petroleum. Valuable jade mines are worked. Other minerals are tin, tungsten ore and silver. Teak forests provide teakwood which is exported. Other exports are rice, silver and petroleum.

COMMUNICATIONS

Length of metalled roads, 3,760 miles; unmetalled roads, 6,770 miles. There are 60 miles of navigable canals. Railway mileage, 1,777.

RELIGION AND EDUCATION

Most of the people are Buddhists with 843 people out of every 1,000 following this religion.

Primary education is free in state schools. Secondary education is not free, although many allowances and free places are provided. A state teachers college was opened in 1947. The University of Rangoon was constituted in 1920. There is an intermediate college at Mandalay. A forest school, an agricultural college and research institute and a technical institute and veterinary college provide special education.

CHIEF TOWNS

Rangoon, capital, population, 500,800; Mandalay, 163,243; Moulmein, 71,181.

CEYLON THE ISLE OF JEWELS

Its People and Its Jungle-buried Cities

This fragrant island off the southeastern tip of India is a land of tea and rubber plantations, coconut palms, mines of precious stones and jungle-hidden ruins of mighty cities that flourished long ago. These cities were deserted by their inhabitants when the Tamils invaded the island more than a thousand years ago. Two of the most important are frequently visited by tourists.

THE ancestors of the now dominant Sinhalese race in Ceylon came from Bengal. Later, Tamil invaders arrived from southern India and for centuries held the upper hand by force of arms. Finally the Sinhalese abandoned the northern part of the island to the Tamils, who remain today. In 1505 Portuguese invaders appeared on the west coast and established a chain of fortified settlements. A hundred and fifty years later the Dutch ousted the Portuguese, but in 1796 were themselves ousted by the English. After becoming a crown colony in 1802, Ceylon progressed through various stages of self-government. Finally in 1948 it assumed full sovereignty and became a member state within the British Commonwealth of Nations.

In Colombo, its capital, the island has one of the finest harbors in the East. It is not a natural harbor, but has been made one at great cost and labor. The best natural harbor is Trincomalee up the northeast coast. Ceylon has low-lying shores, sandy and palm-fringed; but in the interior Mount Pedro, the highest peak, rises to over eight thousand feet. Near it is the health resort of Nuwara Eliya (pronounced Nuraylia), a settlement over six thousand feet above the sea to which white people who live in Ceylon go when the low country gets too hot. The tourist will find it interesting to visit the tea and rubber plantations.

Flowers bloom the year around. When we land at Colombo, it is the color that first attracts attention. The emerald water of the harbor contrasts with the figures of the men in pink or yellow garments lounging along the wharf. One old man in snowy garments, who looks like a priest, is a Sinhalese gentleman. Be-

tween the shafts of a rickshaw is a little man in a loin cloth with fuzzy hair sticking out from under a red fez. These two men are of quite different races and beliefs. The Sinhalese, who are Buddhists, ruled the island before the Hindu Tamils came from India; but even before them were wild men called Veddas. There are still a few Veddas, but they live hidden away in the jungles of eastern Ceylon. The population is largely Sinhalese, but there are also Mohammedan Moormen, the descendants of Arab traders, and a mixed population with Portuguese and Dutch blood in their veins, as well as Europeans.

The Tamils are sturdy, hard-working people. It is they who run in the rickshaws. This is a calling that descends from father to son. We may sometimes see a brown tot who staggers uncertainly as he runs, following his father as the man dodges this way and that. He is training to be a rickshaw coolie.

The open-front shops of Colombo are filled with colored silks and fine embroideries, copper and brass and ivory, to say nothing of jewels like those that dazzled the eyes of Aladdin. Here are stones which have been discovered in the island. They lie in gleaming piles. There are moonstones, which are found chiefly in Ceylon; there are rubies, topazes, beryls, cats'-eyes, zircons and jacinths; there are sapphires that gleam like the tropic sea.

But the pearls of Ceylon are the finest of her jewels. The odd thing is that the fishing season lasts only from one to two months in the early spring. The main pearl fisheries were formerly over on the east side by Trincomalee, but the pearl oyster is changeable in its ways, and year by year the catch declined in value until

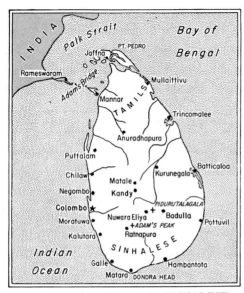

HOME OF TAMILS AND SINHALESE

it dropped to nothing at all. At the same time this particular kind of oyster appeared, as once before, on the west side, in the sand of the Gulf of Manaar, close under the shelter of the chain of islets known as Adam's Bridge, which links Ceylon to India. A valuable pearl bank has also been discovered at Twynam Paar. In 1925 the government opened a pearl fishery, and many Tamils and Moormen earn enough as divers during the short season to keep them the year around. There is, of course, a risk of injury to the lungs, as they dive without apparatus. The Tamil merely holds his nose; the Arab uses a nose clip.

The Ceylon pearl oyster, unlike that of the South Pacific, is hardly two inches in length and has a shell that one may crush between the fingers. The bags of oysters are sealed by a government inspector and taken ashore, where they are counted, the government taking two-thirds and the men one-third of the catch.

Ceylon devil-dancers are well known to everyone who has been in the East. Their costumes and antics were, in the old days, claimed to heal the sick by driving out devils, but now their performance is merely for money. To tempt money from the pockets of visitors, jugglers also

do incredible feats, but the snake-charmers are always the greatest attraction. These men train their pets until the snakes seem mesmerized, and do whatever they wish.

Huge cobras, seven or eight feet long, fix their flickering eyes on their master, and, rising from their coils, sway to and fro to his piping. Finally they coil around his neck and nestle against his cheek, meek and obedient. These men really have some secret power not known to everyone, and they can mysteriously call wild snakes from their holes.

We must leave Colombo and go up country. There are many ways of doing this. The railways are good as far as they go. The roads are excellent. They were begun early in the nineteenth century by a boy named Thomas Skinner, who came out when he was only fourteen as an ensign in the army. He was told by his commanding officer to go off up country and make roads. The roads, when he started work upon them, were mere jungle tracks, but he gave them such sound foundations that they have remained good ever since.

We might go about the island by native boat, for Ceylon is cut up by waterways, especially near the coast, and has many rivers. The bamboo boats, the pretty villages, the wild life on the banks make this method pleasant, though it takes a long time.

The railways are wonderfully built, running in places on terraces cut out of shelving rock. Sometimes the line doubles on itself, so that the engine passes the rear carriages on a higher level, going the opposite way.

The first thing we notice as we leave the plains is the cultivation of paddy, or rice. It is grown on terraces built up in such a way that they can be flooded. Unfortunately, Ceylon does not produce enough rice for its own needs, but has to buy from Burma and other countries.

Higher still we see the tea bushes growing in regular lines. Tea forms one of the largest exports of Ceylon. About five-sixths of it is sent to England. Women pickers wear red head-cloths, ear-

A TAMIL COOLIE PLANTING NURSERY SHRUBS OF TEA PLANT

Tea, which is cultivated all over Ceylon, is a hardy shrub that grows equally well in sheltered valleys or on lofty mountain slopes. Here we see a Tamil coolie setting out in the ground prepared for them the young shrubs that he has taken from the nursery. In about three years the young leaf shoots will be ready for plucking.

Stevens

TEA SHRUBS REQUIRE PRUNING FROM TIME TO TIME

At intervals of about twelve days, pruning is done to make the young leaf shoots abundant, and also because the tea plant, left to itself, might grow into a tree or shrub thirty feet high. It would then be difficult for the women to reach the leaves. The flowers, so like wild roses, are nipped off, that more of the leathery leaves may be produced.

A STIFF BREEZE BELLIES THE SAIL OF A FISHING CANOE

Along the coast of Ceylon sand bars are frequent, and these shallow craft can glide over them easily. Sharks lurk in the water, and they are caught for the extraction of their oil.

OXEN PULL HUGE LOADS OF FREIGHT IN CEYLON'S HARBOR CITY

Colombo, capital and leading port city of Ceylon, is a city of contrasts. Here East meets West, the old meets the new, and modern cars ease slowly past lumbering ox-drawn carts.

© UNDERWOOD & UNDERWOOD

RICE FIELDS provide the principal native food. There are only twenty-five acres to every hundred and eighty people, and Ceylon cannot grow all the rice that she needs because she does not everywhere get enough rain to feed such thirsty plants. Much of her water comes from a wonderful system of irrigation tanks installed centuries ago by a long dead civilization.

THE TEA GARDENS of Ceylon, now the island's chief source of wealth, annually provide many millions of pounds for export, chiefly to the United Kingdom. Those shown above are in the Dimbula district, near Nuwara Eliya. Coffee used to be grown on these fertile hillsides, but fungus attacked and killed the coffee plants, and the tea industry was substituted.

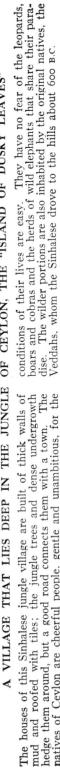

Stevens

A VILLAGE THAT LIES DEEP IN THE JUNGLE OF CEYLON, THE "ISLAND OF DUSKY LEAVES"

The houses of this Sinhalese jungle village are built of thick walls of mud and roofed with tiles; the jungle trees and dense undergrowth hedge them around, but a good road connects them with a town. The natives of Ceylon are cheerful people, gentle and unambitious, for the conditions of their lives are easy. They have no fear of the leopards, boars and cobras and the herds of wild elephants that share their paradise. The wilder portions are also inhabited by the original natives, the Veddahs, whom the Sinhalese drove to the hills about 600 B.C.

rings and anklets. Tamils do this work for the main part.

With tea-growing, planters combine other things, such as rubber. On some roads we see great reddish-brown cocoa pods hanging from the trees like Chinese lanterns. Then there are the shrubs that yield pepper, spices and gingery cardamoms.

The wealth of Ceylon is, however, largely natural and not cultivated. First in importance come the palms, which fringe every sandy coast and love to send their roots clear out under the salt water.

Everywhere we see coconuts and find houses thatched with palm leaves. There is also the palmyra, which flowers but once in forty years, bursting upward in an enormous nosegay of frothy millions of tiny flowers. From this palm are made the palm-leaf books used by the priests, who write on them with a sharp point. There is the talipot palm with long leaves which fold up, so that people use them as umbrellas. A rough sort of brown sugar is made from another palm.

Every village has clumps of feathery bamboos growing alongside the houses.

AMERICAN PRESIDENT LINES

ANCIENT STONE CARVING IN THE DALADA MALIGAWA IN KANDY

A bit of discolored ivory two inches long, supposed to have been a tooth of Buddha, is kept within the Dalada Maligawa, or Temple of the Tooth. It is enshrined upon a pure gold lotus flower and seven jewel-crusted bells fit over it. The Portuguese claim to have burnt the tooth when they captured the city, but many Ceylonese believe the original was hidden.

THE TAMILS OF CEYLON, two of whom are shown here performing a native dance, migrated from southern India to the northern part of the island. A quarter of the population is made up of Tamils and two-thirds of Sinhalese. For hundreds of years Tamil and Sinhalese have battled, but they now live peaceably, though the former are Buddhists and the latter Hindus.

NOSE AND TOE RINGS are worn by Tamil girls who earn their living in the tea gardens of Ceylon. Small and slight, they are none the less hard workers. The Tamils are a Dravidian people who came from India where the language is still spoken by something like twenty million people. They have also spread into Burma and even into Siam.

The forest, carefully tended by the government Forest Department, includes such valuable woods as ebony, satinwood and teak. The last is largely used in the construction of ships, even nowadays when there are so many steel vessels.

Plenty of fruit and vegetables can be plucked by the villagers. Bananas or plantains are a staple part of their diet. There are also limes, oranges, mango-steens, custard apples, papaws (which are like melons) and jack fruit (which looks like so many pumpkins), a cattle feed growing on a small stem straight from the trunk of a tree.

Cattle form the chief beasts of burden, some drawing heavy carts and some pulling lighter two-wheeled vehicles. These latter are trotting bullocks, but they cover no more than four miles an hour, while

© Underwood & Underwood
HINDU TEMPLE IN COLOMBO, CAPITAL OF CEYLON
The native quarter of Colombo is known as the Pettah, and in Sea Street, leading out of its market place, are two Hindu temples, both elaborately decorated with figures of gods and goddesses, elephants and various beasts. It is in Sea Street that the Tamil who deal in rice and cotton, congregate to sell their products.

JINRIKISHAS IN THE BUSY FORT DISTRICT OF COLOMBO

Jinrikishas—man-powered carriages—are used in many cities of the Far East, and one sees them side by side with up-to-date cars. The Fort District—the part of the city that was built within the walls of a colonial fort—is the business section of Colombo. The city is a supply stop for vessels bound to or from the Suez Canal, Cape Town or Singapore.

177

© E. N. A.

THE RIVERS OF CEYLON, with their banks picturesquely overgrown by palms and flowering jungle plants, are not very large and have shifting sandbanks at their mouths, so they cannot be used by ships of large tonnage. But as many of them are connected with one another by canals, they are useful for native transport. Many native boats like these, thatched to give shelter from sun and rain, drift loaded down to the ports, and toil back empty against the swift stream. The warm waters are infested with crocodiles, but men, none the less, take the risk of fording them.

© E. N. A.

AN IMAGE OF BUDDHA seated in meditation reposes deep in the jungle of Ceylon, just where it was carved more than a thousand years ago. This colossal granite figure is but one of the signs of a vanished civilization that has been discovered in Anuradhapura. Another statue, 146 feet long, of Buddha sleeping, can be seen at Polonnaruwa.

A GEM PIT IN CEYLON

Ceylon is an island of gems—sapphires yellow and blue, misty moonstones, crimson essonites and garnets, cats'-eyes, deep green alexandrites and zircons blue, green and brown. Above, workers are gathering gravel in a gem pit. The earth is brought up in baskets and stored in a pile. Later it is carefully washed and picked over in the search for precious stones.

the heavier beasts in the agricultural carts do only two.

In the deep recesses of the forests where the flying foxes play, and monkeys swing from branch to branch, while birds of paradise flash through the green gloom, one travels by jungle tracks that can be traversed only afoot or at best by a slow ox-wagon. Here one may still find wild elephants, leopards, buffalo, Sambhur deer and sloth bears, mongeese and porcupines, to say nothing of snakes, jackals, crocodiles and tortoises, which invade even the irrigation tanks.

The famous Lost Cities were built in the times of the ancient kings. For ages after they had been deserted by the Sinhalese, who fled from the attacks of the

© E. N. A.
QUEER FRUIT TREE OF CEYLON
Jack fruit, though the natives sometimes eat it, is more often used for feeding cattle. The tree is a relative of the breadfruit tree, and the fruit grows on the trunk.

© E. N. A.
A GOOD-NATURED MONSTER
This elephant is one of forty which belong to the Temple of the Tooth at Kandy and annually play an important part in the great festival of Gautama the Buddha.

Tamils, the jungle covered them with living green. There are ruins in many parts of the island, but the two cities visited by people from all parts of the world are Anuradhapura and Polonnaruwa.

The first named was the capital from about 500 B.C. to 800 A.D. Here granite blocks have been carved in quaint and interesting scenes by hands long since dust. Huge dagobas, or mounds like rounded hills composed of uncountable numbers of bricks, rise from the jungle. Granite columns fallen this way and that remain by the hundreds. One might spend days exploring. At Polonnaruwa there are also splendid temples of brick.

181

THIS DEVIL DANCER of Kandy, with his marvelous head dress of jingling brass, believes that he and others of his calling, by dancing themselves into a frenzy, can frighten away the devil that possesses a sick man. At least the Tamils used once to hold such a belief. Nowadays they often dance in the hope of collecting money from interested travelers.

THIS SINHALESE GIRL has the beauty typical of her race, of clear skin, regular features and large eyes. The men of Ceylon, as well as the women, dispose of their long black hair in a knot at the back of the head, and wear the loose robes suited to a hot climate. The Sinhalese also reflect in their jewelry their skill at work in gold, silver and ivory.

About midway between these two cities is to be found one of the strangest places in any country in the world. The huge rock of Sigiri, composed of red granite, thrusts itself up out of the surrounding jungle like a gigantic mushroom. This steep-sided rock is four hundred feet in height. In the fifth century A.D. King Kasyapa, after killing his father and seizing the throne, fled to this refuge from the wrath of his elder brother. For eighteen years he ruled Ceylon from the top of this rock. He had a palace constructed on the top, within which was a great red granite throne which remains to this day, though the palace lies in ruins.

At Kandy, in the center of the island, reigned the last of Ceylon's kings. His throne, supported by dragons of cut crystal with amethyst eyes, was carried to Windsor, where it remains to this day. Many of the nobles descended from the ancient royal house of Kandy are living, and on festival occasions appear in their quaint dress with flat hats and their voluminous skirts caught up by gorgeous jewel-studded belts.

The center of interest at Kandy, however, is the Temple of the Tooth. This contains a curious relic which has accompanied the royal house of Ceylon in all its changing fortunes. The original tooth (whether of Buddha or not) was brought over from India, hidden in the hair of a princess. Whether this identical tooth is still there, or, as some say, was stolen by the Portuguese and has been replaced, matters little. A tooth lies today encased in a series of caskets in charge of the Buddhist priest and once a year is carried in procession on the back of an elephant.

On Adam's Peak, to the south, is guarded a great imprint in stone said by Buddhists to be the impression of the foot of Buddha and by Mohammedans to be that of Adam. Of one thing there can be no question—it is not the impression of anything human: it is six feet long.

CEYLON: FACTS AND FIGURES

THE COUNTRY

An island, in the Indian Ocean, which lies south of India. The area is 25,332 square miles and the population is 6,693,945.

GOVERNMENT

Formerly a British Crown Colony, Ceylon achieved dominion status in February, 1948. By special agreement, the British government retains the right of defense of the island. A constitutional government is headed by the Governor General and Prime Minister. For purposes of administration, the island is divided into 9 provinces.

COMMERCE AND INDUSTRIES

Agriculture is the occupation of about two-thirds of the people, and coconuts, rice, tea and rubber are the chief products. Cacao, tobacco, spices, areca nuts and sugar-cane are grown also. There are numerous cattle and buffaloes, swine, sheep, goats and horses. Mineral products include graphite or plumbago, gems (sapphires, rubies, moonstones, cat's-eyes and other precious and semi-precious stones), monazite and mica. The preparation for export of tea, rubber, coconut products, citronella oil, spices and rice cleaning are the principal industries. Manufacturing such as weaving, basket work, tortoise-shell boxes, earthenware, jewelry, metal work, lacquer work and carving is of minor importance. The principal exports are tea, copra, crude rubber, coconuts, coconut oil, coir, plumbago (graphite), cacao and citronella oil, and the imports are rice, cotton manufactured goods, sugar, beverages, tobacco, coal, iron and steel goods and machinery.

COMMUNICATIONS

There are about 900 miles of railway, and about 13,200 miles of telegraph line and 18,900 telephones.

RELIGION AND EDUCATION

A majority of the people are Buddhists. Hindus, Moslems and Christians rank next in number.
Education is free from the kindergarten to the university. The University of Ceylon was established in 1942 by combining the Ceylon Medical College and Ceylon University College. There is also the Ceylon Technical College with courses in science and engineering.

CHIEF TOWNS

Colombo, the capital, population 361,000; Jaffna, 63,000; Galle, 49,000; Kandy, 52,000.

REPUBLIC UNDER BRITISH PROTECTION

Maldive Islands, 400 miles southwest of Ceylon, are governed as a republic, with an elected president, a prime minister, a senate of 80 members and a lower house. The Maldives are a group of coral islets which produce coconuts, millet, fruit and edible nuts. The people, numbering about 93,000 Moslems, are great navigators and traders.

CITY AND JUNGLE IN MALAYA

Wealthy Eastern Lands and Indolent People

Singapore, Sanskrit for "the Lion City," stands at the crossroads of the East on the ocean highway between Europe and the Far East. It is the main gateway into countries whence comes much of the world's rubber and tin. It stands at the end of a long peninsula which, with a number of islands, makes up the former Straits Settlements and Malay States. The British, who secured control of Malaya in 1824, were the first to really tap the vast natural resources of the country—its tin, rubber, oil-palms and agricultural products. These resources were lost to the world during the Japanese occupation in World War II, but were restored following Japan's surrender in 1945. The Federated and Unfederated States, with two of the Straits Settlements, became the Federation of Malaya in February, 1948, under British protection.

WHEN we speak of Malaya we mean those parts of the southward pointing Malay peninsula that include the states of the former Federated and Unfederated States of Malaya, and the Crown Colony of Singapore (including the Cocos Islands and Christmas Island).

Since the end of World War II, however, the nine states and two of the former Straits Settlements have become the Federation of Malaya, a British protectorate. These are Perak, Selangor, Negri Sembilan, Pahang, Johore, Kedah, Perlis, Kelantan and Trengganu; and the former settlements of Penang and Malacca. The former settlement of Labuan is administered by the governor general of Malaya.

Although we know of these provinces as Malaya, the peninsula is still called Malacca by the peoples on the continent of Europe, after the name of its oldest town. The settlement of Malacca was founded by the Malays, who came from Sumatra as early as the twelfth century. The Portuguese, who occupied Malacca in 1511, found the interior occupied by cannibals and the coast by Malay, Chinese and Japanese spice traders. The Dutch East India Company expelled the Portuguese in 1641 and the English finally secured control in 1824.

Inland, rice, fruit and rubber trees have been planted, and their products are beginning to give the settlement new life. In the shops we can find beautiful examples of basket work. The Malayan forests are famous the world over for producing the finest materials for basket-

making, and in Malacca by far the best of the baskets are made. Malays work slowly, however, and, as they take a month to make a set of baskets, the craft is of little commercial value.

As, with the coming of the Dutch, the trade of Malacca began to decline, Penang, an island at the northern entrance of the Straits of Malacca, which was the earliest British settlement, became the more important place. But no sooner was the settlement of Singapore founded than Penang began to lose its trade. Recently, with the increase of tin-mining and rubber-planting in the Malay States, it has become busy once more, and its beautiful scenery attracts large numbers of tourists. So that now it shares with Singapore the first place among Malayan ports.

We approach Singapore by steamer via the narrow red-walled straits leading to Keppel Harbor which is crowded with the shipping of seven seas. Its waterfront is lined with warehouses, oil tanks from which piers reach out in a fringe for a mile along shore. It is also an important air and naval base and the centre of air traffic from East and West.

In Commercial (or Raffles) Square east of the fort, rickshaws and gharries stand lined up like parked motor cars (though there are also electric cars), their fares fixed by the municipality. European men in white ducks and sun helmets, wealthy Chinese merchants and nearly naked water-peddlers, sailors and tourists of every nationality mingle in the in-

CLASSIC ARCHITECTURE IN SINGAPORE

Although only about one per cent of the population of Singapore is European, sections of the city have a distinctly Western appearance. Victoria Hall, left, and the Municipal Building, right background, are in classic-revival style. They could quite suitably appear in Toronto or Philadelphia. Singapore is big, noisy and overcrowded, with a wonderful harbor.

RICKSHAW A LA MODE

You will get the real flavor of Singapore in the Asiatic districts of the city. If you are too tired to walk, you may rent a tri-shaw, a sort of rickshaw mounted as a sidecar on a bicycle. The open air shops display all sorts of tempting goods. The shopkeepers' signs are probably commonplace, but they have a strange, romantic air to those who cannot read them.

dolent throngs. One is surprised to find how modern and substantial are the Government House, the Hong Kong and Shanghai Bank and the Supreme Court buildings. The British residents have polo, golf and cricket grounds and a race course and live a gay social life after the coolness of evening has swept in from the sea. Here we cannot fail to be impressed by the shipping, for we are at the gateway of the Far East, on the highway from Europe and India to the west, and China and Japan to the east. Ships from all over the world bring merchandise to Singapore, for it is the distributing center for the whole of the Malay Archipelago. At all seasons of the year the port is filled with strange craft: Malays with their fishing boats—the only home of many of them—Chinese junks and sampans, large and small steamers from Indochina and Japan, and great vessels loading cargoes of tin and rubber for the markets of Great Britain and the

United States of America. Besides the tin-smelting, rubber-refining and pineapple canning industries of Singapore, there is a great trade in rattan canes, which are there cleaned and prepared.

As we wander among the shops and markets of Singapore we meet all sorts and types of peoples. The majority of them are Chinese; Malays take second place. Although European and Japanese manufacturers have done away with much of the picturesque native dress, we can still see the stately Malay in his loose trousers, jacket and sarong, or tartan skirt, which is bundled around his waist and reaches down to his knees. On his head he wears a kerchief or a velvet cap, which he would never be without. The Malay considers his headdress even more a point of etiquette than his coat, though it may be only a thin wisp of palm frond tied around his forehead. After the Malays come the Hindus. The tourist will find Hindu jewelers, who sell precious

BLACK STAR

OPERATING TIN MINE IN THE KINTA VALLEY, NEAR IPOH, MALAYA

British Malaya is one of the world's important tin producers, and the output has increased in recent years. The limestone area on the west side of the central mountain range in and near the Kinta Valley is its richest source, and Ipoh is the most important city in the section. Only a few degrees from the equator, Kinta Valley is hot, with a heavy rainfall.

By Burton Holmes from Ewing Galloway

OX-CARTS DRAWN BY ZEBUS IN THE BUSIEST PART OF PENANG

Here placid humped zebus draw creaking ox-carts past fine public buildings in a city equipped with telephones and electric lights, an electric railway and government wireless stations. The island port of Penang (Georgetown) was the capital of the Straits Settlements until 1837, when the seat of government was removed to Singapore.

stones in the rough, and Chinese silk merchants. He can buy beautiful examples of Malay weaving—bright cloths inlaid with gold leaf from Selangor and striped shawls made in Kelantan. Odd pieces of pottery are sent down from Perak and Pahang, and from the former district,

delicate silverware. He can buy embroidered mats and slippers made of fine silk and gold thread, and occasionally he will find pieces of wood-carving, the craft of the people of Negri Sembilan.

We may leave Singapore on a comfortable state railway which crosses a causeway over the shallow strait and winds through the mangrove swamps of the coast, past inland fresh-water swamps, over a way carved out of the jungle and past the jagged limestone cliffs from which about 35 per cent of the world's tin is mined.

Malaya is too near the equator for seasonal changes, though the northeast monsoon blows off the Gulf of Siam from November to March, sometimes so violently as to demolish the bamboo huts of

the natives and do serious damage to the rubber plantations. At Kuala Lumpur it is often 140 to 150 degrees in the blazing sunshine and humid with the sudden downpours that occur toward evening.

The rubber trees, which have largely replaced the sugar, coffee, spice, banana and tapioca plantations, are worked by coolies under white supervision. The trees are planted in regular rows, and European experts superintend the tapping. In Johore, one of the Non-Fed-

Malay States Agency

NO DRESS COULD BE SIMPLER OR COULD BECOME THEM BETTER

The sarong of the Malay woman is the simplest garment imaginable. It is just a length of material, brightly colored and printed in beautiful designs, that is wrapped tightly around the body beneath the armpits, whence it hangs to below the knees. The Malays are a not unattractive people, either in character or in appearance.

HUNDREDS OF SMALL BOATS CROWD A GREAT CROSSROADS HARBOR

Singapore Harbor is one of the busiest ports in the world, handling over 80 per cent of all the imports and exports of the whole Malay Peninsula. These small boats are used chiefly to carry goods produced in the interior to the port city for handling and shipment overseas. So over-crowded is Singapore that many of the people live all the time on their boats.

MALAY FAMILY ON THE RUDE DOORSTEPS OF THEIR AIRY HOME

Even in the deep forest the Malayan builds his house high off the ground. Merely bound together with rattans, it can be built in less than a day. When the community moves, the women carry the babies and household utensils strapped to their backs; the men travel with chopping swords for clearing the trail, and blowpipes with poison arrows.

erated States to the south of the peninsula, nearly the whole of the country is planted with rubber. Rubber is not a native of the East. It comes from Brazil in South America and was introduced into Malaya only as recently as 1876. Yet that country now produces almost half of the world's supply.

Pahang, on the eastern side of the central mountain range, is one of the richest tin-producing areas. The United States was formerly one of the largest consumers of Malaya's rubber and tin. The conquest of Malaya by the Japanese deprived Americans of this source of supply and helped to bring about serious shortages in rubber and tin.

Rattan is one of the important vege-table products of Malaya. The rattan palm has hooked prickles which enable it to climb the tallest trees of the jungle. Their stems are cut into lengths of from five to thirty-five feet, dried in the sun on trestles, till the outer skin is peeled off, then split and exported in that state for furniture making.

If we follow the course of a river from its mouth, we find that it passes through crocodile-haunted swamps and over sand-bars near the sea. Higher up it threads a winding course through miles of forest; nearer its source in the mountains we find it cascading over the cliffs.

Forests of green twilight, their high branches interlocking, deepen the silences of the interior. Certain of the trees grow

A YOUNG MOSLEM IN A STREET OF GEORGE TOWN, PENANG ISLAND

Although the majority of Penang's population is Chinese, many other types of Asians may be seen, among them Malays, Indians and Eurasians. The small island is just west of the Malay Peninsula; and George Town, its seaport, is on the eastern side, with large docks and a ferryboat to the mainland. The climate is hot and humid, and there is a high rainfall.

RUBBER TAPPING IN MALAYA: A PROCESS REQUIRING GREAT SKILL

Rubber trees are usually tapped for the first time in their fifth year. They must be tapped to just the right depth, for the latex—the gummy fluid from which rubber is made—lodges against a thin layer of cells between the bark and wood of the tree. It flows most readily in the cool morning temperature. The average yield of a tree is four or five pounds a year.

to 150 feet or more while beneath them trees half that height intermingle with their stems, and below these lesser trees grows a dense tangle of ferns and creepers, mosses, orchids and other flowering plants.

In the forests there is plenty of big game. Elephants do great damage to the plantations only a few miles north of Kuala Lumpur. The great beasts are captured in "drives" in which the blowing of trumpets and the beating of tomtoms frightens them into stockades, after which men with spears and torches prevent the captives from demolishing their imprisoning walls. There are two species of rhinoceros, and the Malay tapir is common. The Malay tiger is smaller than its Indian relative, and is not very greatly given to man-eating, because game, in the form of deer, is very plentiful.

In the hills north of Perak lives the rare Siamang ape, a powerful, long-armed creature. One old male seen by the writer had an arm span of nearly five feet. There are three anthropoid apes and several gibbons, besides which the wizened faces of several kinds of monkeys peer at one or go crashing away, barking and jibbering. It is interesting to watch the country Malays with the coconut monkeys. They train them as pets, and send them up the coconut trees to pick whichever coconut they point out.

Squirrels are to be found everywhere, some bigger than a cat, other species nearly as small as a young rat. In mentioning rats we name one of the most constant troubles in Malaya, for they exist in enormous numbers, and do great damage to the crops. Bats haunt the vast limestone caves, snakes hunt through

Malay States Agency

MACHINE THAT TURNS A POISONOUS ROOT INTO A WHOLESOME FOOD

The cassava or root of the manioc is a plant native to South America that is cultivated in Malaya. The juice is poisonous but it is driven off by heat and pressure. The material is next dried, while moist, on hot plates till the starch grains swell, sifted, washed, dried in the sun, then partially baked. The result is the tapioca that we know.

the tree tops and undergrowth, crocodiles and tortoises infest the swamps. But there are also hundreds of gorgeous butterflies, song birds, and birds of gay plumage.

The beautiful Argus pheasant is fairly plentiful, and so are several species of pigeon. There are few parrots, but brilliantly colored kingfishers dwell there in large numbers, and the clumsy hornbills are easy to find.

In the interior we come across a round-headed race of Negritos that hark back to the days before men learned to plant crops and pasture cattle. These hunt their meat with blowpipes or trap it, fish, and hunt wild roots and fruits. They make offerings to the spirits of the elements and to their ancestors. As shy as four-footed forest dwellers, these Semangs may be told from the Sakais because they are smaller, darker and frizzly haired. They live in leafy shelters on high poles, and wear loin cloths, with belts of dried grass or ornaments of plaited rattan for the women.

The other aboriginal race of the peninsula, the Sakai people, are superior to the Semangs in culture. In the mountain districts of Perak and southward down to Selangor we find their pile houses grouped together in small villages. They are a sturdy race, with light brown skins and straight or wavy hair. Near the villages there are small cultivated patches of ground where the Sakais grow millet, sugar, tobacco and hill-rice. When they have garnered their crops they move on and make fresh clearings. They use bows and arrows, although they make these chiefly for sale to tourists, but their important weapon is the blowpipe.

BREAD IN MALAYA GROWS ON TREES

Malayans do no farming in the real sense of the word. They have little need to. The breadfruit tree yields fruits which, when picked slightly unripe and baked, supply a food like bananas in flavor but like bread in texture.

The Sakais have many strange religious customs. If we could arrive at a rubber plantation at the time of one of their festivals, we would see them preparing a deep trench about thirty feet in length. In this they burn wood for two or three days, until the trough is filled with smoldering ashes. A number of the men of the tribe fast for some days before the event,

195

then, on the appointed day, walk barefoot down the trench. They do this with the idea that evil spirits will be driven out of them in the course of their uncomfortable promenade. The Sakais' feet are padded underneath with very thick skin, so they do not suffer as much as they would have us believe.

A number of small rivers crawl through the jungle to form the Pahang, which curves through Malaya to the China Sea, bearing innumerable sampans with palm-thatched cabins on its bosom. Were it not for the good roads that traverse the peninsula, it would matter more that the mouth of the great river is so choked by sand-bars as to be unnavigable to the many large vessels of the coast and trans-oceanic trade.

Near its junction with the sea the banks of this stream are dotted with the villages of the Malayans built on high piles, some of them far out over the water where it is possible on a hot day to fish directly from the kitchen porch. The front veranda is the reception room.

The peninsular Malay comes of a mixture of neighboring races and is really courteous and likable. He is olive-skinned and has straight lustrous black hair. His eyes are black or reddish-brown, sometimes slightly almond shaped, and his nose is generally flat and broad; but he has small, finely molded hands and feet, prominent cheek-bones, a square chin and even white teeth. It must be confessed that he is lazy, although when he likes he can work both hard and well. He is a Mohammedan, yet his womenfolk have considerable liberty; and he is more than usually kind to children. Anywhere in the peninsula where we come in contact with men of his race, we are sure to be treated with gentle courtesy, and to find a certain degree of loyalty. One departs favorably impressed with this Eastern land.

SINGAPORE, FEDERATION OF MALAYA: FACTS AND FIGURES

SINGAPORE

The island of Singapore (including Cocos and Christmas Islands), was formerly one of the Straits settlements, together with Penang, Malacca, and Labuan. Penang and Malacca are now part of the Malay Federation, and Labuan is under the Federation's jurisdiction. Singapore has the status of a Crown Colony. The island, 27 miles long and 14 miles wide, is separated from the Malay Peninsula by the Straits of Johore. Area, 220 square miles; population about 980,818. The chief industry is tin smelting, and for many years Singapore produced more than half of the world's supply.

The Cocos or Keeling Islands, a group of about 20 small coral islands, are attached to Singapore. Population is about 1,763. There are large coconut plantations; copra, oil and nuts are exported.

Christmas Island is also attached to Singapore. It has an area of about 62 square miles and a population of about 1,216. Inhabitants are employed by the company that works the enormous phosphate deposits.

FEDERATION OF MALAYA

A Federation of Malaya was established on February 1, 1948, in which the nine Malay States and the settlements of Penang and Malacca were granted the right of local self-government. Control of defense and foreign affairs still remains in British hands, as does ultimate legal jurisdiction.

The Malay States lie on the Malay Peninsula. Four of them were federated once before: Perak, area, 7,980 square miles, population, 962,-400; Selangor, area, 3,167 square miles, population, 723,000; Negri Sembilan, area, 2,550 square miles, population, 272,900; Pahang, area, 13,873 square miles, population, 241,500. Total area: 27,570 square miles; total population: 2,199,800. The products are coconuts, rice, rubber, sugar, pepper, timber, gutta-percha, oils, resins and canes. Mining of tin, gold, tungsten and coal is carried on. The chief industries are the cultivation of rubber and the mining of tin.

The states formerly known as the Unfederated Malay States are: Johore, area, 7,321 square miles, population, 753,900; Kedah, area, 3,660 square miles, population, 561,400; Perlis, area, 310 square miles, population, 71,300; Kelantan, area, 5,746 square miles, population, 444,700; Trengganu, area, 5,050 square miles, population, 227,100. Their area totals 22,087 square miles, with a total population of 2,058,-400. The principal town is Johore Bahru, with a population of about 21,776. Rubber, rice, coconuts, tapioca and tin are the chief products.

The settlement of Penang has an area of 110 square miles and its neighbor, Wellesley, two miles distant, has an area of 290 square miles. Their total population is 454,000. Malacca has an area of 633 square miles and a population of 244,600. Labuan is 35 square miles in area with a population of about 9,000. The total area of the Malay Federation is about 50,700 square miles and the total population is about 5,000,000. The capital is Kuala Lumpur.

LAND OF THE WHITE ELEPHANT

The Independent Siamese and Their Country

The Siamese call their land Muang Thai, the Land of the Free. The word Siam (or Sayam) is probably the same as Shan, the Burmese name for the Lao race, the Shan and the Siamese. Their country, however, is usually called the Land of the White Elephant, for albino elephants are found in its vast forests and are thought by the Siamese to be semisacred. This kingdom of the Far East is one of the few tropical countries that remain in a state of independence, and it shows the combination of an Oriental king with a certain amount of Western civilization. With its mixed population, largely Buddhist, Siam is a most surprising and interesting corner of the globe to visit.

SIAM (Thailand) is a country of southeast Asia. To the east lies French Indochina, to the west, Burma, and to the south, Malaya. Siam's greatest length is about 1,000 miles, and its greatest width, 500 miles. It has a long coast line, about 1,700 miles, and many very fine harbors. The most important river is the Menam ("mother of waters") which has its source in the mountains in the north

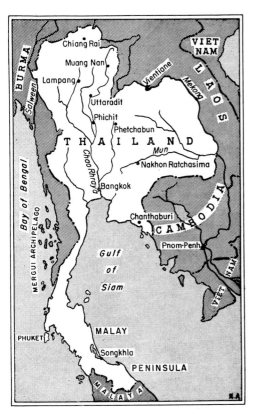

THAILAND, OR SIAM

and which flows 600 miles to empty into the Gulf of Siam.

Some two thousand years ago Mongoloid tribes, the Mon-Annams, and a few centuries later the Lao-Tais, overran the territory we know as Siam, driving the aboriginal Negritos into the mountains. To their Chinese culture, colonists from India added customs and beliefs. In the sixteenth and seventeenth centuries Portuguese, English and Dutch traders successively appeared on the palm-fringed shores of Siam, and the French tried, without success, to secure the kingdom. Destructive wars with Burma followed, in the course of which period the Siamese chose for king a warrior, Phaya Chakkri, who established peace. Though both Great Britain and the United States of America made treaties with Siam early in the nineteenth century, a Chinese monopoly largely prevented foreign commerce until 1851. Then there came to the throne a king who spoke English. The open door followed. Though there was considerable material progress in the years that followed, Siam remained an absolute monarchy until 1932. In that year a bloodless revolution resulted in the formation of a limited monarchy. Siam, which was one of the Allies in World War I, became a more or less unwilling partner of Japan in the second World War.

The traveler in Siam will find many huge walled enclosures called wats, which contain the Buddhist temples, the dormitories of the "bonzes," or student priests, and their school buildings. To them at sunrise come devout women bearing offerings of tea, rice and boiled bamboo shoots. After them flows a stream of worshipers, also holiday-makers. Families will make journeys requiring several days' travel to pray at the wats. At the gates they will be stopped by dealers in gold leaf, for the images in the shrines are covered with gold foil, and the worshipers renew the gold on any spot that may have become tarnished.

The gardens of the wats are the refuges of aged cats and dogs, for it is against the teachings of Buddhism to take the life of any living creature. For the same reason the priests each possess a filter that their drinking water may not harbor any living organism.

The bazaars of Bangkok extend for two or three miles outside the city proper. They consist for the most part of rickety bamboo shops, booths and stands on which odorous dried fish, oil, brass bowls, little carved Buddhas—some no bigger than hazel nuts—primitive looms, sweetmeats, green and blue slippers and toys

are displayed in colorful confusion. Itinerant candy sellers, with bell-shaped umbrellas over their wares, kite-makers and flag-makers mingle in the streets.

When a customer enters a Siamese hair-dresser's booth, the barber shaves his head with a razor and pulls out the hairs of his beard one by one with broad tweezers. There are also traveling barbers who carry with them their whole stock-in-trade, including a chair.

We see tailors in the bazaars, sitting cross-legged at their work. It is not through making clothes that they make the greater part of their profit, but by selling needles and threads.

White elephants are venerated. The Siamese do not look upon these animals as gods, but believe that the spirits of their wisest and noblest ancestors inhabit them. On that account the albino pachyderms used to be tended by the greatest mandarins of the country, and even today they are guarded with the utmost care.

PLOWING THE HARD WAY

The picture was taken after an epidemic of rinderpest had swept through the country, killing a large percentage of the cattle. The loss of draft animals forced upon farmers a battle for survival in its most primitive form. Science is doing a great deal to control such epidemics.

UNATIONS

Charbot

WOMAN OF GOOD POSITION AND HER DARK, SUN-HATTED SERVANT

The chief garment of the Siamese, worn by men and women alike, is the "panoong." The fair-skinned woman on the right is the wife of a petty official. Her servant, clad for work in the rice fields, has been tanned a dark color from constant exposure. But the Siamese are in general paler than the Chinese. The upper class, the Mon, are of Talaing stock.

A GIANT BUDDHA BROODS AMID THE RUINS OF A TEMPLE IN AYUDHYA

Rich in the ruins of early Thai civilization, Ayudhya is one of the world's most historically interesting cities. It was the capital of Siam until it was destroyed by the Burmese in 1767.

B. O. A. C.

SIGHTSEERS AND SHOPPERS MINGLE AROUND THE STREET MARKETS

The shopkeepers must hustle out at dawn to raise their brightly colored awnings and arrange their merchandise, for the street markets are crowded with customers from morning to night.

AVA HAMILTON

BANGKOK HAS SOMETIMES BEEN CALLED THE VENICE OF THE EAST

The canals of Bangkok were once the major means of transportation within the city. Although many wide modern streets have been built, the canals are still used by gondola-like boats.

BANGKOK, THE CAPITAL CITY, lies along both banks of the River Menam near its mouth, and its streets are largely waterways, though there are a few paved roads served by electric cars. The town is actually only about a mile wide but stretches for many miles along the sluggish river, connecting with canals which traverse the plains of Siam to distant towns, as roads would be too often flooded. Even the yellow-robed monks, with their shaven heads and unsandaled feet, go about in boats, silently offering their begging bowls for enough rice to maintain life.

HOUSES MOUNTED ON PILES line the waterways, not only in Bangkok but throughout the country, and almost all goods are transported by water in Siam. This wooden, grass-thatched house is stoutly built and stands firm above the river. Some houses, however, in this strange country are built of light wood and bamboo and actually float upon the surface, and so are the more secure against floods. The floods may be very severe, for in many places the rivers disappear entirely in the dry season, but when the rain comes they are soon transformed into torrents wide and deep.

THE SIAMESE CATTLE THIEF WEARS A YOKE LIKE THIS

The Siamese are, on the whole, a law-abiding race, but when an evil-doer has been caught, a great yoke of bamboo is fastened, like this, about his neck. Then his captors have no further trouble with him, for he is too hampered to struggle or run, and it is useless for him to try and escape into the thick undergrowth of the jungle.

A voyage of about forty miles up the Menam River takes us to Ayuthia, the ancient capital of Siam. It is in the jungles to the north and east of Ayuthia that elephants are most common. Trained elephants play an important role in parts of the country. There are valuable teak forests in Siam, and many elephants are used in the lumber industry. One should see these huge animals lifting, pushing and carrying immense logs and trees.

Curiously, Siamese servants in foreign households, believing it wrong to take life, will sometimes leave a good situation rather than kill insects, and gardeners will abandon their work in preference to destroying a snake.

The Menam is a river of houseboats.

UNATIONS

TRANSPLANTING TENDER YOUNG SEEDLINGS IN A RICE PADDY

Rice is sown first on well-prepared, fertile seedbeds. After the seedlings are 25 to 50 days old, the farmer wades into the beds and gently pulls up the plants. These must be replanted in the paddies and carefully spaced, about 3 plants every 6 inches. The paddies are covered with about 4 inches of water banked in by levees which encircle the field.

POMP AND CEREMONY accompanied the King of Siam wherever he went. Western influence has caused many old-time customs of the country to be discontinued. The inhabitants of the country have always been known as Thai, the Free People, and prefer to call their country Muang Thai. The government has been changed to a constitutional monarchy. Much pageantry still remains. Here outside the royal palace in Bangkok there are men of rank in silver lace, palanquin bearers and ceremonial umbrellas. A white pointed hat indicates that the wearer represents a god.

CHARBOT

THE SIAMESE DRAMA is Indo-Chinese in character. In this Ti Kay or classical play, in which a prince, a princess and a demon invariably figure, the woman's part is performed by a man. The Siamese, a mild people and as apathetic as their rivers are sluggish, love all forms of art, from music to fine architectural carving. They also excel in gold-smithery.

FRUITS OF THE EARTH FOR SALE IN THE OPEN-AIR MARKET OF A LITTLE TOWN OF SIAM

These vegetable sellers have a raised bamboo platform on which to squat and spread their goods. One thing they are certain to have is betel nut, for the chewing of that is universal. The nuts are the seeds of the areca palm, boiled, sliced, dried in the sun and, with a small pellet of lime, wrapped in the leaves of the betel pepper. Siamese people are fond of chewing this, a habit that causes their teeth to turn black. Fortunately—for this practice does not improve their appearance—they have lately taken to smoking cigarettes instead.

The ordinary floating homes are constructed of light wood and bamboo, the roofs being thatched with the leaves of the atap palm. There are rarely more than two rooms in each house, though there is usually an open front with a landing-stage. If they have two floors, the number of steps to the upper story must always be an odd number, for it is a Siamese superstition that an even number of stairs brings bad luck.

The river peddler is a feature of life on the Menam. He goes up and down the stream in a sampan, a boat of Chinese pattern, propelled by a single oar at the stern. No gondolier could be more skillful than a Siamese boatman, as he—or she—contends with the rapids.

The Menam abounds in fish, and the Siamese have many ways of fishing. One consists of erecting in the water, close to the bank, a large wooden wheel to which a wide net is attached and lowered to the bottom of the river. Having done this, men row out in boats and make a wide sweep over the water, yelling at the top of their voices, splashing the stream with long bamboo poles and beating gongs. The frightened fish are driven before them into the net, which the men on the bank draw up by means of the wheel. As the net rises, the boats flock around and take out the catch.

Children are well cared for in Siam. Mothers continue to carry, astride their hips, little ones old enough to walk. Siamese children are taught to be extremely courteous to old people.

It must be borne in mind that Siam is a country where the majority are very

AVA HAMILTON

FISHING AN EASY WAY IN RURAL THAILAND

Thai fishers do not bother with bait. They simply lower an empty net and wait a bit for fish to swim over it. Then they pull the net up and scoop their catch out of its center.

ELEPHANTS OF THAILAND are royal property and are looked after by a special government department. The regal collection of these immense beasts is large, but every now and then, to increase the numbers, a mammoth hunt is organized and wild ones are captured, as shown elsewhere. The huge elephants we see here, with drivers astride their necks, are about to go on a big game hunt. For this reason the howdahs on their backs, beneath the shelter of which sit the hunters, are as light as possible—this is in marked contrast to the elaborate howdahs used on state occasions.

© EWING GALLOWAY

THE WAT PHRA KEO is one of the most magnificent of the many Buddhist temples in Bangkok. The brightly tiled roofs and gilded pinnacles so characteristic of Siam rise against a background of bamboos, banyans and tamarinds. Within the temple burn candles as thick as a man's body, and offerings of rich treasure are built within or under the figure of Buddha.

poor. Boys and girls have to start earning a living at an age when children in Western countries are still at school. The girls usually start as porters, and we may see quite tiny folk going to and fro carrying waterbowls, rice, fruit and sugar-cane.

The national game of Siam is *ragaraga*, or shuttle-ball, as many as ten youths playing this game together. A large ball of split rattan is deftly kicked from one to the other, the players using either heel, ankle or knee to return the ball. So expert are these "footballers" that they will often keep the ball going from foot to foot for an hour on end without allowing it to touch the ground.

In a Siamese bazaar we are sure to find a "guessing-shop." The proprietor of this gambling establishment stands behind a table upon which are a number of melons of various sizes. A pool is made up by a company of guessers, all of whom make bets with the shopkeeper as to the number of seeds inside a given melon. When all the wagers have been made the melon is opened, and he who has guessed nearest takes three-fourths of the money staked; the rest goes to the proprietor.

The old methods of trial have been forsaken. No longer is a prisoner tried by being ordered to eat poisoned rice or to walk barefoot across hot stones, so that if he could eat the rice with impunity, or cross the hot stones unscathed, he might prove his innocence.

In recent years, other changes have been taking place. The most notable has been that of making the government, for hundreds of years an absolute monarchy, into a limited monarchy with an elected assembly, and changing the name, Siam, to the ancient name, Thailand.

When France was defeated by Germany in 1940, the Siamese regained some of their former territories. After the Japanese invasion on December 8, 1941, Thailand was completely under Japanese influence, although in theory her independence was respected by Japan. The people, however, yearned for freedom. A strong underground movement persisted in Thailand and awaited the opportunity to collaborate with Allied forces. The restoration of a national sovereignty was established in early 1946, not many months after the end of the war.

THAILAND (SIAM): FACTS AND FIGURES

THE COUNTRY

Forms part of the extreme southeasterly projection of Asia which also includes Burma, French Indo-China and the Malay Peninsula. It is bounded on the northwest and west by Burma, on the northeast and east by French Indo-China, and on the south and east by the Gulf of Siam. Area, 200,148 sq. mi.; pop. (est.) 17,317,764. In 1945 Bangkok became the commercial capital as well as the administrative capital.

GOVERNMENT

Formerly an absolute monarchy, since 1932 a constitutional monarchy. The king exercises legislative power with the advice and consent of the Senate and House of Representatives, and executive power through a State Council of 14 to 24 members. There is universal suffrage for all persons over 20 years of age.

COMMERCE AND INDUSTRIES

The principal product is rice, which is the national food, but para-rubber, coconuts, tobacco, corn, pepper and cotton are grown. A large area is under forests and teak-cutting is an important industry. There are large numbers of livestock, including cattle, horses, buffaloes and domesticated elephants. Of the extensive mineral resources, only tin, wolfram, tungsten ore and sapphires are mined on a commercial scale. The chief industry is ricemilling. Exports are rice, tin, tin-ore, teakwood, salt fish and rubber and the imports are silk and cotton goods, flour, sugar, vegetables, iron and steel goods, petroleum products, electrical equipment, machinery and automobiles.

COMMUNICATIONS

There are 2,032 miles of state railway and 792 post offices. Length of telegraph line amounts to 6,155 miles. An automatic telephone system was introduced in Bangkok in 1937. Three wireless stations have been built.

RELIGION AND EDUCATION

Most of the people are Buddhists, and there are 19,759 Buddhist temples and 113,644 priests. The Minister of Education is responsible for education. There are a number of American, French and British mission schools. Over 77% of the local schools and 23% of the government schools are situated in temples. There are two universities in Bangkok.

ANCIENT RIVALS OF THE FAR EAST
Jungles and Rice Fields of Indo-China

Indo-China, now a federation of independent states—Viet Nam, Laos and Cambodia—within the French Union, was a French possession before World War II. It consisted then of the colony of Cochin-China and four kingdoms—Laos, Tongking, Annam and Cambodia—under the protection of France. The present state of Viet Nam was formed out of Cochin-China, Tongking and Annam. However there are warring governments for authority in Viet Nam: the Associated State of Viet Nam, whose head is Chief of State Bao Dai (the former emperor of Annam); and the Republic of Viet Nam, whose head is Ho Chi Minh, a Communist, and in which Communists hold the key positions. Southern Indo-China is one of the world's richest rice-producing regions. Tea, sugar, cinnamon and maize are grown in the central area. The northern part is the industrial heart of the country, with rich resources of hard coal and other minerals. Here mining and manufacturing are carried on.

THE FEDERATION of Indo-China, formerly French Indo-China, with Siam forms a peninsula extending into the South China Sea. As a political unit, it has had much internal unrest since the beginning of World War II.

The country, with its mingled Hindu and Chinese culture with an overlay of French modernity, is crossed by a mountain range that provides cool, jungle-clothed highlands in the interior, while after an intermediate forest belt the long seaboard has tropic heat and seasons regulated by the monsoon winds.

The territory appears on the map like a thick letter S which on the north touches Southern China, in which French interests in the Far East are centered, while the lower half of the S curves about Siam. The S is divided between Tongking (or Tonking, or Tonkin), Annam, Laos, Cambodia and Cochin-

© Ewing Galloway, N. Y.

A NATIVE OF TONGKING (TONKIN)

China. Tongking, Annam and Cochin-China are joined to form Viet Nam. This state and the kingdoms of Cambodia and Laos act in most respects as completely independent countries. They all honor the same currency, custom regulations and postage system; and each has self-rule in all matters except foreign and military, under France.

Until the tenth century the greater part of Annam was occupied by the Chams, a people of Hindu culture. But a Chinese invasion of the third century B.C. had resulted in Chinese supremacy. In 968 Dinh-Bo-Lanh ousted the Chinese and founded an independent dynasty. Annam, however, again fell under the yoke of China for a generation early in the fifteenth century. When it was once more free, the real power from that time until the end of the eighteenth century was divided between the family of Trinh in Tong-

SON OF HEAVEN is the title given by the Annamese, the chief race of Indo-China, to their king, who, on state occasions, sits richly arrayed upon a golden throne. His gorgeous **robe** and the great painted dragon, as well as his title, show Chinese influence.

CAMBODIA'S KING is a gorgeous figure, with his jeweled orders, pagoda-like crown and state robes. In the twelfth century his ancestors ruled a kingdom stretching from the Bay of Bengal to the China Sea, a kingdom of which but little remains to-day.

HEAVY LOADS FOR HUMAN SHOULDERS

Peasants in French Indochina, returning from their bargaining in the market, walk barefooted along the narrow roads fringed with dense tropical vegetation. Over their shoulders they carry long poles from which swing their large baskets filled with produce. The principal food crops of Indochina are rice, corn, yams, potatoes, coconuts, sugar-cane, tea and coffee.

THE THREE ASSOCIATED STATES OF INDOCHINA

MOI BABY OVERHEARS ALL THE GOSSIP OF THE VILLAGE

"Moi" is an Annamese word meaning savage, and is applied to the wild tribes of Annam, chiefly of Indonesian origin. They live in the most inaccessible parts of the country and have successfully resisted all attempts to civilize them. The women are very fond of metal bracelets and anklets, like those the women in the photograph are wearing.

A CHARMING AND GRACEFUL WATER-CARRIER IN THAILAND

Thailand is, in the main, a rural country and the people's lives are governed by the planting and harvesting seasons. When times are normal, there is little poverty for the farmers are largely self-supporting. They raise their own food, and weave their own fabrics for clothing. The attractive young farm girl above is carrying water in containers made from bamboo logs.

king and that of Nguyen in Southern Annam, which about 1568 became a separate principality (under the name of Cochin China). Near the end of the eighteenth century rebellion overthrew the Nguyen, but in 1801 one of its surviving members, aided by the French, conquered the whole of Annam, Tong-king and Cochin China. This proved an opening wedge for the establishment of French power in Indo-China.

Annamese the Dominant People

Annam, which now contains the dominant race, was a protectorate of France from 1884 until 1946. In that year, the northern part of Annam and the state of Tong-king united to form the Republic of Viet Nam, under an agreement with France, becoming a free state within the Federation of Indo-China. Cambodia, Laos and Siam bound it on the west. It has a narrow coastal plain from twelve to fifty miles wide, which is backed by the foothills of a range of lofty, forest-clad mountains the peaks of which mark its western boundary. The whole country has an average breadth of only ninety-three miles.

Annam's rivers are many, but are short and swift, and so are of no use for navigation. They are, however, important for irrigation purposes.

The Annamese, who dwell in the valleys and on the coastal plain, came originally from South China. They are small, wiry people, cunning and hard working, and have, since earliest times, been periodically at war with their one-time overlords the Chinese, with the Malay-like Chams who dwell in South Annam, and with the Khmers of Cambodia.

Lacquer Teeth to Preserve Them

Men and women dress alike, in indigo-blue tunics, wide cotton trousers and conical hats. Their feet are bare and their black hair is twisted up into a knot—the men's as well as the women's. Likewise, their teeth are usually lacquered black to preserve them, and their mouths are stained red from the chewing of betel nuts.

Most of them fish or are occupied in the rice fields that provide them with their principal food. They are fond of learning and the children all go to school. Boys too young for school are sent out to tend the big herds of water-buffaloes that are the chief beasts of burden.

There are also many Chinese people in Annam, most of whom are traders. The Annamese, though they do not like these traders, are painstakingly respectful to them and address them as "uncles."

In the jungles that cover the slopes of the inland mountains lives another race of people, the original inhabitants of the country. These are the Mois—a name that means simply "savage." There are many tribes of Mois, all speaking different languages, but little is known about the majority of them, for they live in inaccessible places, unharmed by the fevers that kill all invading races. The Mois are, for the most part, hunters, but they also grow rice in a primitive fashion. The women pierce their ears with thin pieces of bamboo and then replace them with larger and larger pieces until the lobes of their ears hang down over their chests. Then they wear heavy metal earrings.

Chams Once Dominant Along Coast

In olden days Southern Annam was a powerful empire called Champa, peopled by the Chams, the descendants of whom are now found only in the extreme south of the country. The Chams, Mohammedans and Hindus of Indo-Malayan descent, are an indolent people of small stature. The color of their skin varies between dark brown and red-brown, while their hair is black or auburn.

The usual costume of a man consists of a skirt and a long robe; that of a woman, a dark green bodice and a large piece of cloth wrapped around to form a skirt. White, or white striped with red and green are the favorite colors. Both sexes wear the hair long and twist it into a knot at the nape of the neck. Woman here proposes marriage; her children take her name and inheritance descends through her.

Chams never dream of applying soap and water to the little ones; but to appease

A DRAGON USHERS IN THE NEW YEAR, IN SAIGON

Saigon and its sister city of Cholon form a Greater Saigon of more than 1,000,000 inhabitants, mostly Annamese and Chinese. The Annamese profess the religion of Confucius; their language and culture in general resemble the Chinese, and so it is not strange to find New Year's celebrated in the Chinese manner, with dragons parading through the streets.

A RELIEF DECORATING THE TEMPLE OF ANGKOR VAT IN INDOCHINA

Angkor Vat (or Wat) is a magnificent temple in Cambodia in Indochina. Dedicated to Vishnu, it was completed in the twelfth century. Later it was abandoned and its ruins were rediscovered in 1860 in the jungle. After 1908, it was cleared and a moated park now surrounds the ruins. They are the best-preserved examples of Khmer architecture that exist in the world today.

SYRUP BEING POURED INTO COOLING POTS TO CRYSTALLIZE

As soon as crystals of sugar begin to form on the surface of the juice in the purifying pans, the syrup is poured into coolers. When the syrup has been left for two or three days it turns into a mass of sugar crystals and molasses. The molasses is drained away, leaving the moist sugar. This Annamese way of making sugar is naturally wasteful.

the spirits a mother will smear her baby's face with a mixture of flour and saffron, for she believes that the faces of the gods are yellow and they will be pleased at such imitativeness. Should a mother have had a bad dream she will cover her baby's face with soot to hide it from evil spirits.

The Cham equivalent for a kiss is a kind of snort made at the back of a child's neck, just behind the ear, a caress that seems to fill the youngster with delight. The young Chams are but poorly educated. The priests teach them merely the rudiments of reading and writing.

Annamese towns all look very much the same; they consist for the most part of clusters of villages grouped together inside a girdle of walls and moats and defended by a huge citadel, which is often large enough to hold the whole population of the settlement. In the villages the houses, thatched with palm leaves, are built with a wattling of bamboos and mud. The furniture consists of a number of low platforms used as tables in the daytime and as beds at night.

Each village possesses a communal hall which is kept for meetings that correspond to our municipal gatherings. In the dwellings of the Annamese aristocracy there is usually a reception room fitted with a table in the middle, armchairs, a shrine at the back and sleeping stands on either side. These houses are generally constructed of brick or wood, and are roofed with tiles.

Women do all the marketing—both the buying and selling. The venders squat down amid their merchandise and carry on a chattering that seems never to stop, all the time ceaselessly chewing betel, a custom universal throughout the country.

Hué, the capital of Annam, occupied an important position at the mouth of the Hué River. At the beginning of the nineteenth century it was strongly fortified by French engineers and ranked as one of the best defended military posts in Asia. The king of Annam, notwithstanding the fact that he lived in a large, strongly fortified palace in an inner enclosure of the citadel at Hué, had not really much power. For practically the whole administration of the country was in the hands of the French.

Cambodia, an important section of

ANGKOR VAT, CAMBODIA'S MAGNIFICENT RELIC

In Cambodia's jungle are ruins of a once beautiful city, Angkor Thom. It was the capital of the Khmer Empire, a Hindu-Buddhist civilization that flourished more than a thousand years ago. Near by is a resplendent Khmer temple, Angkor Vat. For centuries the Angkor ruins lay hidden and forgotten, but in recent years the jungle has been pushed back and restoration work begun.

Indo-China, is bounded on the north and northwest by Laos and Siam, on the east by Annam, on the southeast by Cochin China; it is washed on the southwest by the Gulf of Siam. It consists chiefly of the very fertile, alluvial plain of the Mekong, a mighty river that has its source in Tibet, and that forms, in its upper course, the boundary between Siam and French Indo-Ch.ina. The Mekong flows through Cambodia from north to south, and periodically floods immense tracts of the country. At the junction of all the navigable waters of Cambodia, there stands Pnom Penh, the capital. The climate is tropical, and much of the land is covered with jungle, in which snakes, tigers and elephants are found. The land is fertile and produces vast quantities of rice, but some parts are so malarial that no one can inhabit them.

For centuries there had been continuous fighting between Cambodia, Siam and Annam. Cambodia had for years continually to pay tribute to the one or the other. During a part of the seventeenth and eighteenth centuries Cambodia was governed by two kings, one supported by Siam and one by Annam, but by a treaty of 1846 the Annamese evacuated the country, and in 1863 Cambodia placed itself under French protection.

The Mystery of Angkor Thom

Where the first Cambodians originated is not certainly known. Centuries before the Christian era, immigrants from the east coast of India introduced into Cambodia both Brahmanism and the Sanskrit language, and the name itself is derived from the Hindu name of the mythical founder of the race, Kambu. But not until the fifth century A.D. did the Khmers as a nation rise into prominence. It is thought that the royal city of Angkor Thom (which means "capital city") was begun by Jayavarman III about 860 A.D. and completed some forty years later. It is pretty well established that the extraordinary temple of Angkor Vat was built early in the twelfth century for the worship of Brahma but later converted to the worship of Buddha.

The Siamese (Thais) were long subject to the Khmers, but about the middle of the fourteenth century they began repeatedly to attack, capture and pillage Angkor Thom until, after a century or so, the capital was abandoned. Indeed, when the Siamese invaded Cambodia around 1340 they carried off ninety thousand captives. Centuries passed. The creeping jungle of banyans and bamboo gradually buried the magnificence of the walled city. Some sixty years ago a French naturalist, after a five-day boat trip through all but impenetrable jungle, discovered the stupendous stone temple near Great Lake (Tonlé Sap) and north of it, the ruins of Angkor Thom.

The Four Faces of Siva

He found Angkor Vat an assemblage of vast, colored sandstone galleries rising to a central pyramid that towered above the palm trees; and Angkor Thom an assemblage of palaces and temples built within moated walls running practically two miles in either direction. There was the royal palace, rising in three quadrangular tiers beneath a central tower and four corner ones, and there was the temple of Bayon, likewise a square structure, with vast galleries and colonnades enclosing a huge tower and beset with half a hundred lesser towers each depicting the four faces of Siva, the Hindu destroyer and fosterer of crops. The walls were carved, beneath an overgrowth of olive and cerise lichens, with the figures of gods, men and beasts, and the inscriptions—obviously derived from the Sanskrit—told of what must have been (for that time) a great and wealthy people of Hindu extraction or at least pupils of Hindu teachers. But as to what had become of that people and that civilization, all was mystery. The French School at Hanoi is excavating at Angkor with a view to learning more of the ancient civilization of the Khmers.

Paved Roads to the Ruins

To-day paved roads lead to the ruins and every tourist in this part of the world tries to visit them. Part of the way these

225

DOZENS OF "LITTLE MAIDS FROM SCHOOL" IN CHOLON, INDOCHINA

The demure little white-robed pupils, fans in hand, go to a French missionary school in Cholon. They appear to have rather mixed emotions at being photographed on their afternoon walk.

roads run through cleared land on which the jungle has been converted to fertile paddy fields. The Great Lake lies in a depression fifteen miles by sixty-eight and in flood time serves as a reservoir for the Mekong River. One finds purple banks of hyacinth and rose-hued rhododendrons, and swamplands brilliant with a rank growth of tiger lilies, which perfume the entire countryside.

The Pnom Penh of to-day presents a neat array of white buildings, parks and a museum of the antiquities of Indo-China which conducts manual training classes. Yet despite such modernity, seven-headed stone cobras guard the bridge, the open-faced shops offer the variable prices of the Orient and Buddhist priests in their long yellow robes mingle with crowds in which the native men and women are dressed precisely alike, in sarongs and pajamas. Peddlers roast bananas over charcoal or cook rice in portable stoves, and at night one hears the tom-tom beating out a rhythm for the drama-dancing

girls, while pipers skirl and bamboo xylophones mingle melodiously.

The civilized Cambodians of the present day dwell on the banks of the Mekong River and around the Great Lake. They are a strong but gentle people, mostly tillers of the soil, but accomplished musicians and poets and lovers of literature, the dance and the drama. Most children are taught by the Buddhist priests in the many temples found in the land. The national costume of both men and women is a coat and a sampot—a straight piece of material, often of beautiful hand-woven silk, which is wound around the waist and loosely caught up between the legs. The average Cambodian prefers to live a lonely life among his rice fields. His house is built on tall piles as a protection against tigers and floods.

The wild tribes of Cambodia are also of the same race as the civilized Khmers. As is the case with the Mois, little is known of them, for they hide themselves from strangers in fever-ridden jungles.

THE ROAD FROM PEKING TO PARIS—VIA DONG-DANG, THAT IS!

Signs in an Indochinese town invite the traveler to stop at Dong-Dang, and point the way to Paris, only 7,000 miles (12,672 kilometers) away, and to Peking, a mere 1,800 miles.

WILD WATER-BUFFALOES TAMED FOR THE PLOW

Water-buffaloes, which are found wild in Laos, have been domesticated, as have the zebus; and while the bulls are used as draft animals in the farming districts, the cows are milked or their flesh is eaten. Large tracts of upland country in Indo-China, especially in the plateaus and certain provinces of Annam, offer conditions favorable to stock-breeding.

Though it has been a century and a half since France first made conquest of territory in Annam, the real beginning of French influence in Indo-China (1862-67) dates from the time when she seized and colonized Cochin China, the river plain down the southern tip of the peninsula which the Mekong inundates from June to October. There is, indeed, a network of waterways, which have been made to communicate with one another by means of natural or artificial channels. The humid warmth is all but unendurable to white men, the more so during the summer season when rain falls almost daily and mosquitoes breed malaria. Domesticated buffalo are used in the rice fields and for general transport, and the forest areas are made hazardous by the presence of tigers, leopards and deadly reptiles. Since the Khmer kingdom, which was at its zenith from the ninth to the twelfth centuries, included most of what is now Cochin China, we have had its earlier history with that of Cam-bodia. Its later history follows that of Annam until the time of French occupation. In 1887 it was united with Cambodia, Annam and Tong-king to form the Indo-Chinese Union which preceded the existing political arrangement. It is interesting in this connection to note that in December, 1924, the governor-general initiated a "congress of the Indo-Chinese union," with extended financial powers, together with an increased share in the government for the natives. Possibly as a consequence of this extension of democracy, there is a larger demand for education than there are at present schools to meet it. Since 1917 French has been taught even in the primary schools.

Saigon, capital of Cochin China, has fine public buildings, a tree-lined boulevard and an extensive port, together with wireless communication with Bordeaux. Its neighbor Cholon is the larger city by reason of its Chinese, who comprise half the population. These live in assemblages of native "villages." Cochin China has

228

not only a good irrigation system but entirely modern rice granaries for its chief crop.

Laos, in the central interior, is a green jungle where tigers fill the natives with real and superstitious terror, elephants are caught and tamed as beasts of burden and alligators infest the streams. Monkeys swing from branch to branch, the prey of serpents whose fetid breath taints the pungent air, rhinoceroses wallow in the tepid mud, peacocks scream with their raucous voices in the watches of the night, and in the grassy savannahs small native horses race as warily as any of the wild folk. Here the teak forests supply a timber for export which has been found so durable that teakwood temples in Southern India have survived two thousand years. The road from Savannakhet to Dongha is the principal route to Annam and is open throughout the whole year.

Tong-king, snug up to the borderline of Southern China, was visited by French missionaries as early as the seventeenth century, though its modern development did not begin until about 1860. The state practically occupies the basin of the Red River or Hong-Kiang, and Haiphong is a busy port from which exports of vast quantities of rice grown on the river delta are sent to China, besides which the city serves as the only outlet to the sea for Yun-nan in Southern China, which reaches it by rail. Sampans and Chinese junks travel up and down the waterways, the wharves are redolent of tropic fruits, coffee and tobacco, pepper, cinnamon, corn, hides and rubber; while ships flying the flags of Great Britain, France, Japan and other countries take on coal, limestone, or bales of such exports as silk and tea, after having unloaded their cargoes of metal tools and machinery, cotton thread and cotton tissue. Huge billets of Laos teak are hoisted aboard by cranes. Fish, too, are sent to China by the thousands of tons; for under French rule both salt and fresh-water fisheries have been developed.

It might be mentioned in passing that for French Indo-China as a whole, the exports so nearly equal the imports as usually to make a fortuitous trade balance.

A great national road now runs from

STREET IN HAIPHONG, ON RED RIVER, THE PORT OF TONG-KING

Haiphong, a harbor town with electric power stations, though twenty-two miles from the sea, is the only outlet for Yun-nan, China, with which it has rail connections. Tong-king exports quantities of rice from the delta lands about the river mouth, as well as maize, hides, raw silk, cotton cloth and cement. It imports metal tools and machinery.

PLYING CHOPSTICKS IN A HOME IN CAOBANG, TONKIN

For a dining table there are mats, and the family eats sitting on the floor. Rice is the main dish, and it is garnished with smaller portions of vegetables, pork or perhaps fish.

230

THE RUE GUYNEMER, STREET OF CHINESE RESIDENTS IN SAIGON

A tricycle jinrikisha stands against the curb, waiting perhaps for a Chinese merchant. Side-
walk stalls are flimsy and cluttered, but the shuttered building behind looks well-kept.

the Chinese border across Tong-king and on the Siamese border of Cambodia, besides which there are motor roads, entirely passable during the dry season, traversing Tong-king and Cambodia on their way to Cochin China.

Tong-king is rich in minerals—coal, iron, salt, copper, zinc, phosphates— mined by natives working under French engineers, while the several towns hum with mill wheels. At Hanoi, the centre of the town is occupied by a lake spotted with islets on which stand colorful pagodas. The University of Indo-China, established in 1917, aims at turning out native lawyers, planters, traders, manufacturers and government assistants. Most

of the attendants are, as it happens, Annamese. There is also a French School at Hanoi, which is making important researches into the native history, language and art, and which has made searching studies and excavations of the ruins of Angkor. There is a European College, a College of Interpreters attended by native students, a cathedral, a theatre and a race-course. But the tourist will be equally interested in the local color, such as that of the many native streets with their wares colorfully displayed in open booths. These local wares include the output of silk and cotton mills, tile and ceramic factories, as well as the lace made by native women in their homes.

FEDERATION OF INDO-CHINA: FACTS AND FIGURES

THE COUNTRY

The Federation of Indo-China, wholly within the tropics, is in southeast Asia, bounded on the north by China, on the west by Thailand and the Gulf of Siam and on the east by the South China Sea. The federation includes the three states of Viet Nam, Cambodia and Laos. Viet Nam, made up of Tonkin, Annam and Cochin-China, has an area of 126,608 sq. mi. and a population of 22,973,000. The area of Cambodia, 69,866 sq. mi.; population, 3,279,000. The area of Laos, 89,320 sq. mi.; population, 1,208,-000. The total area of Indo-China, 285,794 sq. mi.; population, 27,460,000.

GOVERNMENT

According to a treaty of Feb. 3, 1950, the states of Viet Nam, Cambodia and Laos became independent members of the Indo-China Federation and of the French Union. The three states retain self-rule of internal affairs. A French high commissioner safeguards French interests in the federation and establishes Indochinese foreign policy through the aid of a Government Council. Authority in Viet Nam is contested by warring regimes. One is under Bao Dai, the former emperor of Annam; he is supported by the French and his government is recognized by the U. S. and the United Kingdom. The other regime, recognized by the Soviet Union, Communist China and other communist countries, is under Ho Chi Minh, the Communist leader of the revolutionary, anti-French party called the Viet Minh. Cambodia and Laos are each governed by a constitution, which regulates the powers of a king, Cabinet and legislature. Representatives of the French high commissioner advise each of the federation governments.

COMMERCE AND INDUSTRY

Agriculture is the chief occupation of the people and the principal crop is rice. Other prod-

ucts are corn, tobacco, sugar, coffee, pepper, kapok and rubber. Livestock-raising is important and fishing is actively carried on. The chief mineral products are coal, phosphates, zinc, antimony, tin, wolfram, graphite and lead. There are forests of rare hardwoods, bamboo, rubber, coconuts, dyewoods and medicinal plants. The most important industry is rice-milling. In Cambodia, salting and smoking fish is the principal native industry. Raw silk is produced and is woven in Tonkin. The chief exports are rice (about 50% of the total), rubber, fish, coal, pepper, cattle and hides, copra, corn, zinc and tin ore, sticklac and teakwood; principal imports are cotton textiles, metal goods, machinery, kerosene and automobiles.

COMMUNICATIONS

There are nearly 2,000 miles of railroad, much of it government-owned, and an excellent highway system of about 17,000 miles. Telephone line mileage is almost 17,900, and telegraph line mileage is 3,030.

RELIGION AND EDUCATION

Buddhism is the principal religion. The educational system includes public and private elementary and secondary schools for both French and Indochinese. There are technical schools and colleges for higher education at Hanoi, Dalat and Saigon.

CHIEF TOWNS

Saigon-Cholon, 1,179,000, capital of the Federation of Indo-China, is in the Cochin-China area, now called South Viet Nam. Hanoi, 160,000, in the Tonkin area, called North Viet Nam. Hué, 25,000, in the Annam area, now Central Viet Nam. Pnom Penh, 26,000, located in Cambodia; and Vientiane, 28,000, in Laos.

232

FORMOSA, CHINA'S ISLAND PROVINCE

Its Jungle Tribes, Once Savage Head-hunters

Formosa was discovered by Portuguese navigators who sailed along its coast in the sixteenth century. It is a beautiful land, quite mountainous and heavily wooded. Its forests once harbored fierce tribes of head-hunters that preyed on shipwrecked seamen and camphor workers, but civilization has gradually tamed them. Most of the world's camphor trees grow on Formosa, and until artificial ways of making camphor were discovered the island was famous for this product. Japan, in her period of expansion and conquest in the Far East, forced China to cede her the island in 1895, but fifty years later, after World War II, Formosa was returned to China. When the Nationalists were pushed from the Chinese mainland in 1949, they established their headquarters on Formosa with their capital at Taipei.

WHEN the Portuguese adventurers sailed up the China Sea in the sixteenth century, they sighted an island about one hundred miles off the mainland of China. Its dense forests, rocky coast and the high range of mountains that runs down the centre of the island gave it such an enchanting appearance that the Portuguese navigators called in the Beautiful Island—Ilha Formosa.

As we sail along the east coast we cannot help being impressed by the beauty of the scene, the cascades gleaming in the sunlight as they tumble over the two thousand foot cliffs. Every now and then, as we round a headland, we get glimpses of valleys and ravines and perhaps of a tiny native village in a clearing.

Formosa lies in the volcanic chain that extends from Japan to the Philippines. It is one of a long line of islands which serve as a barrier to the Asiatic coast from the typhoon area in the warm Kurosiwo current. It is an oval island ending in a pointed tail at the south. Its area is just less than that of Hokkaido, and like some primeval monster of the deep, its back rises in a hump of mountain ranges. These reach farthest skyward in Mt. Sylvia, 12,480 feet above the level of the sea, and Mt. Morrison, named by the Japanese Niitaka or New High Mountain, 14,270 feet and higher than Fuji. While the mountains are not volcanic, there are steam and sulphur springs on the island. The higher slopes are shaded deep with pines, then a little lower, with gigantic Cryptomerias and Chamæcyparis. Below

six thousand feet the bush is composed of palms, banyans, cork and camphor trees, tree ferns and interlacing creepers, and is perfumed with lilies and gay with orchids. These forests are interspersed with all but impenetrable thickets of rattan or stretches of head-high jungle grass through which creep deadly reptiles and wild beasts. But the hill slopes are more dangerous, for there dwell aboriginal Malay tribes of savage, and often cannibalistic, head-hunters. Along the coast the climate is damp and altogether too hot for a white man, besides being malarial with fever-breeding mosquitoes. Off shore one sees coral and flying fish. The tourist who wishes to visit the tropic beauties of Formosa will find the climate in the north driest and best from October to December and that of the south in February and March.

The island, unlighted and unsurveyed, with its sheer cliffs on the one side and long shallows on the other, has been the scene of many a shipwreck, and until the missionaries came, about the middle of the nineteenth century, Formosa was known to white men chiefly by reason of the many wrecks that occurred along its coasts and the consequent treatment accorded the survivors by both the cannibalistic aborigines and the Chinese. Indeed, when the British brig Ann was lost off Formosa in 1842, forty-three of the fifty-seven persons on board were executed at Taichu. Over a generation later the crew of the shipwrecked Japanese junk Loo Choo was put to death by one of the tribes

EAST CHINA SEA

CHINA

HOKA

Tansui
Keelung
Taipei
Shinchiku
Giran
Rato
Byoritsu
Suo
Gosei
TSUGITAKA
Taichu
Rokko
Karenko

FORMOSA

PESCADORES
ISLANDS
Kagi
NIITAKA
Tainan

Taito

Takao
Heito
Toko
KASHO

SOUTH

CHINA

Koshun
KOTOSHO

CAPE GARAN BI

SEA

Bashi Channel

Formosa Strait

THE ISLAND OF FORMOSA

crossed to Formosa, where he drove out the Dutch and took possession of the island. But in 1682 after K'ang-hi came to the throne he turned it over to the Chinese imperial government and Formosa continued a Chinese possession until the war with Japan in 1894–95. The Japanese administered the island until the end of World War II.

The early Chinese settlers, it seems, ousted the aborigines in no gentle manner from their immemorial hunting and fishing grounds. Wherefore, when the Chinese went to the mountain forests for camphor or rattan, the savage hillmen laid ambuscades for them; and many a pig-tailed yellow head has been dried as a trophy. Little by little the head-hunters have become more civilized until they are no longer the great danger they once were. Many of the groups, however, have not become really friendly, and they continue to live as wild men. This is especially true in the eastern mountains of the island. Green savages, Chin-hwan, and wild savages, Sheng-fan, the hillmen are called. They keep ferocious dogs for hunting panthers, boars, bears and deer. Their thatched huts are usually made of bamboo and have but one small window and a door which it is possible to enter only by stooping. Some of the tribes build their houses half underground and line the interior with slate quarried from the hills.

The principal occupation of these savages is weaving. They cultivate millet, and the stores of grain are in charge of the women, who deal it out on a ration system. Among themselves, theft is almost unknown. They count on their fingers.

Such religion as they profess is confined chiefly to pleasing the God of Rain. They believe that when a man dies he must

of the southern coast, and as the Chinese government declined to punish the culprits, the Japanese invaded the island in 1874, and war was barely averted.

Added to other drawbacks to shipping, violent typhoons occur from four to five times a year during which the wind has been known to blow at a velocity of 125 miles an hour, while the rain falls in torrents. Keelung in the north has known years when there were 242 days of rain.

The island, with its wealth of camphor and other natural resources, has belonged to three other nations in turn. In 1624 the Dutch built a fort on the east coast, near where Anping now stands, and there maintained a settlement for roughly forty years. When the Ming Dynasty ended in China, Chêng Chi-lung, a defeated adherent of the Mings, harried the coast as a pirate, but was finally cast into prison and died. His son Coxinga thereupon determined to leave the mainland and

cross a bridge over a chasm, and that those who have been successful in war will pass easily, as will those who have been industrious and of use to the tribe. Others, who have not been good weavers, will fall in and so will never enter paradise. In troublous times it is the custom for a selected party to go up into a cave in the mountains and there to sing and perform a weird dance. The echoes of their chants are interpreted as the sayings of the gods—indications of what the people are to do.

Among these head-hunters a human skull is regarded as a valuable kind of cup. A man may not marry until he has

WIDE WORLD

A RIVER OF FORMOSA, HEAVY WITH SILT FROM THE UPLANDS

In a dry season, a sluggish Formosan river carries an abundance of mud and gravel from the mountains and narrow plains of its upper course down to the coastal lowlands and the sea.

A REMNANT OF JAPANESE OCCUPATION, NEAR TAIPEI, FORMOSA

This torii, or gateway, leads to a former Japanese shrine not far from the island's capital.   The island, which is separated from the China coast by the Formosa Strait, was under Japanese rule for fifty years.   Its climate is tropical, with ample rainfall.   More than half the people depend on farming, with rice the most important crop and sugar the chief export.

A TEMPLE OF MANY FAITHS IN TAIPEI, CAPITAL OF FORMOSA

The architecture of this Japanese-built temple reflects characteristics of three Oriental religions: Confucianism, Shintoism and Buddhism.   It suggests that the Japanese, during their fifty-year rule of the island of Formosa, tried to adjust differences among their subjects.   Taipei is a modern city, with several industries, and has an estimated population of half a million.

MAIN STREET IN FORMOSA'S MODERN CAPITAL

In his island of safety above the rush of automobiles, bicycles and rickshaws, this helmeted police-
man looks down on all the world. He directs the traffic along the smoothly paved streets of Taipei
(formerly Taihoku) by means of modern electric signals. Although Formosa is still very primitive
in many ways, Taipei is a surprisingly modern city in appearance.

AN EARLY STEP IN THE PAPER-MAKING INDUSTRY

Workers are stripping bark from trees at a pulp and paper factory at Lotung. The peeled wood will be washed, cut up and ground to pulp as the next step in the production of paper.

PHOTOS, WIDE WORLD

CUTTING MACHINE AT A PAPER MILL NEAR TAIPEI

The machine cuts huge rolls of paper into sheets of precise size. Other machines in this factory will fold and glue the sheets into bags, for use at home and for export.

Nippon Yusen Kaisha

ATAYAL VILLAGE BUILT HIGH UP ON A MOUNTAIN TO COMMAND THE VALLEY BELOW

The savages of Formosa are grouped into eight main divisions, of which the Atayals form one of the largest. All these tribes, except the Pepahwans, are exceedingly warlike, so we shall find that most of the villages have been built in strong positions. The villages of the Atayals are small, those in the southern portion of the Atayal country generally containing about half a dozen huts. The houses are constructed of bamboo bound with grass or rush, and are raised upon posts, on the top of which are placed flat pieces of stone or tins to keep out rats.

OX-DRAWN, RUBBER-TIRED WAGONS MOVING INTO THE CAPITAL

From the mountain forests, where oak, cypress, Japanese cedar and other valuable timber trees grow in profusion, comes one of many convoys with sawn lumber for the busy builders of Taipei.

OLD CARS, SHAFTS AND CONVEYERS IN THE SUISHAN COAL MINE

The Suishan mine is inland from the northern port of Keelung and the capital, Taipei, in the valley of the Keelung River. The mine has been improved with the help of foreign loans.

WINNOWING RICE BY LETTING IT FALL FROM BASKET TO BASKET

The wind will carry the lighter chaff away, letting the precious kernels fall to the basket below. This is tedious labor which yields only a few pounds of rice for a day's work.

WOMEN IN MOSQUITO VEILS PICKING TEA ON A PLANTATION IN NORTHERN FORMOSA © Ewing Galloway

Tea growing is one of the most important industries of Formosa. The Chinese introduced the plant and supplied most of the labor even when the Japanese operated the rich plantations and reaped the benefits. Women and children pick the leaves. The picture shows the kind of hats they wear to protect their heads from the heat of the tropical sun. When the great bags are filled, a woman can manage two of them suspended from the ends of a short bamboo. Formosa teas include green and black, the familiar Oolong and Pouchong exported to Java.

presented his intended bride with a number of skulls, for only after a certain number of heads have been placed beneath the foundations of their new house can they take up their residence. The finest form of decoration is not a picture, but the skull of an enemy. The customs in connection with courtship and marriage are curious. The young man takes a bundle of wood to the girl's home and leaves it in front of the door. When there are twenty bundles, he returns. If the wood has been taken in, it is a sign that his suit is accepted. In the marriage ceremony, bride and bridegroom sit back to back on the floor of the hut, dances and various rites are performed, then a slight cut is made in a leg of each and the blood is mingled. They are now supposed to have acquired mutually satisfactory temperaments.

Before setting out on a head-hunting expedition, the hunters consult the omens and follow the movements of a certain jungle bird, supposed to tell them

whether they will be successful or not. When the party has left the village, a sacred fire is kept burning day and night, all weaving is stopped, and the hemp is not even prepared for the loom during the absence of the warriors. If the expedition be successful, the heads are placed in the centre of a circle, food is put into their mouths, and wild dancing goes on all night. The successful warriors have a special mark tattooed on their faces; and boys whose fathers have been famous as head-hunters are also allowed this badge of honor.

Boys and young men must live in a large hut apart from the rest of their fellows until they are warriors or are married. The Formosans argue that this tends to make the men of the tribe hardy and accustomed to shifting for themselves.

Formosa has for long been the greatest camphor-producing area in the world. It has vast numbers of camphor trees, the product of which is valuable in medicine,

Hose

WHERE A SLIP MEANS CERTAIN DEATH IN THE GORGE BELOW

The rattan and other creepers grow profusely in the tropical forests of Formosa, and the aboriginals make frail bridges supported solely by rattan cables. To cross such a narrow, swaying footway, with only a rattan handrail to hold, is a terrifying experience, except for the aboriginals, who are accustomed to walking along the brinks of sheer precipices.

RYUZAN-JI: AN ELABORATE BUDDHIST TEMPLE IN TAIPEI

Dragons and foliage twist and turn around the pillars and flare from the corners of the up-
curved eaves. The structure is a classic example of Buddhist architecture in Formosa.

in the making of celluloid and smokeless gunpowder, in protecting furs from moths and in many other ways. The best forests are situated along the northern hills, where the trees are exceptionally large and productive. Before the coming of the Japanese the method of extracting the camphor was wasteful. Vast quantities of trees were cut down, and only a little camphor was obtained by the crude system of refining. The Chinese had placed Formosa in charge of a viceroy appointed by the emperor, and he had control of all the camphor in the island; but he simply regarded it as a means of amassing a fortune. As a result, the savages in whose territory the camphor trees were found were so ill-treated that they often massacred the Chinese workers, whose

friends then murdered any of the tribesmen they could capture.

The Japanese then introduced scientific methods of dealing with the camphor trade. The trees were felled and the chips taken from them were refined by modern processes, so that there was very little waste. It is estimated that there are still eight thousand square miles of unexplored territory in Formosa, most of it forests of camphor trees. The early Chinese settlers knew the value of the camphor, and they constructed an embankment along the borderline of the native territory as a protection against the raids of the head-hunters.

The Japanese in their turn built a guard line through the forest. This included much of the country that had scarcely, if

Nippon Yusen Kaisha

ATAYAL WOMEN POUNDING GRAIN WITH HUGE PESTLES

The Atayals who live among the high mountains of the interior eat ginger with their food.
as they usually have no salt. They live chiefly on rice and millet, taros (starchy tubers)
and sweet potatoes, venison and wild pork, eaten half raw. Their household equipment
includes wooden mortars, pestles like heavy Indian clubs, and a variety of capacious baskets.

UNDER ARMED PROTECTION: A CAMPHOR STILL IN THE MOUNTAIN FORESTS OF FORMOSA

Formosa is the main source of the world's supply of camphor, and the industry became a government monopoly when the island was in the possession of the Japanese. Wherever the camphor laurel grows, stills **are worked.** The chips are placed in retorts over boiling water; the vapor is piped into earthenware vats cooled by running water and it there condenses in the form of white crystals. Lumps of these crystals are placed in wooden troughs and the yellowish free essential oil drained off and taken to the refineries where it undergoes further treatment.

CHIPPING WOOD OF CAMPHOR LAUREL AT A FORMOSAN DISTILLERY

Camphor is obtained by steaming the leaves, wood and bark until drops of the gum are driven out to the surface. Formosa is the world's outstanding producer of camphor gum and oil.

ever, been explored; for they had found that it was worse than useless to send military expeditions into the territory of the head-hunters. The tribesmen knew every inch of the ground and could prepare successful ambushes, whereas in this guerrilla warfare the Japanese soldier, hampered by his heavy equipment, made poor headway in climbing through the dense jungle.

Every effort was made by means of the guard line to get in touch with the natives and to pacify each tribe by peaceable means. The Japanese even strove to induce the head-hunters to adopt farming as a means of livelihood.

During World War II, the Japanese made Formosa a strong military base; and for this reason it was bombed frequently by Allied planes during the last years of the war. When Japan was defeated, Formosa, without much ado, was returned to China, which was then under the Nationalist Government of Chiang Kai-shek. Consequently, since 1945 Formosa has been involved in the changing fortunes of China.

As everyone knows, civil strife continued in China after World War II ended. Antagonists for more than two score years, the Nationalists and Com-

munists took up their quarrel with even greater vigor than before. The Western world watched with growing dismay as the Communists by degrees gained the upper hand and then, at the end of 1949, succeeded in pushing the Nationalist forces from the Chinese mainland altogether. It was then that the Nationalist Government established itself on Formosa and made the island a focal point in the whole explosive Far Eastern situation.

In 1950-51, the status of Formosa and the Nationalist Government there were matters of considerable controversy, aggravated by the entry of the Chinese Communists into the Korean conflict. The United States, as the world power whose decisions would influence the course of events in Formosa most forcefully, was generally united in opposition to Red China but sharply divided in its views on the Nationalists. Official policy was that the United States would block any attempted Red invasion of Formosa but would not take the island over. However, in the spring of 1951, there were about five hundred United States military advisers helping to train the Nationalist troops in Formosa, and it was announced that they ranked with Western Europe in priority for United States arms.

FORMOSA: FACTS AND FIGURES

THE COUNTRY

An island which lies between the Philippines on the south and Japan on the north with the China Sea on the west and the Pacific Ocean on the east. The area is 13,890 square miles and the population is about 7,617,700. Taipei, the capital, has a population of 504,000. In 1895 Taiwan was ceded by China to Japan. As a result of World War II, Japan surrendered control of the island to Nationalist China.

COMMERCE AND INDUSTRIES

The agricultural products are rice, of which two crops a year are grown, tea, sugar, sweet potatoes, ramie, jute and tumeric. Camphor, the most important product, is worked in the forests. There are active fisheries. Industries include flour milling, sugar, tobacco, ironworks, glass, bricks and soap. Minerals include gold, silver, copper and coal. Most of the commerce is with Japan. The exports are tea, sugar, rice, camphor and coal and the im-

ports are cotton and silk goods, wood and planks, oil cake, petroleum and opium.

COMMUNICATIONS

Roads are being constructed, and there are 2,500 miles of railway. Length of telegraph line is 734 miles and length of telephone line is 2,946 miles. There are about 193 post offices.

EDUCATION

Since the end of World War II, the Japanese educational curriculum has been abolished and one similar to that of the Chinese mainland has been introduced. There are 1,191 elementary schools; 206 middle, normal and vocational schools and 6 universities. Enrollments in all classes have increased sharply since 1945.

DEPENDENCY

Pescadores, or Hokoto Islands, a group of 12 islands lying west of Formosa, is under the Formosan government. Their area is about 50 square miles.

THE LAND OF THE DRAGON

Some Glimpses of China

Far in advance of the Western world, China developed a complex civilization, in which the arts, literature and invention flourished. However, as time went by, it froze into a rigid pattern. The best and only accepted way to do anything was to do it as one's ancestors had. Through these centuries, China was governed along feudal lines down to the smallest village. The great tide bringing about more democratic forms of government elsewhere did not reach China until early in the twentieth century. Though a republic was established in 1912, it failed to unite China. For long years after, internal strife and foreign invasion kept the nation impoverished. Following the war with Japan, from 1937 to 1945, civil war flared up more violently still between the Nationalists and the Chinese Communists. The Reds, grown strong during the conflict with Japan, at last swept the Nationalists from the mainland in 1949. Today the Chinese people are governed by a ruthless dictatorship.

CHINA was for many centuries a far-off wonderland, a place of mystery. To Europeans, during the Middle Ages, it was known as "far Cathay," and many tales of its marvels and magnificence were told by the few travelers who managed to get a glimpse of it. To the Chinese themselves it has been "The Flowery Kingdom." They do not forget that their race was civilized long, long ago, while the people of all northern European nations were savages, so they have always regarded themselves as heavenly people—"Celestials"—and the rest of the world as barbarians.

As far as possible for many years they kept foreigners out of their country. However, as early as 1557, in return for aid given against pirates, permission was granted to some Portuguese to put up warehouses on the end of a peninsula at the mouth of the Canton River. The Chinese, thereupon, built a wall across it to keep the barbarians from mixing with the Celestials. This place, Macao, became a Portuguese colony, and has remained one ever since, but it was not really recognized by treaty as Portuguese territory before 1887.

Traders from England followed those from Portugal, after about a century; but it was not until after war with Britain that, in 1842, Hong Kong, an island off the Canton River, became a British Crown Colony. At that time, five other coastal towns, including two famous ones, Shanghai and Canton, were opened to foreign traders. These were known as the Treaty Ports. For a time Japan held Manchuria and the island of Formosa, as well as Korea. As a result of World War II, Manchuria became part of China and Korea achieved independence. Formosa has become the last stronghold of the Chinese Nationalist Government.

Who are the Chinese, these people who have seemed so exclusive, and what is the land so many millions of them have guarded so dearly? In ages of strength China has included lands on all sides of it, and in times of weakness it has been the domain of foreign rulers. The China under consideration in this article is China proper—the almost circular cluster of eighteen provinces between Tibet and the Pacific Ocean and between Mongolia and the southeastern peninsula of Asia. A section on Manchuria appears at the end of this chapter.

The Chinese belong to the great yellow race of mankind. They are small in stature, their eyes are almond-shaped and frequently slanting, their skin is yellowish and their hair black and straight. Coming into China about 4,000 years ago, though nobody knows whence they came, they drove the people already living there to the mountains of the western provinces, especially Yunnan, where millions of them still exist.

Early Chinese history, like that of other ancient nations, has a long period (over a thousand years) where tradition and fact cannot be disentangled. After this came nearly a thousand years more when development went on in a number

249

THE GREAT WALL OF CHINA, was begun in the third century B. C., but long stretches of it were added hundreds of years later. It is about 1,500 miles long, with a general average height of 22 feet. At intervals were placed towers, 40 to 60 feet high. The wall, built as a protection against savage invaders, was not altogether a success as a means of defence. The section at Nankow Pass, shown in this picture, seems to be in good condition; this is due probably to the fact that at points of special danger the structure was most strongly built and most often repaired.

CHINESE MONKS find quiet in this tree-sheltered holy place, with its pagoda and graceful marble bridges. It is situated on the island of Pu Tu, on which only monks may dwell. The island is especially dedicated to Kwan-yin, the goddess of mercy, who is said to keep a close watch over sailors. As a very great many of the Chinese earn a living on the sea and the rivers, the goddess is most popular, and many thousands of pilgrims visit the island. Some of them even travel long distances in the hope of securing their own safety and that of their relatives.

of separate feudal states more or less under an emperor. Finally a strong ruler of the third century B.C. drew these states together under his firm hand. Soon Shi-Hwang-ti, "the first universal emperor," brought an end to feudal conditions, made canals and roads, and (about 220 B.C.) started the building of the Great Wall, to keep out barbarians. During the feudal period, silk had become an important product, some of the finest bronzes had been made, Confucius (Kung-fu-tze) and other great teachers had lived, and masterpieces of literature had been written.

A Glorious Age in China

Looking over centuries of advancing civilization, during which paper was invented, the first printed book was produced and navigators were beginning to use the compass, we come to the thirteenth century A.D., when Jenghiz Khan and his Mongols overran northern China. His grandson, Kublai Khan, after overthrowing the Chinese rulers, made himself emperor, reigning with great splendor at Peking. But in 1368 the Mongol rule was ended, and the Ming dynasty, last of the Chinese imperial line, held control until 1644. This was a time of notable expansion in porcelain-making. But China now began to lag behind Europe. Shutting her doors to the outside world, the nation lost creative force.

Again came an invading force from the north, Manchu Tatars, some of whom had been living in northern China for centuries. Their leader ascended the throne at Peking in 1644, and at this time the Chinese began to wear the pigtail—a queue, with the front of the head shaven—as a badge of Tatar sovereignty. Nearly three centuries later, during the revolution, queues were cut off in token of release from imperial rule.

An Old Empire Comes to an End

The current of foreign trade thrust into China's ports (as we have already noted) swept the government and the people into the stream of world relations. During the nineteenth and early twentieth centuries, wars, treaties, "concessions" (lands set apart for foreign residents), railways built with foreign capital, reaction to neighboring Japan on one side and Soviet Russia on the other, strong pressure of outside thought and customs—a crowd of disturbing and arousing experiences brought about revolution. In 1911 the Manchu dynasty fell; in the following year a republic was set up. For the sake of harmony the great leader of revolt, Dr. Sun Yat-sen, consented to let Yuan Shih-kai become the first president.

Yuan proved to be highhanded; soon the Kuomintang or Nationalist Party, that had been organized by Dr. Sun, was in revolt. Yuan succeeded in crushing this rebellion, only to face another crisis. In 1915 Japan made her notorious Twenty-one Demands on China—demands that would have reduced that unfortunate country to the status of a satellite state. Thanks to the vigorous protests of Great Britain and the United States, the original demands were greatly modified. Yet in yielding to them, as she now did, China enabled the Japanese to win a foothold in the land.

Yuan Shih-kai died in 1916 and was succeeded by the well-meaning but weak Li Yuan-hung. In the following year China entered World War I on the side of the Allies. She could not contribute much to the Allied victory and did not benefit particularly as a result of the negotiations that followed.

Chaos in the New Republic

In the meantime conditions had become chaotic. The Kuomintang had set up a separate government in the South, with the capital at Canton; the government of the North had become constantly weaker. The governors of certain provinces raised their own armies and became *tuchuns* or war lords. They fought constantly against one another as well as against the governments of the North and South. The devastation caused by civil war made millions homeless; banditry flourished in the ravaged areas of China.

Sun Yat-sen died in 1925. His disciple, Chiang Kai-shek, commander of the Kuomintang army, took steps to unite

MONASTERY OF YUEN FU BUILT IN THE FACE OF AN ABYSS

About seven miles from Foochow in a mountainous wooded district is this wonderful monastery, built at the mouth of a cavern in the face of a precipice and reached by very worn steps. Only three monks live there, but many pilgrims visit the place. Water comes from a spring above through the pipe of bamboo sections on the left.

A YELLOW-ROBED PRIEST looks from his monastery on Pu Tu island. He is one of the priests of Buddha, who pass their lives in prayer and study, and depend on offerings of religious people for food and clothing, and often for a place to sleep. A great part of the population of China follows the teachings of Buddha, although this religion had its origin in India.

THIS HOLY MAN of China is very careful of his own comfort. Although the priests of his order are supposed to go barefoot and in rags, he wears thick felt slippers and an ample robe. This is made of patches sewn together to give it some slight resemblance to a beggar's cloak, but being of padded silk it loses none of its power to keep the wearer warm

CHINESE FUNERAL PROCESSION

The dead are held in the greatest reverence in China, where funerals are as elaborate and expensive as weddings. Unlike Western custom, white is the color of mourning. Although a man may die, he is still considered part of the family and no one takes his place. For instance, the youngest son is still the youngest son even if his older brothers are dead.

all China under his rule. He conducted a fierce campaign against the Communists, who had become influential in the South; then he marched on Peiping (Peking). By 1928 the country was ostensibly united; the capital was set up in Nanking. However, internal strife continued. Chiang engaged in ceaseless fighting against the Communists, who were strong in certain districts; moreover, he had but slight control over certain war lords.

To internal difficulties was added the threat of foreign domination. In the year 1931 the Japanese began to occupy rich Manchuria. By 1932 they had overrun the entire area and had organized it as the puppet state of Manchukuo. Japan continued to extend her influence in northern China. The Chinese did not dare to resist by force of arms, but they seriously hampered the Japanese by organizing passive resistance, while they prepared for future attack.

The Japanese Attack China

At last the Japanese, exasperated, determined to crush China; in July 1937 they launched a terrible attack. China lost her seaports one by one; her capital, Nanking, was captured; and large areas of the coastal provinces were occupied. Yet instead of crushing China, the invasion united the country as never before. The Chinese resisted fiercely. Chungking, in the western province of Szechwan, became the wartime capital. Eventually, the struggle with Japan became a part of World War II; and when Japan finally was defeated, the seized territories were returned to China.

War in China did not end with the defeat of Japan. Hostility between the Communists and Nationalists flared up again. War raged throughout the scarred land until 1949 when the Reds drove the Nationalists from the mainland. What could be salvaged of Chiang's army was moved to the island of Formosa. There the Nationalists prepared for a Red invasion.

At the start of the war in Korea the United States sent a fleet of war ships to protect Formosa. The Chinese Reds, in November 1950, entered the war and almost drove the UN from Korea. Their onslaught was stopped. Yet they refused to talk over conditions of peace that would bring them neither a seat in the UN nor rights to occupy Formosa. Such conditions were not granted. In the spring of 1951 the war still went on.

China's Religions

There are three main religions in China —Confucianism, Taoism and Buddhism. Confucius was a wise man who was born in 551 B.C. and taught a beautiful rule of conduct, similar in some respects to that of Christ. Temples to Confucius are common in China, and his teachings are known throughout the country.

Lao-tse, the founder of Taoism, who lived at the same time as Confucius, taught the way by which mortals should in time become immortal. This teaching has degenerated into a belief in omens and charms, in lucky days, soothsayers and magicians. It includes the worship of idols and of various spirits, such as the god of the city—for every city has its own god—the spirit of the household, the spirit of the mountains, and so on.

Memorial buildings called pagodas, of which there are nearly two thousand in China, are believed to bring good luck to places near by. They are usually constructed of brick. The most famous of them all, the green and white Porcelain Tower of Nanking, had at its summit a gilt ball from which were hung on chains five large pearls, each of which was supposed to protect the city from one of five disasters—floods, fires, dust-storms, tempests and disturbances among the citizens. From the eaves of the nine stories of the building were suspended many bells and lanterns. This beautiful tower, built by the son of the first Ming emperor, in honor of his wife, was entirely demolished in 1853 during the Taiping rebellion.

Buddhism, the third great religion, has its temples, wayside shrines, monasteries, nunneries, and sacred mountains. Shansi, in the north of China, has the sacred Wu-tai Mountains, where there are numerous temples to which pilgrims throng from all parts of China and Tibet in the hope

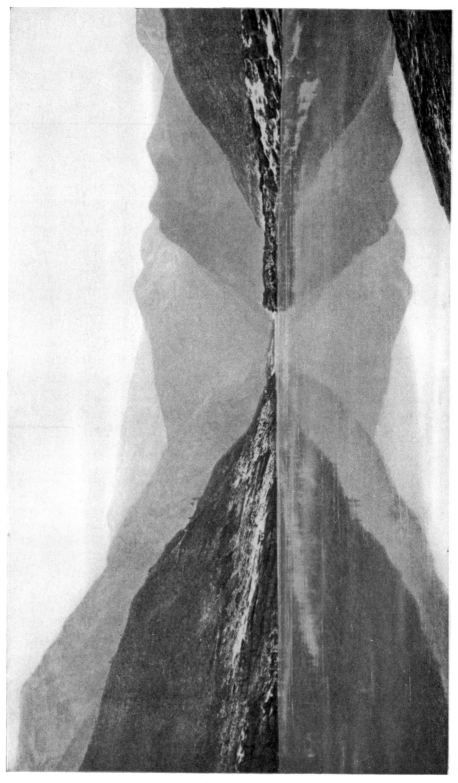

THE YANGTZE KIANG, on its way to the sea, flows through 400 miles of such magnificent mountain scenery as we see here, immediately above the town of Ichang. The river is not always so placid, however, for in places there are gorges with rapids that are very dangerous to shipping. The Yangtze Kiang has many names. It is known officially to the Chinese as the Changkiang, or Great River, popularly as the Blue River; in the districts near Tibet it is the River of Golden Sand; elsewhere it is the White Waters and the Long River. It is over 3,000 miles long.

UNPAVED, ROCK-STUDDED and crossed by streams, this ancient highway runs from Peking, the capital of Communist China, to Kalgan, the "gate" to Mongolia. Long years ago the road was the main route of caravans that carried tea from China to Russia. The road runs through a wild, mountainous region and crosses a bend of the Great Wall. Today there is a railroad between Peking and Kalgan; and Kalgan has become the leading commercial and communications center of Inner Mongolia. Other highways link Kalgan with Ulan Bator and Tolun, farther west.

MISSIONARIES FOUNDED ST. JOHN'S UNIVERSITY IN SHANGHAI

Many schools of all levels were set up by missionaries in China. Young Chinese flocked to them, anxious to add to their classic Chinese education by learning the ways of the West. Since the Communists took over the Government, most of these schools have either been closed or their studies changed to suit the purposes of the Communists.

Courtesy, American President Lines Ltd.

NOISES OF A MODERN CITY VIE WITH TEMPLE BELLS IN SHANGHAI

Here we see both new and old methods of transportation in a busy street which runs through what was called the International Settlement before World War II. Long the banking and trade center of China, Shanghai lost its modern, international flavor in 1949 when the Red Army succeeded in driving Nationalist forces from the city.

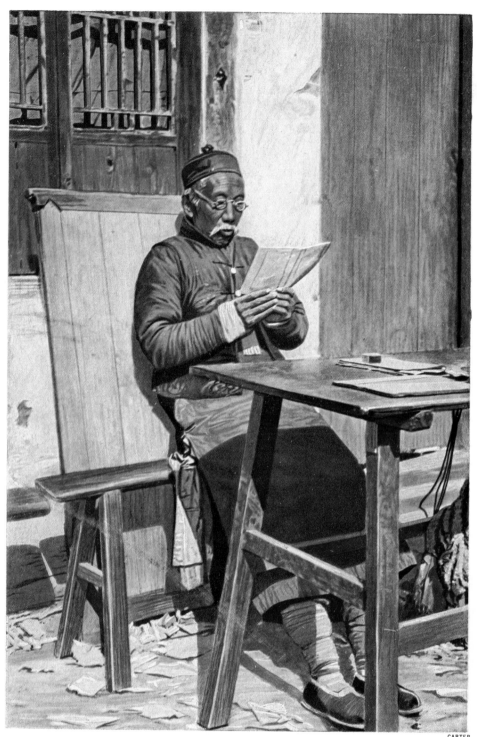

OLD WAYS AND NEW meet in the person of an elderly Chinese of Shanghai. Such richness and color in dress as he displays are frowned on by China's communist overlords. His newspaper represents the "new." Once reading was the mark of the scholar alone; but today so many Chinese can read that daily newspapers are turned out on a mass scale.

A CHINESE ACTOR, in dress that is rich and historically correct, plays the part of the heroine. In modern China, as in the England of Shakespeare's day, women do not appear on the stage, so that men and boys have to take the female parts. Some Chinese plays, usually the most popular, are long, and several days may be needed for their performance.

JUNKS SCUDDING BEFORE THE BREEZE

Chinese rivers and coastal waters are busy highways, with junks and sampans scudding in and out between larger craft. These small craft are fishing boats, water taxis, freight carriers and even homes to countless thousands of Chinese. The junks are flat-bottom affairs, with two or three sails and a small cabin amidships, usually a crude shelter roofed over with mats.

of witnessing the reputed miraculous open-ing of a golden lotus flower. Buddhist priests are called upon chiefly for the cere-monies attending birth, death and burial.

The Worship of Ancestors

The really national religion of China, however, is the old heathen religion of "ancestor worship." When grandparents or parents die the names of the dead, with all particulars, are written on a piece of wood which is known as the ancestral tablet. This is put in a place of honor in the home by the eldest son, who burns in-cense before it and conducts family wor-ship for the departed spirit. The coffin containing the body is covered with a pall —red for men, blue for women—and taken to the family grave. The family follows, led by the eldest son and accompanied by neighbors and friends, the younger rela-tives in white—one of the colors of mourn-ing. At the grave firecrackers are set off and sometimes a theatrical performance is given.

The mourners carry along food, paper money and either models or paper cuttings of the chief objects used in life. These, it is believed, the spirit will need in another world. The Chinese imagine that every dead person has three souls, each of which must be worshiped, at regular intervals, with offerings in the home, at the grave and in the temple of the city god. If this is not done they believe the spirit will be un-happy in the other world and that it will therefore make the descendants of the dead person miserable on earth. Mourning lasts for three years.

Importance of a Son

As the worship of an ancestor must be conducted by a son, people without sons adopt boys, lest they should die with none to worship them. Every rich family has an ancestral hall in which the tablets are stored and family records kept. Here in winter the Feast of Ancestors is held. Wine, fruit and other delicacies are offered at the shrine and are afterward consumed by the family.

Let us look at an old-fashioned home and see how the children pass their lives.

At the birth of a son there is great re-joicing, and ginger is hung at the street door to ward off evil spirits or strangers who might bring the child ill-luck. The new-born baby is wrapped in old clothes belonging to some grown-up, and may be made ill by being fed on a sweet cake.

When the child is nearly a month old his head is shaved. This is a very im-portant day is his life. He is given a name, dressed in fine new clothes, and carried by his father's mother to the temple, where offerings are made and the gods are thanked for the gift of a son. A feast known as the "ginger dinner" is given to friends and relatives. The invitation card is an egg colored red. Men and women do not dine together in China, so the men are feasted at a restaurant, the women in the house. Pickled ginger and colored eggs are always eaten at this feast, and every guest brings a present.

Celebrating the New Year

As the boy grows up he is dressed like his elders in tiny coat and trousers—usually of red, the lucky color. Children's birthdays are not kept up. A baby is counted as one year old at birth, and he adds on another year when the New Year comes in, so the Chinese New Year's Day, which, like our Easter, is a movable date, is everyone's birthday and a general holi-day. Everyone puts on new clothes, fresh red paper mottoes are pasted on the doors, fruits and sweet-meats are placed on the tables and at night there are fireworks. In order to have a free mind, one is ex-pected to have all his debts paid before the day arrives.

On the first full moon of the New Year comes the Feast of Lanterns; on that occasion lanterns of all sorts and sizes, lan-terns in the shape of dragons and fishes, are hung up everywhere in the streets and over the doors. Another feast is celebrated by a family picnic, and in the summer comes a gala day on the water, the Dragon Boat Festival.

When the boy is old enough he will be-gin his education. If he be the son of rich people he will have tutors; or he may go to a school, where, if intended for an

IN NINGPO is the great Tien-how-Kung, or "Queen of Heaven" temple. The roof is the main architectural feature of a Chinese building, and to it, accordingly, the architect gives the greatest part of his attention. The double roof, such as we see in this photograph, with its carved and lac- quered eaves and its ornamentation of dragons and other figures, is held to be a most satisfying artistic device. The town of Ningpo was visited by the Portuguese early in the sixteenth century, but they were soon driven out, and it did not really become open to European trade until 1842.

VIVID SIGNS line a narrow street in Kiukiang, which is a river port city on the south bank of the Yangtze Kiang in central China. Four miles to the south of the city, in a wooded mountain region, is White Deer Cave, where Chu Hsi lived and taught. He was a revered Confucianist philosopher of the thirteenth century.

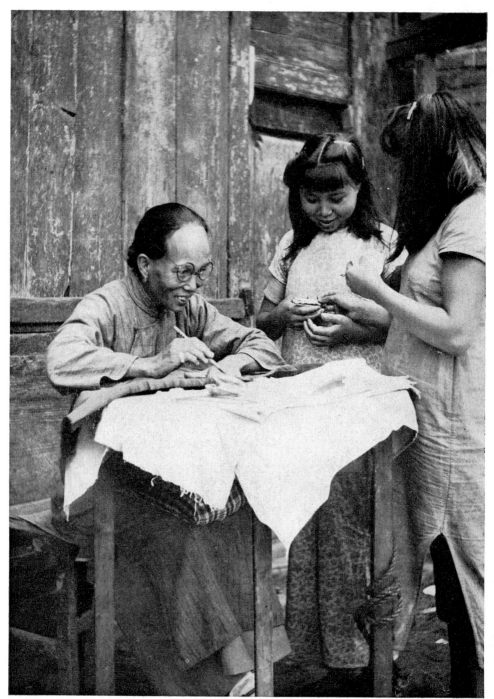

HAND-PAINTED WHILE YOU WAIT

These girls, who look so pleased with the silk handkerchiefs they are examining, have just had them painted by this Kunming artist. Kunming, the capital of Yunnan Province, is the chief city of southwest China. It was of considerable strategic importance during World War II, when it was a U. S. Army air base and the headquarters of the Chinese military command.

official position, he will have to study hard. The ambition of many Chinese boys is to serve their country in some official capacity.

That is the life of a boy of the middle or upper classes. If, however, he belongs to poor people he will get little or no education—hardly a quarter of the people can read—and he will soon become a laborer working in the fields or the factories, early and late, or a coolie (porter) carrying heavy burdens on his back or hanging from each end of a bamboo pole, slung over his shoulders.

Though Chinese parents love their children dearly, and frequently spoil them, a baby girl may be neglected if the family is very poor. When she marries she will become part of her husband's family. Not so very long ago, every little girl of five or six years whose fortune was not desperately poor had her feet pressed into a most unnatural shape and stiffly bound so that they could never develop. Otherwise, she would be utterly out of fashion and could not hope to get a husband. How this painful custom started is unknown, but it is said to have originated with an em-press whose feet were deformed. It is not entirely abolished yet.

The average girl has to work hard. One day her parents sell her to the parents of some young man. Then she receives presents and new clothes and at last the best man comes from the bridegroom bringing with him a red sedan chair—"the wedding chair" it is called—and hands the bride an invitation on red paper.

Dressed in her best, her face covered with red silk, she enters the sedan chair. No matter how hot the day, she is shut up tightly to keep her from evil spirits, and is taken in procession, with much din and rejoicing, to her new home. The bridegroom opens the door of the chair and the bride is carried into the house, where the red veil is removed. Three days of feasting and rejoicing follow with many ceremonials, one being that the bride, who henceforth must obey her husband's parents, has to serve them with a meal and wait upon them.

But, among the most striking changes, where Western influences have been at work in China, is the refusal of young women to fit into the old model. Even

NANKING, CHINA'S "SOUTHERN CAPITAL" BY THE YANGTZE

Nanking, long famous for its art and literature, history, commerce und manufactures, became capital of the empire in the Ming dynasty. Here the first president of the Chinese republic took his oath and in 1928 the city was made capital of the Nationalist government. For long years Japan occupied the city during her period of aggression.

BRIDE AND BRIDEGROOM alike dress in gorgeous costume for the wedding. The young man and his parents arrange the marriage with the parents of the future bride, and husband and wife do not usually meet until the wedding ceremony. The Chinese wife exchanges the life of a servant in her father's house for a similar life of drudgery for her husband's family

PRIDEAUX

GRANDMOTHER AND GRANDSON enjoy the air together. The birth of a boy is always welcome in a Chinese family, and from his earliest days he has infinitely better treatment than a girl. It was once not uncommon for parents to kill a girl baby, or to sell her as a slave after a few years. Some very little girls work long hours in the silk factories.

HONG KONG: FRAGRANT HARBOR

Victoria, city of Hong Kong, is viewed here from Kowloon on the narrow Kowloon Peninsula across the harbor. The city streets sprawl up the mountains which surround the harbor.

when they wear the native costume, they often live very different lives from the women of the past—taking an active part in public affairs, becoming doctors, nurses, teachers, even actors (an unheard-of-thing until our own day).

These changes from ancient ways did not happen overnight but were a long time in coming about. Many factors contributed to China's modern outlook, and not least of these was the work of Christian missionaries from America and Europe. The schools, colleges and universities founded and supervised by these missionaries were among the best in the Orient. They introduced co-education and other features of Western education, such as technical schools for the training of doctors and engineers.

Before the coming of the missionaries in the nineteenth century, China had by no means ignored education. A complicated, exacting system of schooling had been built up over the centuries since before the time of Christ. Bright boys were selected and trained to read and memorize the classics, such as the works of Confucius. After arduous periods of schooling and

testing, the best of the best emerged as "model scholars of the Empire." To them was opened the path to the highest political positions in the land. All China revered the scholar.

The educational zeal of the missionaries found fertile ground. Millions of Chinese sought to better themselves by learning to read and write. Many went abroad for an education, and many stayed in China to attend missionary or newly founded government schools. Even before the Republic was set up in 1912, the Government began to meet the demand. The old examination system was abandoned in 1905; Chinese schools became more and more like models in the United States and Britain. The multitude of the illiterate decreased as modern scholars simplified the long list of characters that must be learned in order to have a reading knowledge of the Chinese language.

After the defeat of Japan, education, like everything else in China, was disrupted by the war between the Kuomintang and the Communists. What has happened since the civil war is hard to determine, but most signs indicate that the

Communist regime encourages education, at least to the extent of instructing the people in the theories of communism. Also, schools are necessary if the Reds are to have the technicians who can build up and man their industries. Missionary schools have been suppressed because, according to the Communists, Christians substitute alien ideas for the interests of the state.

Mineral resources in China are poor when we consider the great size of the country. There is coal in large amounts in Shansi, Shensi and other northern provinces. Iron-ore reserves are low and are of poor grade. Tungsten and antimony are in abundance.

The long rivers, the people and the fields of rice and wheat are the principal ingredients of China's wealth. The country has especially fertile soil, particularly the yellow-brown earth, or loess, of the Hwang Ho basin. Unfortunately, the loess region does not receive as much rain as less fertile areas. The Hwang Ho, which means "yellow river," and is also called "China's sorrow," is often swollen by monsoon rains. It then overflows, wrecking the towns in its path, and rushes on, laden with the "gold" of the loess. Before the river disgorges its rich cargo into the Yellow Sea, it lays down great quantities of loess soil in the densely peopled and heavily farmed North China plain. Fertile earth is thus brought to a region where it is needed most.

The other great river of China is the Yangtze Kiang, which rises in the western mountains, not far from the source of the Hwang. The first third of its course, called the Kinsha Kiang, or "golden sand river," runs southward. After turning east in Yunnan Province, the Yangtze falls through splendid gorges into the central China plain and flows on into the East China Sea above Shanghai. Six hundred miles of the lower Yangtze are navigable.

Silk is one of the things we owe to China, although the Chinese were so anxious to keep the industry to themselves that there was a time when anyone who tried to take silkworm eggs or mulberry-tree saplings out of the country was doomed to die. But about 550 A.D. two pil-

BLACK STAR

HOUSES ARE SCARCE IN HONG KONG, TOO

The buildings that dominate the heights overlooking the harbor are new flats. There is a great demand for housing in the colony. The British race course is shown in the foreground.

273

CANALS INSTEAD OF STREETS are used by the inhabitants of the town of Sungkiang in passing from place to place. A whole family, consisting of grandparents, parents and children, frequently lives in a boat such as we see through the arch of this bridge. No one fears drowning, for children, born and reared on a boat, can often swim before they can walk.

THIS GRACEFUL PAGODA, which was built in 1583 at Soochow, is still in excellent condition, and with its delicate coloring, perfect shape and lovely surroundings is probably the most beautiful in China. The Chinese have a saying that to be quite happy a man should be born in Soochow (sometimes called "the Athens of China"), live in Canton and die in Lienchow.

YOUTHFUL, DEFT, BUSY—A BASKET-WEAVER OF HONG KONG

One of the most useful objects in China and throughout the Far East is the cane basket, which the barefoot boy here weaves with considerable skill and speed. Mainland China, ordinarily the biggest customer for the goods of Hong Kong, was shut off from trade with the British outpost after the Communist Government of China entered the Korean conflict.

be grown on its own little plot. However, many cotton, woolen and silk mills have been built, and there are also flour mills, glass factories and iron works.

Side by side with the silk is another great industry, the cultivation of the tea plant. Tea also we owe to China. It is strange to think of a tealess England, but tea leaves were first taken there in 1645. In China, tea-growing is a family concern. The plant is cultivated in small patches, and women and children pick the leaves.

It is claimed that fine porcelain has been made in China for more than 2,000 years, and even in the Middle Ages "China" ware was celebrated. It is of all descriptions, from fine cups of egg-shell thinness to heavy bowls of a rich green made to imitate jade. There were many factories

Hunter

CHINESE LADY'S DRESS

The loose silk jacket, the pantaloons and the tiny bound feet show that this lady has not abandoned native fashions for foreign, as have most of her country-women today.

grims succeeded in carrying to Europe some silkworm eggs concealed in their bamboo walking staves. Thus the world came to share the precious product.

In the valley of the Yangtze Kiang, and some of the provinces south of it, the rearing of silkworms and the unwinding of the cocoons are carried on as household industries, for China is a land where everything that can be done is done in the home. Most households weave the cotton for the clothes they require, and in the agricultural districts each family tries to live on the food that can

Camera Craft, Peking

A DOORSTEP PHILOSOPHER

With his padded coat on his back, his pot of tea by his side, his pipe in his hand and a whimsical smile for the passing world, this Chinese seems a philosopher, content to take life in the way his ancestors did.

BARREN MOUNTAIN SLOPES stretch away from the town of Shanhaikuan, which is situated on the boundary between China proper and Manchuria. The eastern end of the Great Wall of China, which separated them, reached the seashore near Shanhaikuan, but the part between the sea and the town has now disappeared. From Shanhaikuan the Wall extends far to the West.

THE WALLS OF LIAOYANG were once mighty fortifications, but they have long since yielded to shrub and vine. Liaoyang is one of the oldest towns of Manchuria, dating from around the eighth century. While the Manchus were still a powerful people the town had considerable importance. Today it is a railroad junction and a center of weaving.

THE BARRIER GATE BETWEEN MACAO AND RED CHINA

Macao, west of Hong Kong, is the oldest foreign settlement in the Far East, founded in 1557. With two smaller islands it forms a Portuguese colony. Through the gate, over which flies the Portuguese flag, many thousands of Chinese pass each day on their way to and from China. They are allowed free entry and exit by Macao, which is noted as a pleasure resort.

in China, the most famous being that of King-te-Chen in Kiangsi, which supplied the royal household from about 1370. It was destroyed in the Taiping rebellion of 1850, but has been rebuilt. The secret of the manufacture of the most celebrated variety of this Chinese porcelain is completely lost.

In the south we find that rice takes an important place. It is grown in small patches, flooded artificially with water from the nearest river. After the soil has been churned up into a porridgelike state, seed is sown thickly in a sort of nursery corner. When the seedlings are about twelve inches high, they are pulled up in bunches, separated into groups of four or five plants each, and replanted in the flooded fields. Some of these fields yield three crops a year.

Sugar-cane and cotton are cultivated, and fruit-growing is carried on to a considerable extent. Oranges, which Arabs are said to have brought to Europe, are grown all over south China. Bananas are to be had nearly all the year round; pineapples, cape gooseberries, peaches and apricots are abundant, while palm trees supply several millions of palm-leaf fans annually. But the most useful plant of south China is the bamboo. It supplies the material for the framework for the huts of matting which the poorer peasants call "home," and is also employed in the making of furniture of all kinds, umbrella frames, clothes-lines, tools, etc., and when it has been soaked and pulped it is made into paper. Its dried leaves are made into sunhats and raincoats, and its young shoots are pickled for food.

With such a vast population everything that can be eaten is eaten. Birds'-nest soup, for instance, is a Chinese delicacy. The nests, which are small, and like thin cases of gelatine, are found in great numbers in caves by the sea. They are boiled until they make a thick, white substance which is the first course at every grand dinner. A seaweed called agar-agar, a sea-slug known in Europe as beche-de-mer, sharks' fins and eggs that have been preserved for a long time, are all eaten and enjoyed, while among the poorer people, in times of scarcity, cats and dogs, rats and mice form part of the diet.

A BASKET-MAKER'S DREAM COME TRUE

Although basket-weaving is considered one of the simplest of the arts, it has reached a high degree of perfection in some of the Oriental countries. The Chinese, for instance, use bamboo and rattan to fashion baskets that are unusually fine in quality and beautifully finished. In addition to baskets, this shopkeeper seems to have every possible variety of wood container.

281

HOMEMADE WINDMILL OF A YANGTZE RIVER RICE FARMER

Water from the Yangtze is channeled to farmlands by a series of ever narrowing ditches. Farmers draw the water for their fields from these irrigation ditches by primitive windmills.

THE TERRITORY OF MANCHURIA

At various times Manchuria has been considered a part of China. Manchuria is, however, a distinct region separated by mountains from China proper. The people of Manchuria, the Manchus, once were also distinct from the Chinese, but there has been considerable intermarriage between the two stocks.

The Chinese used to call Manchuria *Tung-san-sheng* (the three eastern provinces)—Liaoning, Kirin and Heilungkiang. Later, when the Japanese wrested Manchuria from China in 1931, they included the neighboring province of Jehol.

In 1945 Manchuria again became a part of China, and this time it was divided into nine provinces—Liaoning, Kirin, Heilungkiang, Liaopeh, Nunkiang, Hsingan, Sungkiang, Hokiang and Antung. Chinese now refer to Manchuria as *Tung-pei* (the northeast). When World War II ended, the Chinese Communists were already in possession of most of Manchuria; and as the Chinese civil war continued, the Communists gradually gained the whole territory.

Many Kinds of Animal Life

Hot in summer and intensely cold during a winter of four months, it has products and animals of both hot and cold climates. The country abounds in bird life, including such edible birds as pheasants, partridges and quails, and in the mountains and on the steppes are found bears, antelopes, deer of many kinds, hares, squirrels and foxes.

The Manchus have small farms where dogs are bred for their thick winter coats and a Manchu girl will often have six or more dogs for her dowry. These dogs are Chows, like those that we keep for pets, just as we do the Pekingese. The latter is in China a very tiny animal, called the "sleeve dog," because it is carried in the wide sleeves of its owner's robe.

The land is rich in minerals, with valuable deposits of gold, silver, asbestos and lead, as well as great coal and iron mines that have been well developed. Much of the coal is carried out of the open mines in large wheelbarrows.

The rivers of Manchuria supply many kinds of fish, including sturgeon and trout and a variety of salmon called the tamara. The skin of this salmon is made into clothing and is worn by the people of a certain district, who are called, in consequence, the Fish Skin Tartars.

Millet the Chief Food

The Manchus are naturally a race of hunters, but when their country was united with China, Chinese settlers introduced agriculture. Corn, rice, wheat and barley are grown, but the principal grain cultivated is millet, which forms the staple food of the working people. The grain is boiled, put into bowls and eaten with chopsticks together with vegetables fresh, cooked or pickled that are added for flavor. From millet is distilled an alcoholic liquor called "samshu," which is sold all over the country. The refuse becomes food for herds of pigs. Millet stalks are used for fencing and firewood, and the poorer people weave them together and plaster them with mud to make houses.

What Is Made from the Bean

By far the most important article cultivated for export is the bean, of which many varieties are grown. Several of these yield an oil which is used all over China for lighting and heating, and the part left after the oil is pressed out, known as "bean cake," is sent south to fertilize the sugar-cane fields. Piled up along railroad tracks or wharves, the "cakes" look like cart wheels or grindstones. Some varieties are ground into bean-flour or used for vermicelli, others are made into a strange sort of cheese called "bean curd." From the soya bean, which is cultivated on about twenty million acres, is made the famous "soy" sauce. The products derived from this plant seem almost numberless and are of astonishing variety. The income from it is enormous.

Besides being linked by the Trans-Siberian railway to Europe, Manchuria has a railway line to Port Arthur (Lu-

PARK IN DAIREN IN THE WINTERTIME

Dairen, much-disputed ice-free port in Manchuria, was declared a free port in 1907. Although it is still technically free, Russia has the right to lease half its port facilities without charge.

HUNDREDS OF SPINDLES OF LINEN THREAD

The girls above are working in the spinning department of a flax mill at Harbin. Plans for the mill area are said to include housing, educational and recreational facilities.

shun) on the Yellow Sea. This port and Dairen, also on the Yellow Sea, give Manchuria access to the Pacific. Much of the interior shipping, which used to be done by means of the rivers or in springless carts that had to go bumping over incredibly bad roads, is now handled by new or improved railroads. In normal times, Manchuria exports considerable farm products, especially those made from soybeans, one of the country's chief crops.

Instead of living on their farms, the Manchus build their little mud and stone habitations in huddled groups or villages. Pigs and chickens share the enclosures with them, and heat is secured by burning bunches of straw or stubble in a "kang," a brick ledge about two feet high in one end of a room. Inside it are flues to spread the heat through the bricks, and on top of it the members of the household sit by day and lie down by night.

In the warmest districts of Manchuria, as well as in certain provinces of China proper, wild silk is obtained from a caterpillar which feeds on oak leaves. From its silk are made the fabrics called pongee and tussah. About four million dollars' worth of this wild silk is produced here every year. Camel's hair and sheep's wool are woven into rugs, but, curiously enough, neither here nor in China is wool used for clothing; padded garments of silk or cotton, costly furs or common skins, according to the rank of the wearer, are used to keep out the cold. For outdoor use in winter the working people wear shoes of tough oxhide stuffed with coarse grass to make them warmer.

The women never bound their feet even though the people accepted some other customs of the Chinese. The Manchurians are no longer mostly wandering herdsmen as they once were, but have become farmers and have intermarried with the Chinese until few pure Manchus remain.

Mukden was formerly the capital; later the Japanese made Hsinking (Changchun) the capital. The People's Government for the Northwest have set up their headquarters at Mukden, however. The fortified city of Port Arthur is a joint Chinese-Soviet naval base.

© Gleason

BANDIT CHIEF'S LIEUTENANT

Formerly hordes of bandits made trade and traveling dangerous. Merchants and insurance companies paid them large sums to get safe conduct for both goods and persons.

There is much beautiful mountain scenery in Manchuria. A peak in the province of Kirin is known as the "Ever-White Mountain" on account of the white pumice stone at the summit. It is the crater of an old volcano. This is said to be the birthplace of Nurhachu, the father of the first Manchu emperor of China, and as such was maintained as a sacred place by the imperial family.

When the Japanese established Manchuria (calling it Manchukuo) as a separate state, they worked to develop the country economically and also to change the attitude of the people. The Japanese knew that a sizable part of the population was made up of recent immigrants from China. In fact, in some years this immigration had been as high as a million individuals—persons who had found no chance for success in overcrowded China and so had chosen to become pioneers in the undeveloped north. The Japanese reasoned that these millions could have no love for the old home, since it had been unkind. Here, the conquerors thought, they could develop both land and people along new lines—Japanese lines, of course.

They sought to make Manchuria a modern industrial state that would in time provide opportunities for emigrants from the Japanese islands, for these, too, were overcrowded. They also saw that a prosperous and well-populated Manchuria (or Manchukuo) would be a fine market for the products of Japanese factories. It would also be a source of raw materials for their factories.

There was much to encourage their dreams. Manchuria is rich in timber, for building, and in minerals of various kinds. For example, it has the most extensive coal deposits known. There is iron ore, also, and great quantities of oil shale from which petroleum may be extracted. Many industrial products can be made from Manchuria's abundant crops of soy beans.

The Japanese, largely with their own capital and under their own management, made an extraordinary start in developing the mines and industries during the few years they were in occupation of the territory. Their defeat in World War II drove them out of the mainland of Asia; but the factories and other installations they had built remain.

The Japanese Policy Is Continued

The Communist Government that was set up soon after the war in Manchuria continued the industrial policies of the Japanese; only, of course, now everything belonged to the state.

In February 1950 Manchuria, by treaty, joined the Communist Government of China, becoming again a part of China.

As you can see by the map, Manchuria

CHINA, WHERE A FIFTH

and Korea have a common border more than five hundred miles long, half of it defined by the Yalu River. Across this border poured great numbers of so-called Chinese Red "volunteers" to fight against the United Nations forces in the Korean War.

OF THE WORLD'S POPULATION DWELLS

CHINA: FACTS AND FIGURES

THE COUNTRY

Bounded west, north and northeast by the Soviet Union, north by the Mongolian Republic, east by Korea, the Yellow, East China and South China seas and south by Indochina, Burma, India, Bhutan, Nepal, Kashmir and Afghanistan, Chinese territory includes the 18 provinces of China Proper (area, 1,373,370 square miles; population, 397,522,237); Formosa (13,780 square miles; population, 6,126,006); Tibet (469,413 square miles; population, 1,000,-000); Sinkiang (660,976 square miles; popula-

287

THE LAND OF THE DRAGON

tion, 4,012,330) ; Sikang and Chinghai (431,987 square miles ; population, 2,997,452) ; 3 provinces of Inner Mongolia (326,792 square miles; population, 5,054,126) ; Jehol (69,491 square miles; population, 6,109,866) ; and 9 provinces of Manchuria (413,306 square miles; population, 38,584,268). Total area, 3,759,115 square miles; population, 461,406,285.

GOVERNMENT

A republic after 1912 and controlled by the Nationalist (Kuomintang) party after 1926–27, China became a Communist People's Republic in October 1949, the Nationalist Government thereafter being confined to Formosa. The People's Republic is based on an Organic Law that sets forth the general aims of communism and the eventual election of an All-China People's Congress. Powers of government—executive, legislative and judicial—are in the meantime vested in a 56-member Central People's Government Council. The council, headed by a chairman and 6 vice-chairmen, has set up a State Administration Council (Cabinet) that manages the ministries and commissions of government.

COMMERCE AND INDUSTRIES

About three-fourths of China's population is agricultural. The average farm is about 3.3 acres and is intensively cultivated. Unaided human farm labor predominates ; there are relatively few draft animals and fewer farm machines. The principal farm products are cotton, silk cocoons, hemp, flax, tea, fats and oils, peas, beans, potatoes, tobacco and sugar. Production of staples, wheat in the north and rice in the south, is insufficient ; both must be imported to meet domestic needs. Of about 150,000,000 head of livestock, 55,000,000 are hogs. Chief forest regions are northern Manchuria and southwest China Proper; teak and tung are the principal trees. Leading mineral products are coal, pig iron, steel, copper, lead and cement; there is also an output of wolfram (tungsten), antimony, tin, bauxite, magnesite, pyrite, gypsum and phosphate. Chief manufactures are textiles, paper, power, machinery and chemicals. Exports: soybeans, hog bristles, tung oil, peanuts, tea and mineral ores. Imports: machinery, gasoline, kerosene, lubricating oil and chemicals.

COMMUNICATIONS

Railways, 13,500 miles opened to traffic; highways, 126,320 miles; state airlines, 55,269 route miles. There are about 7,000 miles of inland waterways. Telegraph lines, 97,360 miles; 673 radio transmitting stations.

RELIGION AND EDUCATION

Ancestor worship, though not a formal religion, is widespread. Confucianism, Buddhism and Taoism are the chief religions. There are also native Moslems and Christians. Missionaries have been murdered, expelled, imprisoned or closely watched as subversives. Communist regime has conducted a vigorous literacy campaign and a program of technical instruction for workers. There are about 37,000,000 pupils in primary schools, 1,570,000 in secondary schools and 128,000 in colleges and universities.

IMPORTANT CITIES

Shanghai, 3,853,511 ; Tientsin, 1,679,210 ; the capital, Peking (formerly Peiping), 1,602,234; Canton, 1,276,429; Mukden, 1,175,620; Nanking, 1,037,656; Chungking, 1,000,000; Pinkiang (Harbin), 760,000; Tsingtao, 752,800; Hankow, 749,952; Talien (Dairen), 543,690.

MANCHURIA

Forms the major part of the North East Regional Government of the People's Republic; area, 413,306 square miles, and population, 38,584,268. Recognized as part of the People's Republic in Sino-Soviet treaty of 1950. Former Japanese commercial holdings, a railroad and the Kwantung ports of Dairen and Port Arthur remained under Soviet control.

KWANTUNG

Formerly Japanese, ceded to China in 1945 while ports of Dairen and Port Arthur were leased to Soviet Russia. According to Sino-Soviet pact of 1950, the cities were to return to China not later than the end of 1952.

TANNU TUVA

Now called the Tuva Autonomous Region as a part of the Soviet Union, it is located in northwestern Mongolia. Area, 64,000 square miles; population, 90,000. Kysyl Khoto is the capital.

FOREIGN POSSESSIONS IN CHINA: FACTS AND FIGURES

HONG KONG

A British Crown Colony, it consists of a number of islands and a portion of the south China mainland at the mouth of the Pearl (Canton) River ; total area, 391 square miles (Hong Kong Island, 32 square miles), and population (1951), 2,060,000. A governor is assisted by executive and legislative councils. Fishing is the primary industry ; there is also shipbuilding and repairs, textile spinning and weaving and manufactures of rubber goods, paint, cement and other goods. United States and colonial-government bans on shipments of war goods—including rubber and oil—to Communist China have caused a drastic

decrease in Hong Kong trade. Railways, 22 miles ; road, 425 miles ; 11 airlines have flights to all parts of the world. About 160,000 pupils in primary and secondary schools; also 2 teachers' colleges and University of Hong Kong.

MACAO

Portuguese province opposite Hong Kong; area, 6 square miles, and population, 500,000. It is under the administration of a governor and has been important for commerce with mainland China. There has been a trade recession due to the embargo of shipments to China. Macao is also famous as a pleasure resort.

288

In Unknown Sinkiang

Life in China's Westernmost Province

We have read of Russian Turkestan in Volume III. Sinkiang includes Eastern Chinese Turkestan, Kulja and Kashgaria. This territory embraces all of the Chinese dependencies between Mongolia on the north and Tibet on the south; but though it extends for six hundred miles from north to south and twelve hundred from east to west, its population numbers less than two million. Turks, Mongols and Chinese, each in turn have overrun this land of the nomad, which forms a strategic wedge into Central Asia. No doubt the Russians are interested in Sinkiang. Its three large cities are in the west near the Russian frontier and Pakistan and India can be reached by journeying over the high passes of the Himalayas. The archaeologist is interested because in the Taklamakan Desert in south Sinkiang are towns buried in the sand from which ancient manuscripts, wall paintings and even many articles of clothing have been recovered.

SINKIANG, or Chinese Turkestan (also spelled Turkistan), is the most westerly province of the Chinese Republic, of which it forms an important part, for it has great mineral and other resources. It is still a land of which little is known. No railway connects Sinkiang with the outside world. It can be reached from Peking only by horseback, camelback or in carts along the trade caravan route through Inner Mongolia.

Sinkiang is divided into two unequal parts by the Tien Shan (mountains). Dzungaria, to the north, is tableland. The larger portion to the south is occupied mainly by the great Taklamakan Desert. So dry is this region that the snow line on the mountains is above 11,000 feet. Streams and rivers formed by the melting snow either disappear in the desert or flow into salt lakes. The Tarim River, the longest stream, ends in Lob Nor basin.

Generally speaking, then, Sinkiang is a land of deserts and sand dunes, though the rivers and streams make a certain amount of cultivation possible by supplying water for irrigation canals. It is bounded on the north by Siberia, on the east by the province of Kansu in China proper and by the Desert of Gobi in Mongolia, on the south by Tibet and the northern frontiers of India, and on the west by Russian Turkestan and Afghanistan. Urumchi (Tihwafu) is the capital, but the most important towns for trade and commerce are Kashgar, Yarkand and Khotan. The climate is the same as that of other regions far from the sea—in summer it is hot and in winter very cold. In the spring high winds are frequent, and raise clouds of dust, enveloping the country in a haze that often takes days to disperse.

On all sides save the east, Sinkiang is hemmed about by mountains which wall it in like a horseshoe. Some of the ice-clad peaks rise to over fifteen thousand feet and it is a difficult and dangerous thing to cross them at any time of year. Just beneath the snow fields are grassy, flower-enameled meadows which are used

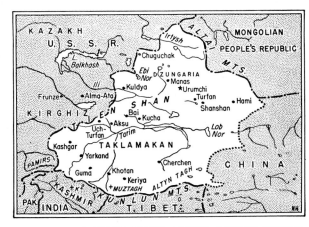

SINKIANG, WHERE WEST CHINA MEETS RUSSIA

A TURKI MOTHER AND HER CHILD BY AN OASIS WALL

At Kara Shahr, a town and oasis near Bagrach Kol, a salt lake of central Sinkiang, a Turki woman prepares to set out on a journey over the bleak foothills of the Tien Shan range.

A GOOD-HUMORED KALMUCK, HIS FAMILY AND STRONG FELT TENT

The Kalmucks, whose tribesmen long ago settled the lower Volga basin in Europe, now roam the rugged uplands of Sinkiang, raising and breeding horses and tending large flocks of sheep.

ON THE WAY TO KASHGAR: TRADERS AND BURDENED CAMELS

Kashgar is the first town that eastward-bound caravans reach after they cross the ranges of central Asia. Even in medieval times there was trade between East and West along this route.

A GATE WITH PEAKED EAVES WELCOMES TRAVELERS TO KARA SHAHR

Kara Shahr is chiefly a horse-raising center, known for the manufacture of saddles. It is on the south side of the Tien Shan in central Sinkiang near a salt-water lake, Bagrach Kol.

291

SWEEPING GRAIN, WHICH HAS BEEN WINNOWED, INTO A MOUND

Wheat is tossed in the pan at the left so that the light chaff is driven off by the wind, leaving the kernels. After each panful is winnowed, it is dumped and carefully swept up.

REPAIRING GRAIN CARTS ON THE PLAIN NEAR URUMCHI

The body of the cart is made of woven straw and it is placed on wooden wheels, which are heavy and cumbersome. It is easy to imagine that the first wheel invented looked like these.

YOUNG RECRUITS ON THE STREETS OF KULDJA, NORTHWEST CHINA

Called up for compulsory military training, these sixteen-year-olds regard their future respon-
sibilities with serious faces.   Kuldja is in Sinkiang Province near the Russian border.

VEILED MOSLEM WOMEN IN A NARROW STREET OF YARKAND

The veiling of women was not part of the original Islamic code, but of later Semitic origin. The rule requiring Moslem women to wear veils and men to wear fezzes is gradually being relaxed.

for summer feeding-grounds by the nomad shepherds. The northern slopes are the best watered. Beneath this upper grass belt comes a sweep of rock-ribbed country cleft by canyons and practically uninhabited. Farther down on the edge of the plain comes a second grassy belt watered by the Tarim and its tributaries and other mountain streams before they evaporate or sink into the sands. They are full-fed in spring and summer by the melting of the snows above and there is therefore no such dearth of water as might be expected on the fringes of the desert. Here the flocks return in winter when the higher meadows are quite exhausted.

The plain itself is unfit for agriculture or human habitation save on the oases, whether natural or formed by irrigation ditches from the rivers. On these oases the cities and trading centers have been built, and to them the camel caravans from India and Russian Turkestan wind over the wind-bitten passes, their banners hoisted on spears, with grain and other things in exchange for the native wool, felts and rugs, jade, silk and cotton. As these oases are from one to two hundred miles of desert or mountain travel apart, there is naturally no strong central government.

There is one other kind of habitable

country in Sin-Kiang—the lakes and reed swamps of the Lop-nor. These are the home of a fisher-folk, the Lopliks. Barring their small numbers, it is probable that all but ten per cent of the population live in the oases. The remaining ten per cent represent the nomadic stockmen.

It is an interesting sight to see the animals being taken on their semi-annual migration. The fine herds of ponies are guided by the younger, more active men, the long-legged camels by the men, the placid oxen by the women and the sheep by children mounted on ponies or oxen. The baby camels are often so unequal to hard travel their first spring that they have to be strapped to their mothers' backs on top of the packs; while the weaker lambs will be thrown across the saddle or tucked into the saddle-bags. Lambs bleat, ponies neigh, cattle low and camels utter their raucous note, while the dust rises in a yellow cloud that can be seen for miles; and at night the cook-fires gleam red beneath a starry sky as chunks of lamb are strung on wire spits and broiled, or other food is prepared before the round felt tents.

The higher meadows have as background peaks of red porphyry and glistening ice hung in white mists, which at times stream in the wind like banners and at times disperse, leaving the great domes and pinnacles to reflect the sunlight. Ice Pass (the Muzart) is itself eleven thousand feet high and down it flows a glacier raked by fissures impossible to cross. The most used pass is that between Aksu, on

A KIRGHIS WITH A GOLDEN EAGLE TRAINED FOR FALCONRY

Falconry is a sport of ancient Oriental origin in which a bird is trained to capture its prey on the wing. The Oriental falconer carries the bird on his right wrist, the European on his left.

A SHELTER FOR CATTLE GETS A WEATHERPROOF ROOF

Flat boards are laid first, then a layer of straw and finally a covering of gravel. This will protect the shed against the torrents of rain that frequently fall in western Sinkiang.

A BAD-TEMPERED HORSE IS TRUSSED FOR SHOEING

The animal is used on the rocky trails and icy passes of the Tekes Valley in the west. In such rugged terrain, a lost shoe could well mean death for both horse and its rider.

the south, and Kuldzha. Such is the Sin-Kiang that greets the traveler's eye.

For twenty centuries its history has been one of control first by China, then by the Turks, then by Mongols and now again by the Chinese. Jenghiz conquered it in the thirteenth century and Tamerlane made conquest of it over a century later. The Chinese acquired it by force in 1758, but in 1862 when the Mohammedan rebellion reached this remote province, the natives slaughtered thousands of Chinese and were free of them until 1876. Now the Chinese call it the New Dominion. This wedge into

Central Asia is of great importance to China, but the influence of Soviet Russia is much stronger in the region than that of the Chinese Government.

Its sparse population, collectively termed Turkis, though the tribes include Kashgari, Kirghiz, Taranchi and others chiefly Mohammedan, shows a greater resemblance to the Iranian stock of Western Asia than to the Chinese. They are light-hearted and cheerful, easy to govern, and without any desire for advancement either educationally or in any other sense. Both men and women are good riders, and if a horse or donkey is not available they

TRIANGLE

CARRYING WATER IN A LAMA MONASTERY IN THE KASH VALLEY

These young novices, members of the Kalmuck tribe in Sinkiang, are preparing to be Buddhist priests. In addition to studying, they must also take care of the manual labor for the order.

are equally at home astride the lumbering ox.

Their houses, low and made of mud, are generally without windows and devoid of architectural beauty. Outside the towns most of the houses have a courtyard and veranda and are surrounded by trees, under which in the summer the women sit and weave the rough but durable white cloth from which they make their wardrobes.

Boots Are Removed Indoors

The people can best be seen on a market day. All roads lead to the bazaar, and they are crowded from early morning by a mixed crowd of men, women and children mounted on ponies or donkeys, all going to the places allotted to the venders of particular articles. A winter market day shows the national costume in its many colors. That worn by the men is a long coat of bright colored cloth reaching to the knees and fastened at the waist by a sash. Men also wear trousers like pajamas. Their coats have long sleeves which may be pulled down over the hands, thus taking the place of gloves. Leather knee-boots, with detachable slippers that are kicked off on entering a house, and a cloth or velvet cap edged with fur—the headgear common to both men and women—complete the costume.

Ladies of fashion wear embroidered silk waistcoats over short coats, which are covered by long coats, and over all are white muslin cloaks reaching to the heels. The women wear lattice-work veils, usually edged with embroidery, which hang down over the face and hide it as required by Mohammedan law. But in midsummer, when heat-waves rise dizzyingly, everyone wears loose white robes.

Camels Sleep Beside Their Drivers

Tea-shops, with floors of mud on which the customers squat on their heels, provide refreshment. The tea-urn sings merrily and there is a tiny china teapot with a bowl for each person. The seller of meat dumplings and small cakes is there to supplement the tea. He takes coins in payment, using his mouth as a purse as he deals out change to veiled ladies or solemn-eyed priests. Hotels are unknown, but accommodation can be had in the inns, or serais, where camels, carts, horses and men are lodged side by side. These inns are merely roofs with mud walls and floors. Nothing is provided for the comfort of travelers, save a cook-fire. When a mounted tribesman with a sword is met, he is known to be on government business and is entitled to free food, lodging and transportation.

The meat market supplies beef and mutton, but horse-flesh is a dainty and commands a high price. The principal articles of food are mutton and rice, with onions, potatoes, turnips and spinach. There are many forms of roast and boiled joints, soups and pilau, or pilav—a mixture of meat and rice flavored with fried onions and other vegetables. Tea is the chief drink and is served with sugar but without milk. However, mare's milk is highly esteemed, the more so when it has been fermented and lightly churned in a colt-skin. It is then called "kumiss." Bread is made in the shape of little circular rolls with a hole through the centre of each. Only two meals are taken by the Turkis.

Good Food Is Plentiful

On market days the restaurants are well patronized. The customer may have tiny meat dumplings known as "mantu," pastry cooked by steam, soups of vermicelli, macaroni and mutton, stews made in curds and whey, doughnuts of fat and flour, salads of carrot, radish and onion chopped fine, mustard and cress.

Fruits of all kinds—melons, apples, pears, apricots, peaches, nectarines, pomegranates, plums, cherries and mulberries—grow in profusion in some parts of the country and appear on the table at the feasts which are popular during the summer months.

The inhabitants of Sin-Kiang are a pleasure-loving race and they have various forms of sport and games, but none is more popular than "baigu," a game, played also in Russian Turkestan, in which the carcass of a sheep or goat serves

Sykes

BOYS STUDYING THE KORAN AT A SCHOOL IN KASHGAR

Practically all that these boys will be able to do when they leave school will be to recite mechanically several chapters of the Koran which they have learned by heart. All are wearing heavily embroidered skull-caps, a popular form of headdress among the young Mohammedans of this district, though the turban is also worn.

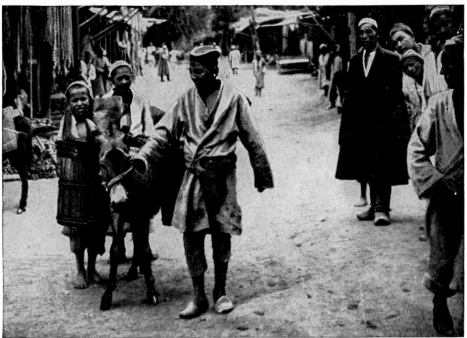

Etherton

THE WATER-SELLER IN THE BAZAARS OF KASHGAR

With two casks of water from the River Tuman slung across his donkey, the water-seller wanders through the sun-scorched bazaars doing a splendid trade. Some of the very narrow streets are roofed to keep the sun out, and in this photograph we can see the awnings of matting which overhang the front of the shops on both sides of the bazaar.

299

A DOMESTICATED YAK, THE MOUNT OF A FRONTIER GUARD

This ungainly looking beast, found in Tibet, Sin-Kiang and parts of China, belongs to the bovine persuasion though its long, woolly hair would seem to relate it to the mountain goat. A rope passed through the animals' nose serves to guide it, and its gait does not matter when it has chiefly to pick a cautious footing up and down rocky steeps.

BOUND FOR KASHGAR MARKET WITH FRESH MELONS

Although so much of Sin-Kiang is arid desert, the soil in the oases at the foot of the mountains around the Tarim basin is highly fertile. Careful irrigation has made the oasis in which Kashgar is situated famous as orchard land, where most of the fruits that succeed in Europe and North America ripen. Melons in particular reach a rare perfection.

300

as a ball. The players, who are all mounted on fast ponies, form in line. There are often as many as 120 players, one of whom is selected from the centre of the line to start the game. He takes the carcass and dashes forward with it, well in front of the eager crowd, swings around in a wide circle and hurls it to the ground. This is the signal for the rest, who set off in full cry. The rider who gains possession of the carcass will have a dozen men hanging on to him: all is fair in this game. A man may beat his opponent's mount, or he may seize a player and unhorse him or compel him to give up the trophy. The din is terrific, for the yells of the players mingle with the thunder of hoofs and the jingling of

stirrups and ornamental trappings; dust rises, leather creaks, horses snort, as the contestants strive to get hold of the carcass and place it at the feet of the principal guest.

At the end of a game players and spectators adjourn for the Turki equivalent of tea and cakes. Dancing then goes on to the music of an orchestra, consisting of a dulcimer, a native banjo and a tom-tom, or small drum. The Turki has, however, his own idea of music.

The system of revenue and taxation shows the methods of Chinese officials in remote parts of the republic. There are official regulations fixing the amount of taxes to be levied, but they depend mostly upon the amban, or magistrate, of the

Miss Ella Sykes

THE BABY'S CRADLE IS STOUTLY MADE IN SIN-KIANG

Built of wood, this mattressed cradle can be rocked without fear of its overturning, because there is a wooden block at each corner. By means of two cloth bands the baby is tied to the cradle so that he cannot fall out; and above him is a bar over which a net may be hung up to keep off flies and mosquitoes.

HAIR STYLES FOR YOUNG MEN

Tunghans of Sinkiang, descended from Chinese and Arab ancestors, preserve many of the customs of both people. The young mother proudly displays her two small sons whose hair is cut to protect them from "the evil eye."

cause suffering, he would accept the remainder in cash—at the then prevailing rate.

Theatricals play a prominent part in the lighter side of life in Sin-Kiang, for they are the national pastime of the Chinese and are much patronized by the Turkis. The scenery is of a rough and ready kind and much is left to the imagination. There are no dressing-rooms for the actors. All changes of costume, the arranging and plaiting of the hair, painting and powdering are done in the open, in full view of the crowd, who treat everything as a matter of course. For the site of the theatre it is usual to take the courtyard of an inn or a point in the street where it is fairly wide, and there the company set up their stage and prepare for the play.

Meanwhile, the street is littered with beams and posts, and pedestrians trip over coils of wire. Gaudy screens, trees and foliage are placed in position, and soon the theatre assumes a size that stops all traffic, which has to be diverted down side alleys. Foot passengers who wish to gain the other end of the street must follow suit or climb under the stage.

particular district, for bribery and corruption are common. An example of this is given in the following true story. A large amount of firewood was demanded. The amban summoned the chiefs and subordinate officials, who were sent out to collect the wood, with the result that the price of wood rose to nearly three times as much, and still not more than half the requisite quantity had been supplied. The people then came forward to say that the commandeering of further stocks of fuel must inevitably cause hardship in the district, upon which the amban showed a fatherly benevolence and stated that, as it was not his intention to

In the Taklamakan Desert between the Tarim (Yakand-darya) and the Khotan-darya rivers is a sea of sand dunes rising from sixty to three hundred feet in height. Here, where frequent dust-storms make animal life impossible save for a few camels, the explorer Dr. Sven Hedin has discovered ruins of the ancient city of Lôu-lan (Shanshan) buried in the wind-blown sand. Dr. M. Aurel Stein has found, near Lop-nor, part of an ancient Chinese wall. Nor are these all of the discoveries that have been made of an ancient civilization long since overwhelmed by the wind-blown sands.

WHERE A LIVING BUDDHA REIGNED

Mongolia, Home of a Once All-powerful Race

When we hear the name "Mongolia" we picture to ourselves a huge desert out of which came, many centuries ago, a vast army of horsemen who overran Eurasia from the China Sea to Moscow and from Siberia to Delhi. But the tables have been turned, and now this interior section of Asia has come under the domination of two of the lands that were overrun—Russia and China. The country is divided into the Tuvinian Autonomous Region of Soviet Russia, the Inner Mongolian Autonomous Region of the Chinese People's Republic (Inner Mongolia) and the Mongolian People's Republic (Outer Mongolia). "Mongolia" now usually means the Mongolian People's Republic, which is, in theory at least, an independent republic. However, it is linked closely, by treaty and economically, to Russia. Soviet troops are stationed there.

SUNSHINE and yellow sands, with the azure of distant mountains piled like clouds on the horizon, that is the scene typical of Mongolia in fair weather. The temperature often rises to 140 degrees at midday but may fall to 70 by night. There are gravel plains and sagebrush but also gentle hills and hollows, sheer red mesas and canyons. The scourge of the traveler is the suffocating sandstorms in which, with a shriek of wind, a solid yellow mass will advance across the unpeopled wastes.

Spring is the rainy season when forage grass grows upon certain areas, though Western Mongolia lies in the broad belt of salt and sand which extends across Asia. This Desert of Gobi or Shamo, once an inland sea, is a plateau of an average height of four thousand feet, though it is broken here and there by slight depressions which give the land an undulating appearance. The grasslands of Mongolia make it possible to breed sheep and cattle. The roads that cross Mongolia are the same great routes that were used by the Mongol conquerors. The Inner Asian trade route to Eastern Turkestan is still the main communication between East and West. It stretches across Asia for 3,500 miles; and much of the way, which lies often through deep and muddy gullies and at times over ten-thousand-foot passes, is too narrow for passing. Caravan leaders must watch the way ahead for miles to see if there is an approaching procession of dust spirals to indicate the approach of another camel train. If there is, the cara-

van must manage to arrive, or wait at some wider place where it will be possible for the two to pass. On the desert itself trees are almost unknown. For a thousand miles from east to west and 450 to 600 from north to south, there are but a few dwarf specimens. Water is found only in wells or occasional small lakes.

The Altai (Gold) Mountains, however, are one of the most fertile regions of Asia, besides being possessed of valuable mineral resources. Timber is abundant in their forests of pine, larch, birch and spruce; and in summer this part of Mongolia is, surprisingly, a paradise of green grass and bright flowers.

The area of Mongolia is probably nearly 2,000,000 square miles, partly under Chinese control. The sparsely peopled land is hemmed in by forbidding mountain walls, those of Siberia on the north and Sin-Kiang on the south, while Western Mongolia is intersected by the Altai Mountains. The mountain walls rob the interior of the moisture of the winds, precipitating it upon their own white summits.

Naturally the Mongols and the Kalmucks and Chinese immigrants who share the grassy uplands are nomads and shepherds, for no part of the desert has ever been placed under irrigation, and practically nothing is raised in the entire million and a quarter square miles save herds of asses, sheep, camels, reindeer and horses. There is gold in Outer Mongolia but it has not been mined. Urga, the capital and only city, is a frontier

ELABORATELY ADORNED GUESTS ATTEND A WEDDING

The Mongols are highly skilled silversmiths. Headdresses similar to the ones above, made of silver and gem stones, with fringe and tassels, are the badges of married women in Inner Mongolia.

emporium for the caravan trade with China across the Gobi Desert, and long trains of camels, plod beneath bulging packs of wool, skins and hides, furs and horns. Since 1917 there has been motor freight service across the desert requiring but four to six days between Urga and Kalgan, China, a matter of five or six weeks' travel by camel.

To-day, it is estimated, a hundred thousand camels are employed, while the entire caravan trade employs over a million camels and three hundred thousand ox-carts. This mode of freighting is enormously more expensive than water or even rail transportation and railroads are a need that will be in part supplied by a new line started in 1930.

Explorations in Mongolia

Roy Chapman Andrews, leader of various Central Asiatic Expeditions of the American Museum of Natural History, has spent much of his time since 1920 in Mongolia. His party used camels for heavy transport only, at least after the first expedition. For reconnaissance work they had a train of automobiles. Their explorations and those of Henry Fairfield Osborn, who was there in 1922, have found this region to be a treasure-house of the life story of the earth. Their belief is that the earliest ancestors of man possibly originated in "Gobia"; indeed, that man existed on earth between two and three million years ago, and that Mongolia was at some time an earthly paradise, possessed of enough rainfall to permit great forests to flourish and with enough winter cold to stimulate man to use his wits to devise means of shelter at that season. Mr. Andrews found a fossil forest where logs, stumps and chips lay preserved as they had fallen, many thousands of years ago. It may have been on the leaves of these trees that some of the largest dinosaurs had browsed.

Skeleton of Pre-Mongol Man

The expedition traced the bed of an ancient stream in which thousands of animals had perished in the Eocene or Dawn Period of the Age of Mammals. They found deposits of fresh-water clam shells, and high dunes on the one-time fresh-water lake shores. They excavated the skeleton of a pre-Mongol man over six feet tall who must have lived in Mongolia long before the time of Tutankh-Amen. He must have been a huntsman, to judge from his implements, and in view of the winter cold and the relics of his activities, he must have dwelt on the sunny side of these dunes in skin shelter huts.

One may say Mongolia suffered four periods of mountain uplift, that which (by erosion) formed the floor of the present Gobi Desert, that which raised the mountains of Northern China, that which raised the Himalayas on the south and that which raised the Altai Mountains in the Central Asiatic plateau.

Colossal Prehistoric Beasts

The succession of life in what is now Mongolia, according to the discoveries of the Museum expeditions, began with a stupendous creature now called the Asiatosaurus, a beast with an incredibly long neck, a small head and fleshy, tapering tail. The next outstanding form was the Deinodont, whose forelegs were shortened to mere feeble appendages, as he had taken to walking on his powerful hind legs in a semi-upright position. There was a Velociraptor, a similar but far smaller form that developed speed in running and so was able to find food and in particular to escape the enemies that he was too small to fight. There was a succession of rhinoceros-like creatures that began as comparatively tiny forms but which became larger and larger till they reached their maximum in the Baluchitherium. Last to develop were the small horse-like Hipparian, the somewhat larger Camelus and the ostrich-like Struthiolithus.

The more colossal of these beasts were, according to Mr. Andrews' theory, unable to find enough food or else, when the climate changed till it became impossible for them to remain in Asia, they were unable to carry their great weight on the long migration to Europe and North America that then became necessary, and

JAGGED PEAKS OF THE TURGUN MOUNTAINS SURROUND A ROCK-STREWN WILDERNESS IN MONGOLIA

Carruthers

Among the Turgun Mountains, some of the peaks of which rise to a height of ten thousand feet, are many such barren tablelands as that shown above, where hardly a yak can find food. Wind-swept and desolate, the glaciers have strewn them thickly with sharp rocks. Below these bleak plateaus, visited only by an occasional surveyor, are sheltered valleys that afford pasture for herds of the hardy yaks, such as we see on another page. These yaks are mainly used as beasts of burden, but are also valued for their flesh, milk and silken hair.

TRIANGLE

THE SOLDIERLY STEEPLES OF THE GREAT LAMASERY IN JEHOL

The Great Lamasery, residence of a high lama, the religious leader of many Mongol Buddhists, is one of several in the vicinity of Jehol. It is modeled after the monasteries of Tibet.

so they perished by the way. The bones of these prehistoric creatures are preserved in the sandstone, limestone, clay and slate deposits beneath the desert sands. And among them has been found a mammal that must have been as long as a sky-scraper is tall. They have called it the Mongolian Colossus. They also excavated in Asia specimens of the forerunners of incredibly large Titanotheres such as dwelt in some past age on the continent of North America. This beast must have browsed on the tops of forest trees. It is, up to date, the world's biggest mammal and a new species, at that.

While it was the inhabitants of millions of years ago who most interested Mr. Andrews, he found some interesting present-day dwellers in Mongolia with which the remainder of this article will treat. He found, for instance, Mongol temple priests who forbade the killing, on cer-

tain spots they hold sacred, of the deadly reptiles that sometimes crawled for warmth into the beds of the explorers during the chill of night. But one should not leave the subject of exploration without a reference to the geologists Berkey, Granger and Morris who have discovered that Gobi is to-day very like the deserts of Utah, Wyoming and other portions of the American desert northward to or beyond the Canadian border.

As to the human dwellers on the Gobi Desert, the nomad Mongols, averse alike to agriculture and organized government, had always raided the more fertile provinces of China, and at the height of their power possessed the best weapons of the world in their day. Their rise forms one of the most romantic chapters of history. They were first consolidated in the twelfth century by the establishment of the so-called Empire of the Great Moguls, and

307

SPINNING YARN IN A WOOLEN MILL AT ULAN BATOR

The city is both the capital and the center of industry in the Mongolian People's Republic. One of its most important manufactures is the production of wool cloth. Ulan Bator means "red hero" and refers to a Mongolian revolutionary leader who helped to establish the communist-led government in the 1920's. The country retains close ties with Russia.

GUARDING SHEEP ON THE PLAINS OF KAZAKHSTAN, EASTERN RUSSIA

Kazakhstan is one of the sixteen republics that make up the Soviet Union. It has a climate that is bitter cold in winter, hot and dry in summer. Nomadic tribes once wandered on this vast pasture land with their sheep and cattle, keeping a sharp lookout for hostile tribesmen. The snow-covered Altai Mountains are shown in the background.

STURDY PEASANT OF THE ALTAI MOUNTAIN COUNTRY

The Altai Mountain Range in the middle of Asia stretches over western Mongolia and Kazakhstan in eastern Russia. The inhabitants of the area, Kazakhs and Kalmucks, are Mongolians, and until recent years some of them were still nomads, living in tents through winter snow and summer heat. They are skilled at weaving wool into felt and rugs.

SIBERIAN COLONISTS WHO NAVIGATE THE RIVER YENISEI ON THEIR CLUMSY RAFT OF TREE TRUNKS

The upper branches of the great River Yenisei flow through northwestern Mongolia, and many immigrants from Siberia laboriously make their way along these streams on rafts rudely fashioned of tree trunks. A voyage on a raft is exceedingly slow, and involves much hard work, but travel by land is almost impossible in this wild country, covered with dense forests interspersed with vast stretches of swamp and rocky ravines. To the south of this zone are the prairie lands from which great numbers of horses are exported to Siberia and China.

A THOUSAND MILES FROM OTHERS OF THEIR KIND, MONGOLIAN YAKS ROAM OVER THE TURGUN HIGHLANDS

The shaggy-haired yak is usually thought to live only among the great mountains of Tibet, but there are also herds of them far away across the Desert of Gobi, in the lofty mountain ranges that form the frontier between Mongolia and Siberia. In North Mongolia there are also gigantic sheep, as big as donkeys, with enormous curling horns, beavers, sables and gazelles, reindeer, horses, asses and snow leopards, and, farther south, great, woolly Bactrian camels. The best of the wild horses are driven over the eastern frontier and sold to the Chinese.

SOVFOTO

A MONGOLIAN CATTLE-BREEDER ASTRIDE HIS SHAGGY PONY

The ponies that rove the Mongolian plains are sturdy animals that can race with surprising speed. It was such steeds that carried the dread hordes of Genghis Khan. The raising of livestock is the chief activity of the nomadic tribes—mainly Khalkhas—of the Mongolian People's Republic. In addition to horses, cattle, sheep, goats and camels are bred.

AN EARLY MORNING SCENE IN A VILLAGE OF INNER MONGOLIA

The covering on these hovels is coarse wool felt. Much of the land in this part of northern China is more suitable for grazing than for farming, and that is one reason why these people have been nomads, tending sheep and cattle since bygone times. Many of them raise camels and horses. Inner Mongolia shares with the Mongolian People's Republic the vast desert area called the Gobi.

313

Adam Warwick

A MONGOLIAN PRINCESS IN FULL REGALIA

Royal lineage and regal adorning grace this Mongolian princess in her bejeweled and beaded headdress that rustles with soft clash at every movement of her head. The full cheeks and narrow eyes are typical.

fourteenth century Tamerlane (Timur), who was the most amazing conqueror the world had ever seen, for one summer he sacked Moscow and the next he stood at the gates of Delhi.

When at the height of their fame the Mongols were Mohammedans. Had they so remained, they might even now retain a prominent place among the nations of the East. Their downfall, which followed soon after the rule of Tamerlane, was due largely to the introduction of Lamaism, a form of the Buddhist faith which forces all sons save one of every family to enter a monastery. Lamaism was introduced from Tibet toward the end of the thirteenth century and rapidly gained adherents.

When the Mongol Empire fell apart, a portion of it came under Russian, and a part under British domination, while Mongolia itself—as we know it to-day—became a Chinese province.

Treaties were established between China and Russia as early as 1689 and goods entered European Russia by way of the Siberian steppes. By a later treaty (1725) the frontier city of Miamchen in Mongolia became one of two gateways for the Chinese trade, while Siberian Kiakta became the other. Then in 1912 Mongolia was declared to be an integral part of China.

But that Russia would like to have Mongolia has been evidenced by certain episodes of the recent past. Since the Chinese Revolution in 1911, Mongolia has tried again and again to win freedom from China. Coveted by both China and Russia, it has since been shuttled back and forth between the two nations, and perhaps the end is not yet. In 1911, for instance, San-to, the Manchu Amban at Urga, resisting Russian influence, strove

soon thereafter, their empire stretched from the Sea of Japan to the Adriatic Sea. It was then that the Mongols came near to dominating the Old World. Under Jenghiz Khan in the thirteenth century an army was organized which penetrated the Great Wall, ravaging and plundering the Chinese provinces; and Jenghiz Khan later conquered most of Inner Asia, sweeping westward as far as where Odessa now stands, capturing what later came to be known as Moscow, invading Poland and Hungary and capturing Budapest.

Later in that same century Kublai Khan dominated the scene of action, and in the

to promote Chinese trade and immigration, but for this the Mongol princes shortly succeeded in ousting him. In his place as ruler, they set up the Urga Hutukhtu (Living Buddha). At this juncture Russia came forward, promising to aid Mongolia in maintaining her independence from China. By agreements signed in 1913 China did for the time recognize Mongolian independence, at the same time that Russia recognized Chinese overlordship in the disputed territory. By an agreement between the three countries in 1915 there was to be a Chinese resident general at Urga, the capital, but Outer Mongolia was to remain independent, under the protectorate of Russia. But in 1919 the Chinese took advantage of the disorder that followed on the heels of the Russian revolution to try to increase their power in Mongolia. They were driven out of Urga in 1921, at which time Red troops organized a government at the capital city. One complication was removed in 1924 when the Living Buddha died. At once there was a revolution and the Mongol People's Republic was set up. It is under Russian influence.

Inner Mongolia, made up of Chahar, Ningsia and Suiyuan, was occupied by Japan during the war. It was made an autonomous region of the Chinese People's Republic in May of 1947.

The Mongol dress, a study for an artist, is like a long and ample dressing-gown of varied color, fastened at the waist by a sash. Beneath are shirts and coverings according to the period of the year. For headgear the rider of the plains has a rounded, turned-up hat, the centre rising to a cone-shaped crown of red, yellow or ochre. For the feet he has leather boots reaching to the knees, al-

ways two or three sizes too large, for as the winter advances successive layers of felt socks are added. Stuck in the girdle is the long pipe without which a Mongol never moves, flint and metal to supply the want of matches, and a riding-whip.

With the women the dress is somewhat similar, with their very long sleeves well padded at the shoulders. The hair and its careful dressing is the feminine strong point. It is plaited and threaded through a flat framework curved outward like the horns of a sheep, these terminating in a silver tip covered with beads and other ornaments. They wear earrings of turquoise and other precious stones easily

Adam Warwick

A MONGOLIAN PRINCE IN IMPERIAL GARB

This princely descendant of the great Tatar khans, Jenghiz and Kublai, sits proud in the consciousness of ancestors whose power was a terror and whose names were feared through all the bounds of Asia.

procurable in this land of minerals while strings of beadwork and necklaces adorn the neck and shoulders. The boots are, of course, far too large for their tiny feet, but then provision must be made for extremes of temperature, and, moreover, they are receptacles for the pipe and tobacco, riding-whip and the brick tea and even the drinking-cups.

Goats' Hair Felt Tents

The home of the Mongol is a large felt tent, a semi-circular construction on a lattice framework with an opening at the top for light and the escape of smoke. The felt covering the framework is made from goats' and camels' hair. The difficulties of house-moving are reduced to a minimum, for the family range themselves around the inside of the tent and, lifting the structure bodily, walk away.

The contents of a Mongol larder are easily supplied, for they consist of milk, mutton, cream and a form of cheese made from goats' milk. The Mongols drink copiously and often of fermented mare's milk, which they keep in leathern bottles in exactly the same way as the Jewish patriarchs or their nomadic forbears did centuries before them.

The conservative Mongols treasure the romantic theory of the bride being carried off from her father's tent. A wedding is a great event, especially when the belle of the encampment is the prize. Arrayed like a princess, the slant-eyed young woman with her flat yellow face and stiff black hair, mounted on a fiery charger, gives the lead in a breakneck race to the young men who aspire to her hand. To ward off undesirable lovers she uses her heavy whip with force and accuracy, and a well-directed slash across the eyes puts the unwelcome suitor out of action.

A Savage Custom

The customs of the Mongols are often remarkable. Instead of burying the dead in the usual way, the body is put out on a knoll in the vicinity of the camp, and there left to the tender mercies of dogs and birds of prey. Should the remains not be disposed of within a few days the deceased is considered to have led a wicked life, since even the dogs are shocked and refuse to touch the body. The sequel to this discovery is the chastisement of all the members of the deceased's family with the idea of saving them from a similar fate.

Among the Mongol lamas, or priests, who comprise forty per cent of the male population, the medical profession is favored, since it affords an opportunity of acquiring wealth and position. Their medical practice is, unfortunately, founded on superstition and witchcraft. There are quaint observances respecting doctor and patient. One is that the medico lives in the patient's tent until the sick person is either cured or dies. Payment of the fee incurred is a question of results.

The Mongols have strange ideas concerning the origin of complaints from which they may be suffering. They will declare with all sincerity that the deity is angry with them and has visited them with a fever, a cold or whatever it may be, because they have inadvertently cut a stick from the stunted trees surrounding a monastery, or because in digging a hole in the ground they have destroyed life in the shape of worms and insects.

Hard Lot of a Mongol Prisoner

The prison system and mode of punishment in Mongolia are similar in their cruelty to those of the Middle Ages in Europe. Here offenders are placed in an oblong box measuring about five feet by two and two feet in depth—very like a coffin. There, chained and manacled, they are left to pass weeks, sometimes months and not infrequently years, according to the seriousness of the crime. They can neither stand up nor lie down, but must perforce assume a semi-crouching posture, so that their limbs become shrunken and useless. They are taken out for a few minutes daily and food is passed to them through a small hole in the side of the box. For covering at night a totally inadequate sheepskin coat is provided when the thermometer drops to 20 degrees below zero.

A Peep at Peking (Peiping)

Once the Paris of the Orient

Under various names and dynasties, Peking served as the capital of China for a thousand years. After an interval of twenty-one years, from 1928 to 1949, when the city was called Peiping, it again became a capital, this time of the Chinese Communists. On its battlemented walls, its palaces and in its streets, invader and conqueror have left their mark. Much of its old-time splendor and romance disappeared after the revolution of 1911, though Peking remained the cultural center of China, with a number of universities. It was often called the Paris of the Orient. The city's most characteristic color is gray, from the dust that settles on streets and roofs when the frequent dust storms of winter bring yellow-gray loess from Inner Mongolia. In this chapter we tell you about some of the ancient glories of Peking.

OF all the cities in the world Peking is, perhaps, the most remarkable, with its huge walls, its historic past and its curious mixture of things old and new. It has a history that few cities can equal. It dates centuries before the Christian era, for a city existed here or near here about 1100 B.C. In the course of time this spot came to serve as a provincial capital; then, after other centuries of change, the city was named Chung Tu and was made the royal residence of the Tatars. From them it was taken by the Mongol leader, Jenghiz Khan, and rebuilt by his grandson, Kublai Khan.

The name Peking, which means Northern Capital, dates from the third Ming emperor, who moved the seat of government there from Nanking, the "Southern Capital," where the court of his two predecessors had been established. In the year 1928, some five hundred years later, the Nationalist Government shifted the seat of power back to Nanking, changing the name of Peking to Peiping. At the end of 1949, the Chinese Communists made it their capital, as Peking once more.

It may be said with truth that the history of China is contained within Peking, for here reigned the emperor, known as the Son of Heaven. His word was law, and he was believed by his subjects to rule over everything beneath the sun and to have no earthly rival. Therefore, as all states and countries throughout the universe were regarded merely as his vassals, their emissaries could be received at the Chinese court only as inferiors.

The present city is very much the same as the one created by the Ming emperor Yung Lo, who reigned from 1403 to 1425, but he built on the foundations laid by the great Kublai Khan. The Manchu emperor Ch'ien Lung did much to improve Peking during the latter half of the eighteenth century. The city is situated in a plain that extends southward for about seven houndred miles and eastward to the Gulf of Chihli, ninety-one miles distant. Forty miles to the northwest is the Great Wall. The soil of the plain is so light and so loose that we are vividly reminded, when the wind raises the dust, of the story that the city was carefully located on the driest spot in the province.

It is from the walls that we can get the best impression of the city. They are about twenty-four miles in circumference, approximately forty feet in height and enclose four cities. Since the fall of the monarchy in 1911 and the substitution of a republic, parts of these cities have fallen into dilapidation. Of the four, three form a nest: first comes the Tatar City, in the heart of which lies the Imperial City, enclosing in its turn the Forbidden City. Each of these is surrounded by its own walls. In the central enclosure—"forbidden" ground to all foreigners until the Boxer rebellion in 1900—are the palaces and exquisite pleasure gardens of the former emperors and their households. Here for a thousand years lived the royal masters of China, unseen of common mortals.

In the Imperial City were the residences of princes and high officials. The whole

CHINESE JUGGLERS PERFORMING THEIR TRICKS IN PEKING

Anything unusual soon attracts a curious crowd in China, and here an appreciative audience occupies the roadway while it watches two jugglers. The man to the right of the centre is swallowing a sword, and his partner is calling upon passers-by to stop and see this marvelous trick. Obviously the half-naked performer can have nothing up his sleeve!

Carter

LITTLE CHINESE ACROBAT READY TO DELIGHT THE CROWD

Almost as soon as he could walk, this little fellow was made to practice various acrobatic feats so that his limbs might become used to assuming unusual positions. His father was probably an acrobat, and his grandfather as well, for trades and professions run in families in the East. A collection is usually taken before the performance commences.

THE LOWLY FRANKFURTER SPEAKS EVERYBODY'S LANGUAGE

In far-off Peking, one of China's most ancient cities, a street merchant happily watches a tray of simmering frankfurters as he waits for passing customers. Peking was once the capital city of the mighty Kublai Khan's empire. The emperors of the Ming Dynasty finally made it their capital, too, and they gave it its present name, meaning "northern capital."

A WINDOWED GATE OF BRICK IN THE CITY OF MANY GATES

Walls surround both the Inner, or Manchu, City and the Outer, or Chinese, City on the south.
Those around the Inner City are fifty feet high, broken by huge gates and defense towers.

area surrounded by the mighty walls of the Tatar City is much older than the Chinese City, which joins it on the southern edge and in which are the shops and the homes of most of the population of Peking.

For a long time no one was allowed to walk on the walls, because it would have been an act of great disrespect on the part of the observer to look down upon the emperor and the palaces in which he lived. It was only after the war between the Chinese and the British and French, in 1860, that an order was given permitting foreigners to enjoy the privilege of walking along the top of these ramparts. This was a great advantage, since the roads are often ten inches deep in dust during the summer, and in winter are masses of mud and slush so deep that carts are often bogged up to the axles.

There are many wonderful buildings in the old city; but one of the most interesting is the Observatory standing on a site first used by Persian astronomers at the court of Kublai Khan. It is probably the oldest astronomical observatory in the world. We know that hundreds of years before astronomy came to be studied with care by Western men of science, the Chinese

EWING GALLOWAY

ONE OF THE WATCH TOWERS OF TATAR CITY

Outside the walls of the Imperial City is the imposing Drum Tower. It and the companion Bell Tower, in imperial days, sounded the two-hourly change of the watch. A water clock and sticks of incense kept the official time.

had evolved a system of their own, which led them to believe that the earth was the centre of the universe, and that the sun, moon and stars moved round it and gave it warmth.

In the seventeenth century Jesuit priests came to the city from Europe, and made known the wonders of Western astronomical science, which the Chinese endeavored to apply to their own system. They worked out eclipses and forecast them with great accuracy, but the results of science were hard to reconcile with the

traditions of the race. For centuries the people had been taught that the only efficient method of counteracting the dreadful consequences of an eclipse was to assemble all the priests, nobles, and astrologers and to beat drums and other instruments to frighten the dragon that was trying to devour the sun.

Near the Observatory we shall find the ruins of the famous Examination Halls, where examinations for official posts were held for centuries. The higher positions in the civil and military service were filled only from among those who had passed the examinations held here, and this system was the leading feature of Chinese administration. The possession of a literary degree was not only a distinction but also a passport to an official appointment. The final examinations, which occurred every third year, were presided over by the emperor in person, and the candidates were all those who had successfully come through eliminating trials previously held at the various examining centres in the provinces.

The Examination Halls contained about 10,000 cells, each nine feet long by four feet wide, into which light and food were admitted through a narrow grating in the wall. Every candidate was thoroughly searched before entering to make sure that he had with him nothing that might assist

him in the coming ordeal. He was then given a cell, locked in and left there during the time (perhaps a week or more) required for the examination.

The questions were so hard that many of the more highly strung candidates went mad under the strain. No one could hope to sit for this final examination until he had spent years in intense study, and if he should make the slightest mistake in composition or the fault of misplacing a character, he knew he would not pass and would not be allowed to present himself for examination again. Many of the questions set at the examinations were taken from the works of Confucius, who lived more than 2,400 years ago and whose teachings have greatly influenced the Chinese race during all these centuries.

The centre of foreign life and activity

Camera Craft

BUYING A CRAB IN PEKING IS A WEARISOME BUSINESS

Crabs are much liked by the Chinese, and we may see baskets of them by the wayside in Peking. In one of our markets the buying of a crab need not take more than a minute, but the Chinese love to haggle over the price of everything that they purchase, and the completion of such a simple transaction as this may occupy half an hour.

CHINESE TINKER BUSY AT HIS TRADE IN A QUIET CORNER

In Peking traveling tinkers ply their trade in the streets, carrying about with them fire, hammers and portable stoves, and thus saving overhead expense. This man goes to the houses in one street and collects all the kettles and pots and pans that need mending, then he retires to some quiet corner where he can work undisturbed.

SAWING TIMBER FOR A BUILDING IN THE CITY OF PEKING

Many of the buildings in Peking are constructed mainly of wood, so that carpenters and their assistants are people of considerable importance. Instead of using a sawpit, these workmen have erected a contrivance that makes it necessary for one of them to work in a very uncomfortable position. As the work progresses, they must move the supports.

323

LIFELIKE LAUGHING BUDDHA

In the neglected Buddhist temples about Peking there are many works of art depicting Buddha as partaking of human emotions. Buddhism is now decaying in China.

but to the public the gates remained closed until 1924, when the former emperor was at last sent forth from within the walls that had so long guarded an imperial residence. After that a permit would gain admittance for the humble as well as the notable visitor.

In the city of to-day, in strong contrast with the structures and methods of times long past, we find motor cars and newly built roads on which they can run smoothly, electric lights, a water supply system, modern banks and hospitals, and a police force modeled on Western lines. Probably the Japanese instituted many changes during their years of occupation of the area; but, basically, life and its habits do not change much in China. The people still live much as they did. A Chinese official is inadequately paid and

in Peking was the Legation Quarter, an international colony where the foreign representatives lived. This quarter was below the Tatar Wall in the southern part of the Tatar city, on land allotted for the purpose after the Boxer troubles. Here are all forms of architecture, because each nation endeavored to set up a portion of its country, with its own particular style of architecture, within the walls of Peking. Each nation had a separate compound for its own buildings, and no foreigners, with the exception of missionaries, were supposed to live in any other part of the city. At one time the quarter's walls and gates were guarded.

The imperial splendors of the Forbidden City, with its artificial lakes and beautiful trees, though they have lost some of their lustre, still suggest in their very names the mystic wonders of a fairy world. There are, for instance, the Jade Rainbow Bridge, the Palace of Earth's Repose, the Throne Hall of Purple Effulgence and the glorious Dragon Throne of the Son of Heaven. Foreign ministers were first given audience within these royal precincts after the uprising of 1900;

GUARDIAN OF A TAOIST TEMPLE

Such fierce-looking images as this are to be seen at the entrances of Taoist temples to frighten away evil spirits. Many observances have been borrowed from Buddhism.

SUMMER PALACE OF THE MANCHUS, SIX MILES WEST OF PEKING

A broad lake mirrors the sylvan Western Hills and the ruins of the magnificent palace sanctuary of Tz'u-hsi, Dowager Empress and one of the last of the Manchu rulers. Tz'u-hsi was the power behind the imperial throne for almost fifty years, acting as regent first for her son and then for her nephew. She died in 1908; the Empire fell after the revolution of 1911.

APARTMENT OF THE DOWAGER EMPRESS IN THE SUMMER PALACE

The exquisite woodwork of the entrance to the Empress's apartment in the Summer Palace, though losing the bright sheen of its lacquer to the wearing effects of time and weather, still suggests the splendor of the court in the old days. In the court the statues of two cranes and an elk remain, inanimate witnesses to the last days of a wily and strong-willed woman.

has to do the best he can to make both ends meet, and this largely accounts for the bribery and corruption that have existed. The custom of "squeeze" was a well-established one, and there is some question as to just how successful the Communists have been in eradicating it.

At one time, a police-watchman in a Chinese town was entitled to a small weekly sum from every shopkeeper and house-

© Ewing Galloway

BEAUTIFULLY SCULPTURED GATEWAY OF THE YELLOW TEMPLE

North of the Anting Gate, which is in the north wall of the Tatar city, lies the Huang Szu, or Yellow Temple. The building is so named because of its yellow tiles, though green and blue tiles have also been used. The temple comprises two structures, the earlier erected in 1651. Here were entertained grand Lamas and Mongol Princes.

holder in his ward. The sum was usually paid promptly, for if there was any failure in payment the police had their own way of bringing the recalcitrant citizen to book.

Chinese police administration made no provision for the poor and those in want, and we must not imagine that there are no beggars in Peking. On the contrary, there are gangs of them. As these beg-

TEMPLE OF HEAVEN WHITHER THE EMPERORS CAME TO WORSHIP

In the Outer City of Peking is the Temple of Heaven, erected in 1420, where the emperors offered prayers on certain occasions. This picture shows one of the beautiful buildings and the stairway of approach. The triple roof is covered with blue tiles, and the steps are of white marble. The carved ramp in the center is for the use of spirits only!

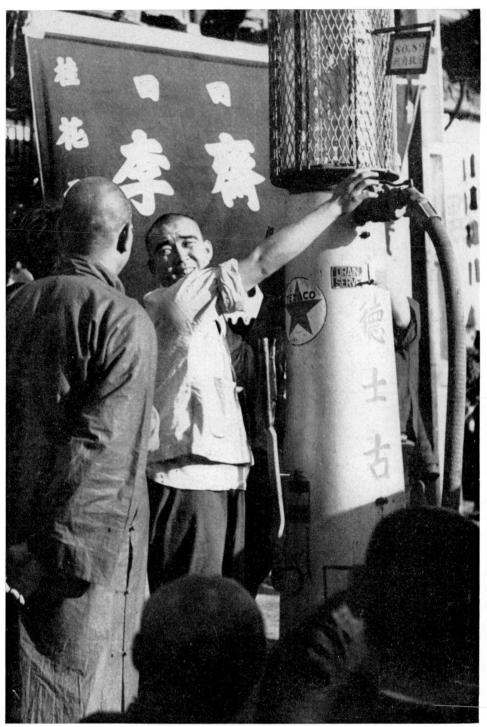

A GAS STATION STRIKES A MODERN NOTE ON ANCIENT STREETS

The tank was left over from the days before the Communists came to power and is still put to use. There are cars for officials and some trucks for the rapid transportation of goods.

gars might be a danger to the state, they are placed under the control of a headman, who is held responsible for the good conduct of his ragged army. He reports periodically to the governing authority and arranges with shopkeepers and householders for the payment of certain sums so as to save merchants and traders from being pestered during business hours. Should there be any refusal to give the amount in question, the beggars soon bring the refractory one to a more reasonable frame of mind.

A party of dirty men will appear and demand alms, and their offensive presence is quite enough to keep away all intending customers. No one can get anywhere near the shop, traffic is held up and all business is at a standstill. If the shopkeeper should continue in his refusal, his resistance is met by an increase in the number of beggars, who press their demands for charity until nothing can be heard above the din. Finally the merchant is forced to submit, and the beggars then retire with flying colors.

A Theatre in the Street

The native, or Chinese, city is most interesting, for there we see the real life of the people and come in contact with their pursuits and amusements. The Peking people, in common with all Chinese, are fond of theatricals. The plays are mostly historical and deal with the sayings and doings of sages who died more than two thousand years ago. The costumes are authentic, fitting exactly the time and personages of the play, and are often costly.

In walking through the streets we occasionally come across a theatre, not in a building but in the open street. There is no scenery; but a few benches, bamboo poles and flags are used in a traditional way to suggest the scenic background. The illusion is helped by the symbolic gestures or postures of the actors. Imagination does the rest. There are no dressing-rooms for the actors. All the changes of costume, the arranging and plaiting of the hair and painting and powdering of the complexion are carried out in full view of the audience.

It is in the streets of the essentially Chinese part of the city that we see the shops, the restaurants and the everyday life of the people. Houses and shops are all of the same pattern. The shopkeepers place their counters in the roadway, and often the space available for traffic is so small that carts can pass only in single file. There are shops containing the beautiful silks for which China is famous, others with lacquer work or vegetables and fruits; here and there are restaurants where we may taste the various foods which are distinctly Chinese.

Delicacies for the Palate

Let us go into one of these eating-houses. We shall have small dishes containing fresh and dried fruits, sliced ham, hard-boiled eggs, morsels of chicken, melon seeds and sundry other tit-bits. There are also soups and sharks' fins served in thick sauce. We can order wild duck and cabbage, pigeons' eggs stewed with mushrooms, dried fish of various kinds, sea slugs from the waters around Japan, pork crackling, chicken with ham, ducks'-egg soup, stags' tendons, bamboo roots, as well as the shoots of the young bamboo, stewed lotus, pickled or preserved eggs, fermented eggs, boneless chicken or ducks stuffed with little pine needles to give them a fine flavor. Beef we shall not find, because it is considered a sin among the Chinese to kill and eat animals that are used as beasts of burden.

Then there is the traveling restaurant which a man carries about on two wooden stands secured to a long bamboo pole that he slings over his shoulder. When he meets a customer he chooses a corner and there ladles out the meals.

Old and New, Face to Face

Peking, as we have already seen, presents a mingling of ancient and modern; mule litters of the most ancient type stand alongside the latest motor cars; telegraph and radio bring news from all parts of the world. The famous Peking Gazette, the oldest journal in the world, which was formerly the one newspaper, contained only what the imperial court considered

PEKING'S HALL OF CLASSICS is an old Imperial university, and the emperor used to sit in the main hall to preside over examinations or explain the old literature. In the grounds are tablets upon which have been carved extracts from the thirteen Chinese classics. They were set up by the famous Chinese emperor Ch'ien in the eighteenth century.

TWO FEARSOME DRAGONS guard the entrance to one of the buildings within the Forbidden City. When China became a republic, some of the halls and palaces were used as government offices and barracks. Many of them, however, have remained empty since the day in the year 1924 when the young emperor received orders to leave the Imperial Palace.

It advisable for the people to know. With the spread of new ideas and the increase in readers of newspapers and other periodicals the prejudice against change has more and more to fight, but it has not lost its hold.

For instance, there was a project to develop the rich coalfields in the province of Shansi, but the priests and people were against it, because they argued that the area to be tapped was the home of the mighty dragon Feng Shui, the guardian of hidden treasures, who destroys anyone offending him. If the coalfields were opened the sleep of the dragon would be disturbed, and he would come out and spread fire, death and pestilence through the land. So the dragon slept on, and the coalfields remain untapped.

Many and varied are the sights in Peking, for it is the centre of Chinese life. Its quaint streets and shops, its temples, its wonderful walls and palaces are reminders of history and romance. We may visit the Great Hall of Audience where the emperor, on his birthday, used to release 10,000 birds from huge cages, so as to bring good luck; and the Temple of Heaven, whither once a year he took a scroll on which were written the names of executed criminals. This scroll he burnt there, so that the ashes could go up to Heaven and make it known that he had done his duty. The wonder and delight of these places and of many others in the storied city of the Celestial people surpass all expectation when we walk within its old, old walls and recall its past.

Camera Craft

OLD MEANS OF TRANSPORT PASSING BENEATH OLD WALLS

Camel caravans from Mongolia and Siberia still bring merchandise to the city as they have done for centuries. The Peking of to-day was built upon the foundations laid by the great Kublai Khan, grandson of Jenghiz Khan, a little to the north of an older city that was captured by the Mongols in 1215. The earlier city was known as Chung Tu

IN CHERRY-BLOSSOM LAND

Tradition Lingers in Modern Japan

When the world was created, Japan, the most beautiful of all places, was the first country to be made. So lovely was it that the gods considered mere man to be unworthy to rule over it. The Sun Goddess, therefore, sent down Ninigi, her Heavenly grandchild, and he became the first ruler of Japan. The people believed the present emperor to be his direct descendant and they the descendants of Ninigi's attendant gods. From a feudal island kingdom, Japan grew into a great empire, until her ambitions were dashed by the outcome of World War II. After the war the Emperor publicly renounced his claims to divinity—told his people that he was not a god. The Land of the Rising Sun has been stripped of its conquests and is now hardly larger than when Commodore Perry opened its doors to the world in the middle of the last century.

JAPAN is a large chain of islands stretching north and south for three thousand miles along the east coast of Asia, from which it is separated by the China Sea. There are four large islands and about four thousand islets, of which only some 550 are inhabited.

As we travel from north to south, we pass the four largest islands, Hokkaido, or Yezo; Honshu, the main island; Shikoku and Kiushiu, all mountainous and forest-clad. From Kiushiu there extends the long chain of the fifty-five Luchu Isles.

Japan used to be much larger, but, as a result of World War II, she lost much of the territory which she had gained through many years of conquest and expansion. The Kurile Islands and southern Sakhalien Island, for instance, were returned to Soviet Russia; Korea became a republic. Formosa and the Pescadores Islands were returned to China, and Japanese mandated islands in the South Seas were placed under trusteeship of the United States.

The natural loveliness of the country is formed to a large degree by its mountains and by the beautiful streams and lakes which are found in all the highland districts. The huge volcano, Fujiyama, is easily one of the most beautiful mountains in the world. It stands by itself in a plain, some seventy or eighty miles from Tokyo, and is partially encircled by a chain of lakes.

The mountain is wonderfully symmetrical and usually capped with snow. It is regarded as sacred by the beauty loving Japanese, thousands of whom make a pilgrimage to the crater every summer. If we climb the steep sides we shall find everywhere shrines built to the spirits thought to inhabit Fuji; and from its slopes we can view plains, lakes and distant peaks.

Both mountains and streams are terrible as well as beautiful, for the people suffer severely from the volcanic activities of at least fifty active craters. Small, barely perceptible earthquakes happen about four times a day in one part or another of Japan. Every now and then, also, a severe earthquake occurs that does enormous damage to life and property, as does the periodical flooding of mountain streams, which often ruins the crops in low-lying country.

The Japanese once held that the magnet loses its power during an earthquake or even immediately prior to one. In ancient times they attributed earthquakes to movements of a tortoise, on which the earth rests, or to the flapping of a large subterranean fish, which, when it wakes, wriggles about and causes the vibrations, Even today during a severe earthquake masses of people can be seen, robed in white, some of them on their knees, attempting to appease the wrath of the gods or demons responsible for the disturbance. A fierce god hidden in the entrails of the earth, the god of the earthquake, receives very sincere worship, because his dreadful convulsions are a scourge against which man cannot fight.

MIYAJIMA THE SACRED on which no one is allowed to die, is a mountain-island that rises from the still waters of the Inland Sea. Forests of pine and maple and grassy glades cover the mountain slopes, and down the ravines fall cascades, with never-ceasing music. The island is dedicated to the three daughters of Susa-no-o, the Sea-King. There are three temples. One temple stands on the shore, another on the hill above and a third on the highest peak, eighteen hundred feet above the sea. The island is well worth the tourist's time.

FUJI THE PEERLESS (as Fuji-san-Fuji-yama, to give it its authentic title, is called) whether we see it from north, south, east or west, is never anything but lovely, at all seasons and at any hour of the day or night. It stands in the centre of a plain surrounded by less lofty mountains. To the south of it stretches the sea. To the north five lakes lie at its foot, from all of which wonderful aspects of the sacred mountain can be obtained Thousands of pilgrims climb up to its crater in the summer when it is bare of snow

335

Although we know little about Japan earlier than the middle of the fifth century, Japanese historians claim that their present dynasty is more than twenty-five centuries old. It was founded by Jimmu in 660 B.C. Jimmu was the direct descendant of the Sun Goddess, who sent her grandson from Heaven to rule the most beautiful place on earth— Japan. He and his successors were, and indeed still are to a certain extent, looked upon not only as sovereigns, but as divinities. For thirteen hundred years they were the actual rulers of the land; then from the eighth until the twelfth century, though the emperor still ruled in name, all the power was in the hands of one family of nobles, the Fujiwara.

During this period the empress was always chosen from this Fujiwara family and the grandfather of the emperor was regent with absolute power while the emperor was a child. If an emperor showed any independence he was forced to abdicate and his young son was placed upon the throne.

To keep the aborigines in subjection a professional military class developed, and the leaders were rewarded with grants of land. A complicated feudal system developed and the power of the Fujiwara was lessened. The great chiefs ruled their lands, but constantly quarreled with one another. The general of the army, known as the shogun, came to be the real ruler, though he paid all the outward forms of respect to the Emperor, whose descent from the gods was supposed to make it improper for him to deal with earthly matters. It was not until 1868 that the power of the shoguns was overthrown and the authority of the Emperor was acknowledged.

Buddhism and Shintoism

During these centuries Buddhism had been introduced, and a high civilization had come about. Painting and poetry developed to a high degree, and many industrial arts flourished. In textiles, embroidery, carving, painting and pottery the Japanese attained a high degree of beauty. But the oldest religion of the Japanese,

one still professed by many, is Shintoism, a combination of ancestor worship and nature worship. Since Shintoism regards people as naturally virtuous, each man's conscience is his best guide, and there is no explicit moral code. It assumes a continued spiritual existence after death, believes that the surviving spirits of one's ancestors may ward off evil, and its followers therefore propitiate them with ceremonials. Shintoists pay their deepest reverence to Amaterasu, "the Heaven-illuminating goddess," and Shinto shrines are simple wooden huts such as the first Japanese settlers built. In the seventh and eighth centuries, however, Buddhism was introduced from China. The Emperor and his court were soon converted and so were the bulk of the people. Chinese civilization and culture, Chinese art and learning spread to Japan and rapidly influenced the whole nation.

European Exclusion Act

In 1542 or 1543 the Portuguese discovered Japan by accident and later came to trade. The Spaniards and the Dutch followed them. They were welcomed by the Japanese people and for some time traded profitably. Christian missionaries came, too, and made many converts. These conditions, however, did not last, for early in the next century Christianity was forbidden and stamped out with the greatest cruelty, and all foreigners were driven from the country. In 1636, chiefly out of hostility to the Portuguese, a law was passed that declared that no European might land in Japan and that no Japanese might leave its shores. One exception was made to the former decree: the Dutch were allowed to keep a trading station on Deshima, an island near Nagasaki.

Feudal Isolation

For the next two hundred years Japan remained entirely cut off from the world. During this period no boats big enough for foreign trade were built and all the existing large ships were destroyed. The only vessels allowed were small coasting boats used for fishing. The only indus-

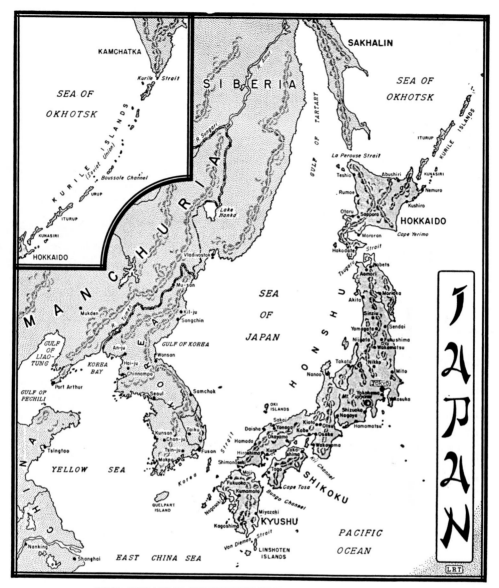

THE GREATLY SHRUNKEN EMPIRE OF DAI NIPPON

According to an old Japanese myth, Amaterasu, Goddess of the Sun, once let four dewdrops fall from her sceptre. As they dropped into the sea, they formed the four chief islands of Japan— Kyushu, Shikoku, Honshu and Hokkaido. Honshu, the largest and most important, is considered the "mainland" of Japan. There are hundreds of much smaller islands along the coasts. The chain takes the shape of a shallow semi-circle, embracing the Sea of Japan. Southern Kyushu has a tropical climate, hot and damp; while Hokkaido is almost at the other extreme of weather. Winter is often bitter, with heavy snows, on Hokkaido. This island is the home of a dark, hairy people, the Ainus, thought to be the first inhabitants of Japan. Defeat in World War II meant the loss of a much greater area that had been gobbled up in the 1930's—Manchuria, Korea, the Kurile Islands, the Bokoto (or Pescadores) Islands, Formosa, the southern half of Sakhalin (Karafuto) and, of course, the seized portions of China itself. As this map shows, the Japanese islands are deeply indented, and the bays thus formed give the country many fine harbors. They are especially important to a country that is so dependent on trade, because Japan does not have the resources to provide its people with all they need.

337

YOUNG WOMEN of Japan wander about the sunny gardens as bright and dainty in their gaily printed kimonos, wide sashes and painted sunshade, as the flowers they have come to admire. Her sleeves are a Japanese woman's pockets, and in them she carries her hand-kerchief—made of paper—her case of chopsticks, her looking-glass and sometimes her fan.

CHERRY TREES are sure of a prominent place in a Japanese flower garden, for they are grown primarily not for their fruit but for their blossoms. Wherever there is a clump of cherry trees, there, in April, we will find a group of beauty-worshipers sitting in contemplation and perhaps taking tea under clouds of the perfumed pink flowers.

tries were those carried on in the homes of the people, such as weaving, dyeing, embroidering, metal engraving, pottery-making and wood-carving, which were all beautifully executed.

It was not until the middle of the nineteenth century that Japan's rapid development began. The United States sent Commodore Perry, in 1853, with a large and formidable fleet to carry proposals for trade between the two countries. Townsend Harris, the first United States consul-general in Japan, secured the opening of Nagasaki in 1857.

The Japanese are adaptable and they now perceived that if they were to evade the fate of India they must exchange certain aspects of their Oriental civilization for Western material and intellectual progress. They paid European experts to enter the cities and instruct them in all forms of manufacture. Thousands of elementary schools were opened all over the country. To-day there are also six great universities—Tokyo, Kyoto, Tohoku, Kyushu, Hokkaido and Osaka.

An Era of Westernization

An era of progress began in 1868, and the young Emperor even embodied the national change of spirit in a so-called Charter Oath. The first railroad came in 1870 and there are over fifteen thousand miles of rails within the Empire. Factories were erected along modern lines. There is coal in abundance, and also hydroelectric power. During the first World War, when Japan had to depend upon her own manufactures, she expanded her trade on a huge scale on the mainland of Asia and in the Pacific. Neutral countries turned to her for supplies and she gained a considerable share of the world's markets. Everything manufactured in Europe was faithfully copied by the Japanese and was produced with the aid of cheap labor in her factories, though the standard of excellence is not always as high as it might be. Japanese families became newly rich, and with the general prosperity a democratic movement sprang up which has resulted, with the extension of suffrage, in the

quadrupling of the electorate. At first, Japanese exports were carried almost exclusively in foreign ships. However, Japan increased her merchant marine until it could handle almost half of her output. Before World War II, the flag of Japan could be seen in nearly every port. Her trade with Manchukuo ranked high. Her trade with the United States, before the two countries went to war in December, 1941, ran into many hundred million dollars annually.

The effect of this sudden change to Western ways is marked, for naturally many of the peasant folk from the agricultural districts have made their way to the towns, seeking work in the factories and harbors. Nevertheless the main industry of Japan is still agriculture.

Japan has comparatively few raw materials and her own people cannot buy much of what is produced. The military clique in the government insisted that Japan needed more territory to furnish raw materials and a larger market. To satisfy these demands, Japan annexed Korea and Formosa, and established the puppet state of Manchukuo.

The Japanese believed that they could manage China better than the Chinese themselves. They encroached on Chinese territory and encouraged rebellion. From 1937 they waged an undeclared war in China and set up a puppet government in the territory they captured. The Chinese moved their capital to inland Chungking. There they had to undergo unbelievable hardships while resisting a superbly equipped and wholly mechanized invading army. Japan was finally beaten in 1945.

Japan's Multimillionaires

It was mainly the money of one house, the Mitsuis, which financed Japan in her adaptation to Western ways. The house consisted of eleven families governed by a written constitution to which the members swore by the "august spirits" of their ancestors. The Mitsuis ranked among the richest in the world. Their wealth came from various enterprises. They imported cotton from the United States of America

JAPANESE FISHERMEN REPAIRING TEARS IN PURSE SEINES

The purse seine is used to catch large schools of fish. After the school is encircled by the net, a rope at the bottom is drawn like a purse string, making a bag to hold the fish.

and also locomotives, canned meat and other commodities. They also had offices in New York City with several hundred employees. They had banks, coal mines, and engineering works, and made electrical machinery, quake-proof steel chimneys and parts for railroad bridges. The Mitsui was one of the so-called "Eight Families" of Japan, called the Zaibatsu or "wealth cliques." The head of the house was Baron Mitsu whose private fortune was said to rival that of the emperor. One important member of the family was the first woman financier in Japan and instituted modern banking methods there. She helped found the Women's University and, though born a Buddhist, adopted Christianity when she was past sixty. The Mitsuis commemorate the fact that the founder of their line was digging a well when he found the money for his start in life.

Pilgrims of Penance

Pious folk make pilgrimages to shrines of the gods, as acts of penance and supplication for favors.

Groups of mountaineering priests gradually established definite series of pilgrim itineraries. Pilgrimages were undertaken as acts of penance and accomplished by stiff climbing. The pilgrimage to the thirty-three sanctuaries of Kwannon is one of the most popular. The majority of the thirty-three sanctuaries stood, and still stand, on hills or precipices—in accordance with the conception that the deity Kwannon looks down with compassion from on high upon the human world.

The pilgrim-bands to Kwannon are small, often just a family. They wear white robes, on which they receive stamps of the various sanctuaries, and, while marching, they chant hymns supposed to have been revealed by the respective deities of the places. At the places of pilgrimage acts of penance are performed, such as fasting, bathing in waterfalls, and sleepless prayer. On the way the pilgrims subsist on alms, and when they die, they are tenderly buried by the villagers. These acts of protection to the pilgrims are considered of great merit themselves.

A noteworthy feature in some of these

341

BUSHBY

A TIME-WORN TORII of camphor wood, most beautifully designed, is the entrance gate to the ancient Shinto temple on Miyajima, the sacred island. There is a day in every year when a long procession of boats crosses the Inland Sea and passes through this gateway, bringing thousands of pilgrims to the water-lapped steps of the temple. This, built on piles, seems at high tide to be floating upon the water. When the tide is out we may stand on dry ground beneath the torii, and feed the graceful little deer that haunt the island.

STEPPING-STONES are a feature rarely omitted in the lovely temple gardens of Kyoto. The beauty-loving Japanese invariably have a stream or a lake in their gardens, for they realize that the picturesqueness of the drooping clusters of wistaria and upright spikes of purple or yellow iris, and of the gay kimonos of their wives and children, is doubled when seen mirrored in the quiet waters. They often build bridges most inconveniently arched simply for the sake of their reflection. In the water swim great red-gold carp and ancient tortoises.

WIDE HATS AND PLEATED SKIRTS FOR THE GION FESTIVAL

One of the most colorful pageants held in Kyoto is the Gion festival. Members who take part wear crisply pleated street-length skirts and wide disc-shaped hats tied under the chin. The folding fan is also part of the costume. It is said to symbolize prosperity as it is slowly and carefully opened out. The Gion religion is an offshoot of Shintoism, the chief Japanese cult.

344

pilgrimages is that they are practiced as a kind of initiatory ceremony introducing young people to religious mysteries when they are entering adult life. Most pilgrimages of this kind are mountaineering trips over dales and precipices, paying homage at the sanctuaries erected here and there and finally worshipping the chief deity enshrined on the summit. The pilgrims are guided by trained leaders, who are mostly regular mountaineering priests and who direct the ceremonies. The most famous of the mountains visited are Kimpu-sen in Yamato, Ontaké in Shinono, and the well-known Fuji.

One of the most prominent pilgrimages is to the temple of Isé dedicated to the sun-goddess. Every spring groups of pilgrims composed of young men and women make a journey of many days to it and pay homage to the supreme deity of Shinto. This pilgrimage to Isé has nothing austere in it, but is merely a pleasure trip. Yet sometimes a form of maniac frenzy takes possession of many of the young people who start on the journey without any money or provisions but are well provided for by alms. These pilgrimages assume more and more the character of pleasure trips.

Weston

THE COLOSSAL BRONZE BUDDHA AT KAMAKURA

The Daibutsu was erected here at Kamakura, a little southwest of Yokohama, in the thirteenth century. A legend has it that the statue sailed across from China and chose this spot as its home. Neither earthquake nor war has harmed the gigantic bronze figure although the base now must be heavily braced.

THIS SERVANT OF BUDDHA will sit thus, in his brocaded robes, for hours seeking self-mastery through introspection. He is one of the Zen sect, which comes nearer to the Buddhism of India than to any of the other sects in Japan. Its priests have always been learned men. The faith was introduced from China about the twelfth century.

CEREMONIOUS POLITENESS is one of the attributes of the Japanese of all classes. Reverence to parents and to the aged is, indeed, taught them by their religion. Here we see a hostess in her house of paper and wood and cool matting greeting her guest. It is considered correct for both to kneel on the floor and bow several times to the ground.

A FARMER'S WIFE CARRIES A HEAVY LOAD

Her burden is compost—decayed vegetable matter used for fertilizer. However, chemical fertilizers have been introduced into Japan. Now that farmers can buy their land they are keenly interested in keeping the soil fertile.

Kaisha, one of the largest steamship companies in Japan.

We find traces among the upper classes of Japan of the Korean settlers who came in prehistoric times to the west coast. They are people with slender figures, long necks, acquiline noses, slanting eyes, oval faces and delicately formed hands. Occasionally we see a Mongolian type of Japanese whose figure is short and whose face is broad, with a flat nose and wide mouth.

The race of people who are perhaps the most important in the formation of the Japanese as we know them today are those who came from the south. They are believed to be Mongolian in origin, like those who came from Korea, but who, after long wanderings through China and Malaya, have a large admixture of Chinese and Malay blood. They are small in stature, with small hands and feet. They have generally good features, but their skin is darker, their noses are broader and their eyes straighter than the aristocrats from Korea.

In character the Japanese are industrious but gay and pleasure-loving. They are frugal people, content with little and wonderfully adapted to endure hardship. Obedience and reverence are instilled into them from childhood, as also are gentleness and politeness. So courteous are rich and poor alike that Japan has been called "the Land of Gentlemen." Another valuable quality that they possess is perseverance in attendance to detail.

The Japanese house is a fragile affair, made for the most part of thin, sliding, wooden frames upon which paper is stretched. The only solid part is the roof. There is only one floor, divided into rooms by partitions which can be slid back and forth as desired. The floor is covered with matting, and the only piece of fur-

Pilgrimages, whether of an austere religious character or combined with pleasure, are much in vogue even today. Many pilgrims can be seen in the country districts marching along in the costumes that have been customary for pilgrims for centuries.

Osaka is fond of sports. At the Koshien Ball Ground not far outside the city is a great stadium, and Japan has played a worthy part in world athletic events. Even a few women have gone in for track and field sports and swimming contests. The city is beginning to have ballrooms for social dancing, though joruri (ballad-drama) has lost none of its popularity as a drawing-room pastime.

The passenger airplane service established by Tokyo and The Osaka Asahi operates daily in fair weather. Here, also, is the headquarters of the Osaka Shosen

niture regarded as essential is a tiny charcoal stove. There is sometimes, however, a low stand, which supports a beautiful piece of china containing a spray of flowers, and a low screen may stand upon the floor. At meal times diminutive tables are brought, but no chairs are needed because everyone sits upon his heels on the floor. Everyone sleeps on the floor, too, between padded quilts. The women, whose hair is often so elaborately dressed that it is dressed only once or twice a week, do not use a pillow under their heads. Each has a hollow block of wood into which her neck fits. While this leaves the head unsupported, it preserves the coiffure.

The costume of Japanese women is a brightly colored kimono with the broad sash tied at the back. The business men are, to a certain extent, adopting the Western business suit. That is to say, they wear it during the day while at work, but upon returning to their homes in the evening exchange it for their loose, full-skirted national dress. On entering a house everyone takes off his shoes and leaves them at the door.

Recently Japanese women have been receiving more consideration, but for centuries they have been regarded as the servants of their fathers and brothers and, later, of their husbands. This is especially so among the upper classes. With the peasants, among whom the women do much of the work, they are held to be more nearly man's equal.

The throne was once the prize of a wrestling match between twin brothers. For wrestling is a sport which the Japanese probably favor above all others. Twice a year big wrestling matches are held in Tokyo in an amphitheatre which holds thirteen thousand people. The

BLACK STAR

SORTING OUT THE PRIME SILK COCOONS

After the silk cocoons have been dried, they have to be sorted. If the silkworm inside is crushed, the cocoon becomes stained; and if a bad cocoon is left in the pile it stains others and makes the silk too weak for spinning.

wrestlers as a class are taller than the average short-legged Japanese man, but also heavier. The tourist will know them by their top-knots of black hair. A wrestler is victorious when he can get so much as the top-knot of his opponent to touch the ground.

Jiu-jutsu, the art of self-defense, is really quite different. Here the winner turns the opponent's strength to that opponent's own disadvantage, with the result that he dislocates his shoulder or otherwise puts himself out of commission. Jiu-jutsu, also called judo, is taught in many of the schools. Baseball is played by students, who send teams as far away as Hawaii and the Philippines. There are the track meets of the Far East Olympics, and tennis is popular. It is said that the members of the royal family like

A LOVE OF FLOWERS is a leading characteristic of the Japanese and every month has its special blossom that rich and poor will travel miles to see. June is the month of the iris, and then everyone in Tokyo will go through the Mukojima Avenue of cherry trees, which they visited in April, to the acres of iris in the gardens of Hori-Kiri.

WESTON

BABY CARRIAGES are seldom seen in Japan. The cradle crowd is usually carried picka-
back by their mothers or their older sisters. These girls are still wearing traditional Oriental
kimonos. In the larger Japanese cities, however, women frequently follow Western styles
and are as interested in the latest fashions as Western women are.

351

to play tennis. Japanese children play with kites, tops and shuttlecocks as they race about the streets in clogs and kimonos. Indoors they wear straw sandals and little girls have lessons in arranging flowers. The Japanese, as a nation, have a natural love of beauty, and this causes them to make long pilgrimages, sometimes hundreds of miles on foot, to see some particular beauty spot of their land, such as a certain avenue of blossoming cherry trees. In the early months of the year the plum trees, trained into graceful shapes, are covered with white and red flowers. A little later the cherry trees are a wonderful sight with their seas of pink blossoms. Scarcely have they ceased to flower when the wistaria blooms, then the purple iris, azalea and peony. These are followed by the white flowers of the lotus and by the national flower, the chrysanthemum.

Hunter

AN ABORIGINAL OF JAPAN WHOSE PRIDE IS HIS BUSHY BEARD

When the Japanese first came to Japan, they drove the original inhabitants north into the island of Hokkaido. The latter's descendants are the hairy Ainus, a primitive tribe of hunters and fishermen who grow luxurious hirsute adornments. Indeed, the moustaches are often so heavy that their owners wear "lifters" on them at meal times.

CHILDREN JOIN IN THE CELEBRATION OF MEIJI'S BIRTHDAY

Before Emperor Mutsuhito died in 1912, he had literally transformed Japan. The rich were devoted to him and gave up immense estates to help him abolish the centuries-old feudal system. He encouraged industrialization and progress. The people called him Meiji, which means "Enlightened Prince," and his birthday is still celebrated every year.

ON NEW YEAR'S DAY the façades of Japanese houses are decorated with fir boughs and bamboo, besides which, each displays a symbol of good fortune. This one has an orange, a lobster and a piece of charcoal tied in a fringe of grass. Gifts are made and calls paid. Witness the bows of inimitable courtesy that are being exchanged.

THE WISTARIA comes out when the cherry blossom falls. Then all Japan visits the fragile tea-houses that fringe so many of the lakes in the temple gardens. There one may sit beneath a canopy of hanging purple blossoms—sometimes a yard or more in length—or stand among the leaves of the purple iris, and watch the reflections in the water.

COCK OF THE WALK FROM KOCHI WHO, WITH SOME ASSISTANCE, CAN A STRANGE TAIL UNFOLD

The cock bird of this special breed of fowl, known as Kochi, instead of molting in the usual manner, grows its tail and hackles for an indefinite period. The bird in the photograph measures over twelve feet. Outside Japan such abnormal growth of the sickle feathers, as they are called, is seldom obtained by breeders, though four or five feet is not an uncommon length for the embellishment of the bird.

OPERATING A LOOM FOR WEAVING SILK BROCADE

Silk was once Japan's leading export. But as artificial fabrics became popular, the demand for silk decreased. Now many of the factories produce only nylon and rayon materials.

HILL

KYOTO is a city of a thousand temples. One of the best known is the Yasaka Pagoda.
If we climb the ladderlike stairs and reach the balcony around the top, the entire
city will lie maplike at our feet. In midsummer the sun-drenched streets will be roofed
over with matting and in the all but dried river bed temporary houses will be erected.

358

HILL

THERE IS A GARDEN to every Japanese house. It may be but a few feet square, or it may cover an acre or two, but it is always artistic and well cared for. Where people have means, there is almost sure to be a stream with lotus flowers and a bridge or stepping-stones, stone lanterns and fir trees and a miniature Fuji-yama with a shrine upon it.

359

A NEW HIROSHIMA ARISES FROM THE RUBBLE OF DESTRUCTION

On August 6, 1945, the second atom bomb destroyed four square miles of Hiroshima, which had been an important city since the seventeenth century. Immediately after Japan surrendered on August 14, 1945, plans were made to rebuild the city. Three months later the streets had been cleared of rubble, and today Hiroshima is once more a thriving modern community.

SHORE LINE AT AKASHI ASHIMMER WITH LAYERS OF FISH

The fisherman is spreading thousands of tiny fish out on mats to dry in the sun. Akashi, a
fairly large city, is on a strait between the Harima Sea and Osaka Bay, and these waters teem
with the finny creatures. Part of the catch is dried, as here, and another big portion is canned.
The Japanese depend mainly on fish dried, canned or fresh for protein food.

361

Tiny trees, grown in china pots, are popular for house decoration—dwarf pine trees or maples that grow no more than a few inches high even after a hundred years.

When so little of this mountainous land is arable, every acre that can be used is cultivated intensively. The average farm consists of but two and a half acres, and one acre must feed four persons. The islands contain a population of seventy million, and that number is increasing at the rate of not far from a million a year. To feed them, Japan must supplement her own resources by importing wheat and flour from both Canada and the United States.

As one rides through Japan on the leisurely narrow-gauge trains, where travelers relax with fans and carpet slippers, one views a patchwork of rice fields emerald in summer, malodorous from the excessive fertilizer used. In a land where farm animals are rather uncommon, most of the labor is performed by coolies and their wives and children. These level the fields for irrigation, bank them about so that the water will not drain off, plant and

BLACK STAR

ONE OF THE BUSY DOCKS IN THE BUSTLING HARBOR OF YOKOHAMA
An ocean-going freighter, anchored in deeper water, looks down on a jumble of fishing craft.
Japan is so overcrowded that many families make their homes on these fishing boats.

weed, and when the grain turns to the yellow of autumn, harvest it with a hand sickle. They thresh the straw by beating it over a barrel or drawing it across steel teeth, and finally husk it in a hand-mill, at which stage they have the wholesome natural brown rice chiefly eaten by the non-flesh-eating natives. To give it a polish they employ a log mortar or a small power mill. In the south two crops a year are grown. The water is ditched from reservoirs fed by the mountain streams, and the government maintains seed and fertilizer experiment farms.

Farther up the slopes of the mountains the rice fields give way to terraces of wheat and barley. Near Kyoto tea is grown. Little is exported, however, for practically the whole of the crop is used by the Japanese themselves.

As the farmers have so small an area for cultivation, they have to eke out their living by handicrafts and manufactures. Some of them make baskets, others carve wood, but nearly all cultivate the silkworm. In each house we hear the rustling noise of silk-winding and find rows and rows of cocoons put out on trays to dry.

SKILLED CRAFTSMEN AT WORK IN A LACQUER SHOP IN KYOTO

As many as twenty to thirty coats of lacquer may be applied on the justly famous Japanese lacquer ware. The lacquer is obtained from the sap of a tree popularly called the "Japanese varnish tree."

Long accustomed to despotic rule, it is only since World War II that the individual Japanese has been given much chance to think or act for himself. And even now, although the "feudal" loyalties of the Japanese have been somewhat modified, there is still a strong feeling of nationalism. The emperor is no longer the executive and the judicial head of the nation—the legislative bodies and the courts no longer function as his representatives and make no reference to him. Even though his office remains hereditary, his functions are merely ceremonial.

However, the popular feeling toward him is reported to be as strong as it was before the end of the war.

The Allied Powers ceased to control Japan on April 28,.1952, when the treaty, signed at San Francisco in September 1951, went into effect. According to a defense pact with the United States, however, United Nations troops remained, in order to carry on the war in Korea and also to defend Japan until she is able to muster her own armed forces. Japan, greatly reduced in size and power, became once again a free and sovereign nation.

JAPAN: FACTS AND FIGURES

THE COUNTRY

Japan, as constituted after defeat in World War II, consists of four islands, Honshu (mainland), Hokkaido, Kyushu and Shikoku with a total area of 142,275 square miles and a population of 80,216,896. The islands lie in the Pacific Ocean off the coast of China. By the terms ending World War II, Japan was forced to surrender her other seized lands, including Manchuria (Manchukuo) with an area of 503,013 square miles and a population of 43,200,000; the southern half of the Sakhalin Island, the Kuriles, Korea, Formosa, and the mandated islands in the Pacific, the Marshalls, the Carolines, the Ladrones and the Palaus, former German possessions.

GOVERNMENT

Under the constitution of 1946 the emperor has no executive power. This is exercised by a prime minister and a Cabinet, chosen from the Diet, or Parliament. The Diet makes the laws. It consists of a House of Representatives and a House of Councillors. Members of both bodies are elected. On April 28, 1952, the peace treaty, signed at San Francisco, California, in September 1951, became effective. The treaty brought Allied occupation to an end and made Japan once more a sovereign nation.

COMMERCE AND INDUSTRIES

About three-fifths of the arable land is cultivated by peasant proprietors, the rest by tenants. More than half the land is used for growing rice, the chief food of the country. Wheat, barley, rye, tobacco, tea, beans, peaches, pears, apples, grapes, persimmons and mandarins are also produced. Mulberry trees are widely grown, and the annual output of silk is huge (three-fourths of the world's total). The country possesses a variety of minerals including gold, silver, copper, lead, zinc, iron, chromite, white arsenic, coal, sulfur, salt and petroleum.

After agriculture and the making of silk, the principal industries were the manufacture of woolens, cottons, paper, pottery, vegetable oil, leather and matting.

The vast family trusts under which Japan was able to mobilize her financial and industrial strength to wage war were dissolved under the orders of the Allies.

RELIGION AND EDUCATION

Japan has no state religion and all faiths are tolerated. The principal forms of religion are Shintoism, with 85 sects, and Buddhism, with 12 sects. There are 110,500 Shinto shrines, 100,000 Buddhist temples and 2,000 Christian churches, with 16 Protestant denominations represented. The Roman Catholics have an archbishop and three suffragan bishops.

Elementary education is compulsory up to the age of 15, and free. There are 200,714 primary schools, 11,533 middle schools. Japan has 6 universities and 39 other schools of university rank. Thirty-six are co-educational. The universities: Tokyo, founded 1877; Kyoto, 1897; Tohoku at Sendai Sapporo, 1918; and Osaka, 1931. Illiteracy is only 10% in the nation. English is the language of commerce and a required study in the high schools. Military training in the schools was abolished in 1945 after Japan surrendered to the Allies.

CHIEF TOWNS

In normal times there is considerable foreign trade. The most important ports are Yokohama, Kobe and Osaka on the Pacific coast of the main island, and Nigata on the Japan Sea coast, the port of transshipment for Vladivostok.

Populations: Tokyo, capital, 6,019,133 (1949); Osaka, 1,102,959; Yokohama, 624,994; Nagoya, 597,941; Fukuoka, 252,282; Yawata, 151,378; Hiroshima, 137,197; Kokura, 131,688; Kyoto (1940), 1,089,726; Kobe (1938), 967,234.

TOKYO, THE PHOENIX CITY

Capital of a Beauty-loving People

Like that fabulous bird, the phoenix, which, every five hundred years, burned itself on a pyre of aromatic gums, and arose from the ashes in new vigor and beauty, Tokyo has more than once been destroyed and then has arisen with renewed life. Ruin from the skies descended upon it in the war; but it is once again showing its indestructability. One thing war has not touched—the glimmering beauty of Tokyo's mountain, Fujiyama. The city unfolds like a gorgeous fan to welcome the ships and to allow visitors their first glimpse of "No Two Such"—the name of Fuji as written in Chinese characters. As a native poet wrote of the lovely mountain: "One glance, and you would give your province; another and you would barter your kingdom."

THE city now known as Tokyo was founded in 1456, but under another name. For four hundred years it was called Yedo. In 1590 it became the capital of the Shoguns, powerful feudal lords who really ruled Japan, while the emperors lived at Kioto. It was not until 1868, when the Shogunate was overthrown and the modern Japanese empire was established, that the city's name was changed to Tokyo and it became the sole capital. In 1940 Tokyo was the third largest city in the world, surpassed only by New York and London. It was, and is still, an important industrial city, and through its seaport, Yokohama, at the entrance to Tokyo Bay, it has access to all the seas of the world. The city has long been a curious mixture of the modern West and the ancient East. There are broad, paved streets, gas and electric light, a modern water supply system, streetcars and even a subway; but there are many more narrow, winding streets, large areas of paper-and-match-wood houses, and other reminders of the days of the Shoguns.

Every city set up by the hand of man possesses its distinctive smell. An un-grudging and enthusiastic liberality characterizes the smells on some of the canals in Tokyo. Were Tokyo more compact, and could one get a bird's-eye view of it, it would bear some likeness to Venice or Bangkok, for canals cross and recross it. Only the fine sea breeze, the "saving grace of the city," minimizes to some extent the mingled odors of dampness, soap, fish,

pickled radish and other less pleasant substances which assail the noses of natives and visitors.

Then there are the crowds, and with them comes the noise that only an oriental city could produce; the sound of thousands of wooden clogs, or *getas,* beating their tattoo on the pavements. It somehow suggests perpetual motion, like a river rattling the pebbles along its banks—a noise not unmusical, but unforgettable. It becomes the background for the piles of glowing silks, the superb materials spread out for the great ladies of the town; it goes with the endless displays of pottery; it sounds natural in the flower shops, because you remember that you have heard the same sound on the paved walks of the public parks and gardens.

The *riki* is still the dominant vehicle in native Tokyo, for manpower is even today cheaper than gasoline. In the roadways the "hai-hai" of the jinrikisha bearers accents the honk of motor horns; the patter of the bearers' padded stockings beats a rhythm to the hum of automobile engines. The rikisha man removes his pudding hat and mops his head with his towel as he lowers the shafts of the rikisha for a moment's rest. Then he is off and away again.

There are also bicycles — apparently thousands of them, whizzing in all directions, their riders often carrying bundles and even three-tiered trays of bowls of soup. There seems to be nothing that can not be carried by a Tokyo cyclist, and

PHILIP GENDREAU

WINDOW SHOPPING ON THE GINZA

The Ginza is the Fifth Avenue, or Rue de la Paix, of Tokyo. Though Japanese are fast adopting Western dress, the picturesque kimono is by no means out of fashion.

these men ride as if they were part of their machines.

The Ginza is Tokyo's great shopping center and promenade. Everyone goes there, to see and be seen, or perhaps to spend a pleasant hour loitering before the windows of the tempting shops. The foreign visitor goes to the Ginza again and again, to buy some fruit for breakfast, or a fine cultured pearl, or yards of silken damask or a bit of old carved ivory. Whatever his purchases, the traveler will bring away also a store of kaleidoscopic impressions. There is no better way to observe a cross section of Tokyo life than to stroll along the Ginza.

Tokyo after Dark

To all but the initiated, Tokyo after dark is a big, dusky village, and to some visitors it is even a dull one. To hobnob for hours with a few boon companions over a tiny pot of weak, sugarless tea, while puffing a tobacco pipe with an incredibly tiny bowl seems to fill the men of Tokyo with boundless content.

They have also Napoleon's ability to sleep anywhere, in any position and at any time. Before World War II young men loved to clatter along the streets in their wooden clogs, singing, utterly unconcerned with the rest of the multitude. Now the joyous singing is gone. The long years of war and more than six years of occupation have turned the thoughts of all—but especially of the young—to stern realities. There is wonder about what the future will hold for the individual. There is dissention, even among close friends, on such subjects as politics and foreign relations. In more respects than one Japan is standing at the crossroads of her national life; and nowhere is this fact more apparent than in Tokyo.

The city is full of cafés, always crowded. In former days prosperous men gave geisha parties, rather solemn affairs at which geisha—professional entertainers—danced their ceremonial dances. *Sukiyaki,* the main dish, was customarily prepared by the host, who, with his guests, sat on the floor. Warmed *sake,* a wine made from rice and served in thimble-sized

Photo, Rev. Walter Weston

TASSELED WISTARIAS FRINGE KAMEIDO'S SILENT POOL

Grace and beauty are realized in the Shinto shrine of Kameido-Tenjin, Tokyo. The grounds include a pond crossed by this semicircular bridge and framed in wistarias trained on trellises. The sight is exquisite in early May when the myriad purple flower clusters, some of them as much as ten feet in length, hang over the surface of the pool.

BOYS PLAY AT WAR

A deserted bomb shelter provides a "play" battle field for these youngsters of Kanoya. Under Allied control, Japanese youth will not be trained for war.

cups, punctuated the mouthfuls of *suki-yaki.*

Today there is very little of this sort of entertainment. The cafés are crowded, their principal patrons being "mobos" and "mogas." The Japanese love to abbreviate. Mobo is the abbreviation for modern boy and moga for modern girl. These westernized young people, with their modern clothes and freedom of manner, are an interesting proof of the influence that Europe and America—especially America—have had upon the younger generation in Japan.

The loveliest and most characteristic thing about Tokyo is its gardens, both public and private. Somehow the smoke and noise and odor of the city do not penetrate the gardens, which look unchanged by time. The beauty-loving people of Tokyo are seized with a species of flower-madness. The blossoming of the plum trees, harbingers of spring, begin the flower season, and man, woman and child hasten to the gardens to drink in this loveliness. Then there are the iris, and of

POSTWAR CROWDS FLOCK TO THEATRES IN TOKYO

As in all war-ravaged countries, people in Japan, so long starved for entertainment, throng to the newly opened theatres. Here is a scene in much-battered Tokyo showing a crowd which caused a near-riot in an attempt to cram into the Takarazuka Theatre.

A DINNER PARTY IN JAPANESE STYLE

These ladies of Japan show us how dinner is served in their homes. Dressed in Kimonos, they sit or kneel on the floor before low tables. Some of the dinner service has a modern and Western appearance, but the rice bowls and chopsticks are in keeping with the Japanese setting. Sukiaki is a favorite dish, a mixture of meat and vegetables. Tea, of course, is the beverage. In all likelihood, a fish course is also served.

course, the wistaria and cherry blossoms.

The real glory of a cherry in blossom is when you see it like a white mist—there is only a suggestion of pink. Behind the cherry trees, giving a somber background that sets off their shining delicacy, are splendid pines and yews, so dark a green as to be almost black. The Japanese have a saying: "As the warrior is king of men, so the cherry tree is first among flowers."

To the blossoming cherry branch add a flower of verse! One may often see a young girl, her black hair brushed until it shines like a wet seal, attaching a poem to a tree so that those who come to enjoy the flowers may also read her work.

Although, as we have said, much of Tokyo was destroyed in the war, one may still catch glimpses here and there of cool gardens. There are bits of lovely moss-grown walls with wistaria-veiled arbors; garden pools, lush with iris standing waist-high, or

crowded with lotus cups. In the more open spaces are seen the masses of the flame-like azaleas, and always the curious, crooked dwarf pines. A sense of peace and tranquility steals over the sojourner

THE SHOE STORE IS OPEN

A shoe vendor spreads his wares on a clean cloth, and he is ready for business. As we see, the stock here is limited to sandals, and does not show us other forms of Japanese footwear, such as wooden clogs.

369

in a perfect garden, even one which has suffered from wartime neglect. The gardens are the last strong-hold of the feudal aristocracy, also, perhaps, the last strongholds of the ancient beauty of the capital.

If one wanders about Tokyo one may come suddenly upon winding, narrow passageways that lead in and out among quiet houses, gateways through which can be glimpsed lovely miniature gardens, and tea houses where one

International News Photo

LIFE GOES ON IN TOKYO

This Japanese mother parks her youngest baby on her back, papoose style, while she bathes an older child. This scene is in the poorest section of Tokyo.

stays awake night after night listening to the deep, thrilling notes of the drums spreading their triple warning of fire throughout the city. Fire has always been a hazard in the wood-and-paper cities of Japan. The winds of Tokyo, described as "propitious for kite flying," are also propitious for spreading fire. At one time in the city's history fire was called the Flower of Yedo. In the old days fires were of daily occurrence in winter and spring. In

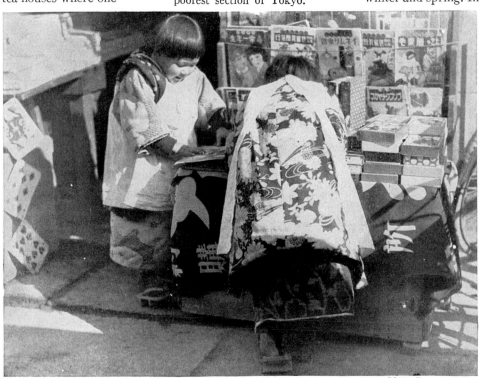

Philip Gendreau, N.Y.

LITTLE JAPANESE GIRLS INSPECT A BOOKSTAND

The books and games on this stand look much the same as those which children have in our country. We notice in the picture the padded clothing which the little girls are wearing as a protection against the cold weather. White aprons are worn over the kimonos to keep them clean when the children are at play. Wooden clogs save the expense of shoe leather.

GEISHA GIRLS DANCE IN FOREST SCENE Philip Gendreau, N.Y.

The name geisha means "a person of pleasing accomplishments," and was given to the professional dancing and singing girls of Japan. The training of the true Geisha or singing girl began often as early as her seventh year, and her period of service was only terminated by marriage. It is possible that the many changes in postwar Japan may bring an end to this ancient Japanese custom.

1601 and again in 1657 flames swept over Yedo, reducing the entire city to ashes.

As recently as one hundred years ago the arsonists, if caught, were crucified; but even this draconic measure of fire prevention does not seem to have done much good. Today the people are learning elementary precautions against fire; but until the buildings are constructed of materials less flimsy than paper and thin wood, danger will be ever present.

In 1923 more than half Tokyo's buildings were destroyed by the earthquakes and the fire that followed. More than 150,000 people perished, and, partly because of the country's poverty, it took nearly seven years for the city to be completely restored. In 1942 General Doolittle's bombers heralded a new kind of destruction, in the first dramatic air raid over Japan in April of that year. The city was bombed many times in the later years of the war and roughly three-fourths of its area was in ruins at the time of the surrender. The biggest burned-out patch straddles the important Ueno railroad station. The imperial palace, hidden within walled acres of gardens and lakes, groves and pavilions, was so damaged as to be uninhabitable, and when war ended it was found that the emperor had been living for some time in a building designed for an air raid shelter. Beautiful as it was, this palace will be missed less than almost any of the other Tokyo targets, for scarcely any of Tokyo's millions of inhabitants had ever seen beyond the outer walls of the imperial domain.

Perhaps the most significant change that the war has brought to Tokyo is the revolutionary change in the relationship between the people and their emperor. He is no longer a sacred symbol kept aloof from the people who were governed in his name. Instead, as the link between the democratic conquerors and the Japanese people, he is quite likely to be seen driving or walking about the streets of the city just as the American president and the British kings have been doing for centuries. It is difficult for the western mind to realize what an important move in the direction of democracy this has been. It remains to be seen how the people of Japan will react to this opportunity for self-rule. The regime inaugurated under General MacArthur may find a solid, permanent foundation among the Japanese masses.

The re-birth of Tokyo is both actual and inevitable. It is a matter of concern to many nations, especially to those whose lands border on the Pacific Ocean.

JAPANESE SURRENDER ON BOARD U.S.S. MISSOURI

Four years of violent warfare, which began at Pearl Harbor, came to a decisive end in this ceremony on board the mighty battleship U.S.S. Missouri, at anchor in Tokyo Bay. The warship served as a stage for the surrender, in which, for the first time in her more than 2000-year history, the Land of the Rising Sun capitulated to an enemy, and lost her chance for world conquest.

THE LAND OF THE MORNING CALM

Korea, One of the World's Oldest Kingdoms

The name the Japanese gave Korea long ago—Land of the Morning Calm—has always had a rather bitter irony. Strife has devastated the peninsula many times in the past, and never more so than in the middle of the twentieth century. Though the latest conflict does not have the official label of "war," it has placed Korea, once remote and little known, in the center of the world stage. Like a pebble tossed into a pond, the invasion of South Korea by the North Korean Communists in 1950 has sent out waves that have spread to the farthest shores. Suffering the horrors of modern warfare, Korea has become the proving ground of the United Nations' power to halt aggression as well as the Western world's ability to meet the threat of communist domination.

KOREA (Chosen) is a peninsular tableland, about as large as the mainland of Japan, that extends southward from Manchuria, between the two naval bases of Vladivostok and Port Arthur. Viewed from the deck of a steamer cruising up the east coast, it is seen that an unbroken chain of rocky mountains runs down this side. Islands dot the shores. Some of these islands rise several hundred feet above the blue of the sea and are lush with vegetation. The largest island, Quelpart, south of Korea, has an old volcanic crater rising to a height of over six thousand feet. Traces of its former activity can be seen in the quantities of pumice stone which are found all over the island.

Korean history can definitely be traced for over three thousand years. It was founded about 1100 B.C. by a Chinese statesman, Ki-tze (now a legendary hero), who settled at Ping-yang. For centuries a high degree of civilization existed, a Korean language developed, and movable type was used in printing years before the Gutenberg discovery. Japanese settlers came, but also Japanese corsairs who raided the coast towns.

But the ancient kingdom did not enjoy unbroken peace. The Mongol, Kublai Khan, repeatedly invaded the territory. Then in 1419 a Yi ruler determined to destroy the Japanese pirates and fitted out a Korean fleet with a view to attacking the island of Tsushima. which was their stronghold. Though he failed of his objective he did later establish trade relations with Japan through the Daimio who ruled the island.

At the end of the sixteenth century a Japanese ruler, Hideyoshi, tried to capture Korea as one move in his advance on China. He took city after city, till at last the Koreans appealed for aid to the Chinese. Though the Japanese were driven out, they left the country in ruins, took many Korean craftsmen home with them as prisoners, and Korea found herself vassal to China. She deteriorated rapidly under this state of affairs.

The Koreans now forbade strangers to land on their shores, they successively repelled France and the United States of America and persecuted Christian missionaries with their converts. But on the advice of the Chinese statesman Li Hung Chang, Korea finally established trade relations with Japan, the United States, and other countries.

Now it happened that China had, about a generation previously, lost two huge provinces in the northeast to Russia: she was therefore the more reluctant to lose her hold on Korea and in 1894 China and Japan went to war over this key territory. The Chinese were defeated and agreed to recognize the independence of Korea.

Japan had by now secured a foothold on the mainland of Asia. This Russia found distasteful and compelled her to abandon. Russia, in the meantime, was advancing into northern China. Taking advantage of ill-feeling between certain Japanese officials and the Korean king, Russia secured valuable concessions in

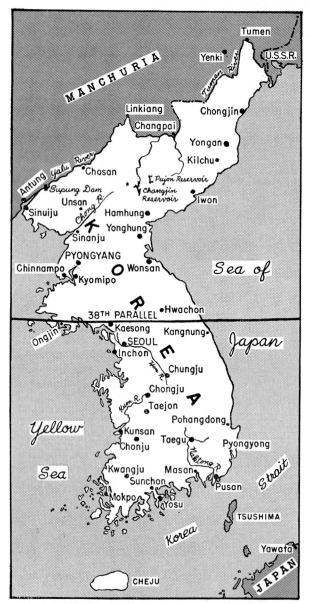

KOREA, THE ANCIENT CHOSEN

ished friendly relations with Korea and in 1910 Japan annexed the country under its ancient name of Chosen. But while the Japanese did much to further material progress, the Koreans deeply resented attempts to force the Japanese language and institutions on them.

Following the ouster of the Japanese government in 1945, the country was occupied jointly by United States and Russian forces. It was decided that Korea, once a kingdom, should have a free and independent democratic form of government.

However, rival factions disputed for control of the country. In May of 1948, two elections were held. The first took place in Soviet-occupied northern Korea and resulted in the formation of a communist form of People's Republic. The second election, in southern Korea, named the Korean Republic. The second election was recognized by the United Nations. Later, the Korean Republic adopted a constitution which also was recognized by the UN. The events that followed are discussed later on in this article.

The climate of Korea is dry and bracing in spring and fall though there is abundant rain in summer. It is never extremely hot or cold. Korea escapes the floods, droughts and typhoons that so often bring disaster to China and Japan; and there are no destructive earthquakes. The light sandy loam of the river plains produces two crops a year.

Land is easy to procure. Any native may become a farmer; he has only to reclaim and cultivate unoccupied land, and in three years the land becomes his own. His agricultural implements, however,

timber, ports and fisheries. As a result, in 1904 Japan declared war on the Tsar and by the next year had driven Russia out of Korea. By a treaty between the two warring countries, Korea was promised autonomy, while Russia surrendered to Japan the disputed foothold on the mainland and at Port Arthur.

The Marquis (later Prince) Ito as Japanese Resident-General now estab-

HOPEFUL KOREANS REBUILD THEIR HOME, NEAR CHINJU

Sixty per cent of the city of Chinju and its suburbs had been destroyed when the United Nations forces recaptured it in 1950. Chinju is in the South Keisho Province, in the cotton-growing region of Korea. It is only fifty-five miles from the seaport of Pusan. In the background is a typical Korean roof, with up-curved gables and up-curved ridgepole.

NO IDLE HANDS HERE

A South Korean farmer spreads wheat grains on a mat to dry in the sun. He will plant them in late October after the rice crop has been harvested. While the northern section of Korea endures extremes of heat and cold, the south, tempered by ocean breezes, allows a long season for agriculture. The valley of the Naktong River is able to produce two crops a year.

375

are the same as those his ancestors used. He tills the land with a primitive wooden plow shod with iron, and digs with a large shovel. This is worked sometimes by as many as five men; the blade is pushed into the ground and men haul on ropes attached to the shaft, and so contrive to break up the ground.

Rice, the chief crop, is threshed by beating the ripe ears against a log so that the grain falls on to the hard mud threshing-floor. To remove the unwanted husks the Koreans throw the grain up into the air on a windy day, so that the husks are blown away, while the heavier grain falls to the ground.

The Koreans, like the Japanese and the Chinese, sometimes make use of the cormorant to help them catch fish. The fishing colonies have to meet the difficulty of disposing of their catches. Along the beaches thousands of fish may be seen put out to dry in the sun. Nowhere are such beautiful lobsters found.

The Koreans believe that the air is full of good and evil spirits. Even stones and trees are reverenced as the abode of spirits. Hills and mountains are looked upon as gods who must be appeased with gifts and pebbles are carried one at a time to the top of high mountains as offerings to the god who is supposed to dwell within. We may often see trees covered with colored rags, which are tied there by devoted Koreans and left as presents to the tree spirits.

McKenzie

PROUD MOTHER OF KOREA

Korean parents are very proud of their children, especially of the boys. The little jacket and voluminous trousers are part of the attire of Korean women.

Wicked spirits are thought to be kept away by noise. A rough wooden scaffold, with a bell suspended from the top, is erected outside a house, and poor people are always glad to get an empty oil can with a stone inside. Certain animals are supposed to be wicked or good spirits. The Korean tiger, a magnificent beast, but nearly extinct, is held to be a great wizard. One of the Koreans' favorite stories tells how a thief once rode a tiger into his village. A Korean mother was nursing her baby in a mud hut when the thief broke into the adjoining stable and hid until it was safe to steal the woman's cow. A tiger had also hidden in the stable, waiting to eat the poor woman.

The baby began to cry, and the mother told her that a tiger would eat her if she were not quiet. As this did not quell the baby's cries, the mother said: "Quiet, little one, here is kokum!" (sweetmeat). The child's tears stopped at once.

The tiger, who had overheard the conversation, said to himself: "What is this fearsome 'kokum' that frightens the child into silence when my dread name has no effect?" At this moment the thief slipped the halter over his head, thinking it was the cow. The tiger was terrified, imagining that he had been snared by the 'kokum,' and all night the thief rode his strange steed till he reached his own village at dawn. When the tiger saw how he had been deceived, he was ashamed and slunk off into the

A KOREAN FARMER WEARING HIS PADDED WHITE WINTER GARMENTS

While some Koreans have adopted Western dress, most of them still wear the costume that developed under their kings, at least at home. This is white or pale blue, and the garments are fastened with ties instead of buttons. The farmer above wears a padded turumaki—a loose coat that reaches below the knees—over a short, padded jacket and loose padded trousers.

PUBLIC NEWSPAPERS ON AN OPEN-AIR BULLETIN BOARD

Even under normal conditions, newspapers and radios are still scarce in Korea; and most of the people get their news of local happenings and world events from public newspapers such as these, which serve hundreds. The wall notices are one indication of the fact that many more Koreans have been learning to read (and to write) in recent years.

jungle, but the thief lived to boast of his ride. Many such superstitious stories about the tiger are related in Korea.

The basic religions of Korea have been Confucianism, Animism (the belief that all natural objects have souls) and Buddhism. However, all of these faiths have been declining, particularly since 1945,

as has ancestor worship. In 1948, it was estimated that almost 700,000 Koreans were Christians. In the past most religious observances were concerned with the propitiation of wicked demons. To keep these away, large sums were paid to professional sorceresses, of whom, at the end of the nineteenth century, there were

UNATIONS

BEATING CLOTHES WITH A STICK TO MAKE THEM SNOW-WHITE

For hundreds of years, while Korea was still a kingdom and forbiddingly remote from the world, the people wore white or pale blue clothing. Even today, when it would seem to be a hopeless task to keep garments immaculate, many Koreans still cling to the old costume. But as long as a Korean housewife has a clear stream nearby and a stick, she will attack dirt with vigor.

over one thousand. The Christian religion was introduced to Korea in the eighteenth century by a Roman Catholic priest and for some time was hotly resisted; converts were persecuted and priests tortured and killed. Since 1882, however, the teaching of the Christian religion has been allowed and, more recently, even encouraged.

The Koreans are taller than the Japanese, well made, with oval faces, high cheek bones and narrow eyes. The usual dress of the men is a plain white cotton robe, simply made. No needles or thread are used in the construction of Korean clothing: it is cut out and stuck together with glue. When washed it is simply unstuck, dried and stuck together again.

Summer undershirts of laborers are of airy, woven rattan. Stockings are of cotton wadding. Korean men wear curious little sailor hats perched on the tops of their heads, unless they are undergoing their three years of mourning for a parent. In that case they appear in mourning-hats with brims that rest on their shoulders. Korean gentlemen almost universally carry fans, and often they ride on palanquins made to rest on one central wheel to relieve the coolies of their weight.

Korean women pluck their eyebrows and redden their lips, but are kept in considerable seclusion. They marry very young and are considered successes when they have brought sons into the world. They are then called "the mother of" so-and-so.

A Korean wedding is strange; the couple do not see each other until the ceremony. When the bride is first led into the presence of her husband her eyes are sealed up and she does not speak. Even after marriage the Korean woman must be silent for a long time.

The one-story houses are made of mud and beams, and usually thatched. The floors are made of dried mud, which is stamped down and covered with oiled paper. The making of oiled paper is a large industry in Korea, for the windows

WIDE WORLD

JUST ANOTHER DISPLACED PERSON—WITH NO PLACE TO GO!

Trudging along a rocky road, a refugee carries with him all that he has left in the world—a pitifully small load—on his own back and tied to his pony. He may find shelter for a night; but his land is so blasted from years of warfare that he can have little hope of a bright future. Elsewhere in the world, too, oppression still creates a tragic toll of exiles.

KOREAN FARMERS LABOR LONG AND HARD WITH PRIMITIVE METHODS

This scene in the village of Kamjyun-ri, not far from the port city of Pusan, shows a Korean peasant woman drying red peppers in the sun. Korea is largely an agricultural country, rice being its most important crop. Barley, wheat and other grains, tobacco and cotton are also cultivated. Deep-sea fishing is a gainful calling of many on the eastern coast.

of the houses are also made of it and the same material is used as a lining for clothing. Koreans like "kimshee," a combination of turnips and sauerkraut; also a certain kind of seaweed cooked in oil, and occasionally, dog flesh served with a peppery relish. The rich drink honey water flavored with orange peel and ginger.

Seoul, the chief city, was founded by Emperor Yi Taejo as Hanyang (Fortress of the Han) in 1392, and it was the capital of the Korean rulers until Japan an-

nexed the country in 1910. On August 15, 1948, Seoul was made the capital of the Republic of Korea.

The city lies in a small valley, on the banks of the Han River, hemmed in by granite mountains, none more than 3,000 feet high. As Seoul is only a few miles south of the 38th parallel, the dividing line between North and South Korea, the city was a main objective in the invasion that began in June 1950. Battle lines have crossed it several times, the chief

BUDDHIST MONKS PERFORM THEIR RITES IN A SOUTH KOREAN TEMPLE

These two devout men, who minister to a Buddhist parish in South Korea, are father and son. Their fine old temple, erected in 982 A.D., miraculously escaped serious war damage. Loyally they have carried on their time-honored traditions. Buddhism is followed by a small percentage of the Korean people today, although it was once all-powerful on the peninsula.

382

bridge across the Han has been destroyed, and today Seoul is a melancholy ruin.

Long ago it was completely surrounded by a wall, pierced by eight gates. One of these was called the Gate of Elevated Humanity and another the Gate of Bright Amiability. Until 1950 sections of this wall remained. Within the city there was another wall, enclosing the five hundred acres of ground on which the royal palace stood.

Among several ancient temples there was an elaborately carved marble pagoda, dating from the thirteenth century, and

a bell tower containing a bronze bell dated 1468. This bell had an especially lovely tone, which the Koreans explained by the following fable. The emperor ordered a bell-maker to fashion, on pain of death, a bell with a clear tone. Although the artisan tried, he was unable to do this until his daughter, who had a beautiful voice, flung herself into the molten metal from which the huge tongue was to be cast. The bell used to be rung at sunset and at dawn. At sunset all the men had to come indoors, for then it was the women's time to enjoy the open air.

UNATIONS

KOREA'S GREATEST HOPE FOR THE FUTURE IS HER CHILDREN

These youngsters are playing around an ancient stone image in the village of Mi A Ri, near the city of Seoul. They are as fascinated by wild flowers as children are everywhere, and they welcome the summer in spite of the searing sun. This portion of west central Korea is circled by low mountains; its summers are hot and humid, and its winters are severe.

The recent history of Korea is a far cry from legends or a serene evening stroll. Though the Koreans had to yield to the might of Japan in 1910, they never gave up hope of independence. In 1919 there was a rebellion, which the Japanese put down with great cruelty. A few Koreans escaped to other countries, partly to secure an education and also to enlist the sympathy of the outside world in Korea's plight.

With Japan's defeat at the end of World War II, she was stripped of all her acquired territory, including Korea. For a time, Russian forces occupied Korea north of the 38th parallel (which divides the country practically in the middle), and United States forces the area south of it. Though these forces were later withdrawn, the parallel continued to divide the country politically. Two independent governments were established: the Korean People's Republic, in the north; and the Republic of Korea, in the south.

North Korea, led by Communists, came into the Soviet sphere of influence, while South Korea had strong ties with the Western powers. Friction developed between North and South Korea and burst into flame when North Korean forces crossed the parallel on June 25, 1950. The United Nations (Russia was boycotting the Security Council at the time) considered this a clear case of aggression and called on member nations to help South Korea. Most of the forces involved in the conflict that followed have come from the United States.

By October of 1950, UN troops had reached the Yalu River, the boundary between North Korea and Manchuria, and hope arose in the Western world that the North Koreans were about to be defeated. Instead, Chinese Communist soldiers appeared in ever increasing numbers and began to push the UN forces back. By the late spring of 1951, however, the tide had turned again. Suffering terrific losses, the Communists had been forced to retreat and the battle lines had moved back to the parallel.

To this extent, one of the aims of the United Nations seemed near achievement —to drive the aggressors north of the parallel; but to establish a "free, independent and democratic Korea" still presented many difficulties. The Koreans will need help for some time to come.

KOREA: FACTS AND FIGURES

THE COUNTRY

A peninsula in Northeastern Asia bounded on the north by Manchuria and Siberia, on the east by the Sea of Japan, on the south by the Korea Strait and on the west by the Yellow Sea. Korea includes many islands along the south and west coasts. The area is 85,266 square miles and the population is 25,120,174 (1944).

GOVERNMENT

The government is divided. The communistic "People's Republic" set up in North Korea on May 1, 1948, is not recognized in the south, where a Constitution of the Korean Republic was adopted July 12, 1948, and its first president elected under UN supervision July 20, 1948.

COMMERCE AND INDUSTRIES

The country is almost entirely agricultural, with rice, barley, wheat, beans, and grains the chief crops. Cattle of good quality are raised and whale fishing pursued. Silkworm-raising is carried on. Gold, copper, iron and coal are abundant. The principal exports are rice, beans, peas, and pulse, hides, cattle, silk, cocoons and gold, and the imports include cotton goods, silk goods, machinery, kerosene oil, grass cloth, sugar and coal.

COMMUNICATIONS

Interior transport is by pack-horse, oxen, rail, motor cars and by river. Before the outbreak of the Korean war in 1950, there were 1,676 miles of railway in operation. Length of telegraph line was 5,496 miles and telephone line, 5,991 miles.

RELIGION AND EDUCATION

A large number still follow ancestor worship and Confucianism. There are also Buddhists and Christians. There are technical schools, industrial schools, a university in Seoul, and 18 special colleges. An adult-education campaign against illiteracy has been launched in South Korea.

CHIEF TOWNS

Population, 1946: Seoul, capital of South Korea, 1,141,766; Pusan, 400,156; Taegu, 269,113; Inchon, 215,784. The city of Pyengyang, capital of North Korea, had a population of 285,965 in 1940. Later figures are unavailable.

INDEX FOR VOLUME IV

Color Plates in Volume IV

INDEX FOR VOLUME IV

(General Index for entire work of 7 volumes may be found at the end of Volume 7)

A single star before a page number marks an illustration; two stars are placed before color-plates. The repetition of a page number, first without a star, and then with a star, shows that there is an illustration on the page, in addition to an important text reference.